# Mechanics 2
## for Edexcel

WITHDRAWN

CAMBRIDGE
UNIVERSITY PRESS

...ematics Project

**SMP AS/A2 Mathematics writing team** John Ling, Paul Scruton, Susan Shilton, Heather West

**SMP design and administration** Melanie Bull, Pam Keetch, Nicky Lake, Cathy Syred, Ann White

The authors thank Sue Glover for the technical advice she gave when this AS/A2 project began and for her detailed editorial contribution to this book. The authors are also very grateful to those teachers who commented in detail on draft chapters.

CAMBRIDGE UNIVERSITY PRESS
Cambridge, New York, Melbourne, Madrid, Cape Town, Singapore, São Paulo

Cambridge University Press
The Edinburgh Building, Cambridge CB2 2RU, UK

www.cambridge.org
Information on this title: www.cambridge.org/9780521605403

© The School Mathematics Project 2006

First published 2006

Printed in the United Kingdom at the University Press, Cambridge

*A catalogue record for this publication is available from the British Library*

ISBN-13    978-0-521-60540-3 paperback
ISBN-10    0-521-60540-7 paperback

Typesetting and technical illustrations by The School Mathematics Project
Illustration on page 64 by Chris Evans

The authors and publisher are grateful to London Qualifications Limited for permission to reproduce questions from past Edexcel examination papers. Individual questions are marked Edexcel. London Qualifications Limited accepts no responsibility whatsoever for the accuracy or method of working in the answers given.

# Using this book

Each chapter begins with a **summary** of what the student is expected to learn.

The chapter then has sections lettered A, B, C, … (see the contents overleaf). In most cases a section consists of development material, worked examples and an exercise.

The **development material** interweaves explanation with questions that involve the student in making sense of ideas and techniques. Development questions are labelled according to their section letter (A1, A2, …, B1, B2, …) and answers to them are provided.

**D** Some development questions are particularly suitable for discussion – either by the whole class or by smaller groups – because they have the potential to bring out a key issue or clarify a technique. Such **discussion questions** are marked with a bar, as here.

**K** **Key points** established in the development material are marked with a bar as here, so the student may readily refer to them during later work or revision. Each chapter's key points are also gathered together in a panel after the last lettered section.

The **worked examples** have been chosen to clarify ideas and techniques, and as models for students to follow in setting out their own work. Guidance for the student is in italic.

The **exercise** at the end of each lettered section is designed to consolidate the skills and understanding acquired earlier in the section. Unlike those in the development material, questions in the exercise are denoted by a number only.

**Starred questions** are more demanding.

After the lettered sections and the key points panel there may be a set of **mixed questions**, combining ideas from several sections in the chapter; these may also involve topics from earlier chapters.

Every chapter ends with a selection of **questions for self-assessment** ('Test yourself').

Included in the mixed questions and 'Test yourself' are **past Edexcel exam questions**, to give the student an idea of the style and standard that may be expected, and to build confidence.

# Contents

# 1 Projectiles

In this chapter you will
- learn about the motion of a projectile (a particle moving in two dimensions acted on by gravity)
- solve problems about projectiles, including those involving release at height

---

**Key points from Mechanics 1**

- The constant acceleration equations for motion in one dimension are

  $v = u + at$

  $s = \frac{1}{2}(u + v)t$

  $s = ut + \frac{1}{2}at^2$

  $s = vt - \frac{1}{2}at^2$

  $v^2 = u^2 + 2as$

- The acceleration due to gravity is approximately equal to $9.8 \, \text{m s}^{-2}$.

---

## A Motion of a projectile (answers p 118)

**A1** A ball is thrown vertically upwards from ground level with an initial speed of $15 \, \text{m s}^{-1}$.

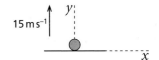

(a) Describe the motion of the ball.

(b) What is the acceleration of the ball?

(c) Use the constant acceleration equations to find

    (i) the height of the ball above ground level after 1 second

    (ii) the speed of the ball after 1 second

(d) Use the constant acceleration equations to find an expression for

    (i) the height of the ball above ground level after $t$ seconds

    (ii) the speed of the ball after $t$ seconds

(e) (i) What is the speed of the ball when it is at its maximum height?

    (ii) Find the maximum height reached by the ball.

A ball is dropped off the edge of a cliff. It starts from rest and moves vertically downwards. The only force acting on the ball is its weight, so the ball has a constant acceleration vertically downwards of magnitude $9.8 \, \text{m s}^{-2}$.

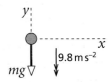

**A2 (a) (i)** Use the constant acceleration equations to find an expression for the displacement of the ball at time $t$ seconds.

**(ii)** Complete this table of values for the displacement of the ball.

| $t$ | 0 | 1 | 2 | 3 | 4 |
|-----|---|---|---|---|---|
| $y$ |   |   |   |   |   |

**(b) (i)** Use the constant acceleration equations to find an expression for the velocity, $v_y \, \text{m s}^{-1}$, of the ball at time $t$ seconds.

**(ii)** Complete this table of values for the velocity of the ball.

| $t$ | 0 | 1 | 2 | 3 | 4 |
|-----|---|---|---|---|---|
| $v_y$ |   |   |   |   |   |

An object that is thrown, dropped or launched into the air so that it moves under the influence of gravity alone is known as a **projectile**.
The last two questions involved projectiles that moved vertically in one dimension. We will now extend this into two dimensions.

The projectile will be modelled as a **particle**, an object that has mass but whose size can be ignored. The effects of air resistance and spin are considered negligible. If these effects are not negligible, then there will be forces other than weight acting on the particle, and it will not move as a projectile.

 **A3** Suggest some examples of situations which can be modelled as projectiles. Suggest a situation which cannot be modelled as a projectile and explain why.

Consider the motion of a ball which is kicked off the edge of a cliff so that it moves with an initial horizontal velocity of $10 \, \text{m s}^{-1}$ as shown.

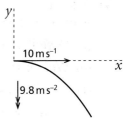

The horizontal and vertical components of the ball's motion can be considered separately.

There is no force acting on the ball horizontally, so the horizontal component of the velocity remains constant.

The only force acting on the ball is its weight, so the ball has a constant acceleration of $9.8 \, \text{m s}^{-2}$ vertically downwards and the vertical component of the velocity is not constant.

**A4 (a)** Show that the horizontal component of the displacement, $x \, \text{m}$, of the ball at time $t \, \text{s}$ is given by $x = 10t$.

**(b)** By substituting the known values into $s = ut + \frac{1}{2}at^2$, show that the vertical component of the displacement, $y \, \text{m}$, of the ball at time $t \, \text{s}$ is given by $y = -4.9t^2$.

If **i** and **j** are taken as the unit vectors in the horizontal and vertical directions respectively, then the components of the displacement can be combined and written in vector form.
The displacement, **s**, of the ball at time $t$ is given by $\mathbf{s} = 10t\mathbf{i} - 4.9t^2\mathbf{j}$.

**A5** (a) Show that $s = 30\mathbf{i} - 44.1\mathbf{j}$ when $t = 3$.

    (b) Complete this table of values for the displacement of the ball.

| $t$ | 0 | 1 | 2 | 3 | 4 |
|---|---|---|---|---|---|
| $\mathbf{s}$ | | | | $30\mathbf{i} - 44.1\mathbf{j}$ | |

    (c) Plot these points on graph paper, using a scale of 1 cm to 10 m, and join them to show the path of the ball during the motion. Label the points where $t = 0$, $t = 1$, and so on.

**A6** (a) Explain why the horizontal component of the velocity, $v_x\,\mathrm{m\,s^{-1}}$, of the ball at time $t$ s is given by $v_x = 10$.

    (b) By substituting the known values into $v = u + at$, show that the vertical component of the velocity, $v_y\,\mathrm{m\,s^{-1}}$, of the ball at time $t$ s is given by $v_y = -9.8t$.

    (c) Show that the velocity, $\mathbf{v}$, of the ball at time $t$ can be written in vector form as $\mathbf{v} = 10\mathbf{i} - 9.8t\mathbf{j}$.

    (d) Complete this table of values for the velocity of the ball.

| $t$ | 0 | 1 | 2 | 3 | 4 |
|---|---|---|---|---|---|
| $\mathbf{v}$ | $10\mathbf{i}$ | | | | |

    (e) Using a scale of 1 cm to $10\,\mathrm{m\,s^{-1}}$, add the velocity vectors to the graph drawn in A5(c). Draw each vector from the point on the graph with the corresponding value of time.

It can be seen from the table of values and the graph that the horizontal component of velocity is constant throughout the motion as there is no force acting on the ball in that direction.

The vertical component of velocity is continuously increasing downwards because of the weight of the ball.

Hence the direction of the velocity of the ball is changing throughout its motion.

**D** **A7** (a) Compare the tables of values for the displacement of the ball found in A2(a) and A5(b). Explain the reasons for the similarities.

    (b) Compare the tables of values for the velocity of the ball found in A2(b) and A6(d). Explain the reasons for the similarities.

**K** Projectile motion takes place in a vertical plane and the path is in the shape of a parabola.

The horizontal component of a projectile's velocity is constant.
The vertical component of a projectile's velocity changes throughout the motion due to its weight.
The magnitude and direction of the velocity of the projectile change throughout the motion.

**A8** A ball is thrown with an initial velocity of $(10\mathbf{i} + 15\mathbf{j})\,\mathrm{m\,s^{-1}}$, where $\mathbf{i}$ and $\mathbf{j}$ are horizontal and vertical unit vectors respectively. The only force acting on the ball is its weight, so its acceleration is $9.8\,\mathrm{m\,s^{-2}}$ vertically downwards.

(a) (i) By considering the horizontal and vertical components of the motion separately, find an expression in terms of $\mathbf{i}$ and $\mathbf{j}$ for the displacement, $\mathbf{s}$, of the ball from its starting point at time $t$.

(ii) Find the displacement of the ball when $t = 0, 0.5, 1, 1.5, 2, 2.5$ and $3$.

(iii) Plot these points on graph paper and join them to show the path of the ball during the motion.

(b) (i) By considering the horizontal and vertical components of the motion separately, find an expression in terms of $\mathbf{i}$ and $\mathbf{j}$ for the velocity, $\mathbf{v}$, of the ball at time $t$.

(ii) Find the velocity of the ball when $t = 1$, $t = 2$ and $t = 3$.

(iii) Draw the velocity vectors for these times on the graph drawn in (a)(iii) to show how the velocity of the ball changes during the motion.

---

### Example 1

A ball is thrown with an initial velocity of $(4\mathbf{i} + 6\mathbf{j})\,\mathrm{m\,s^{-1}}$.
Find the magnitude and direction of the velocity after 1 second.

### Solution

*Consider the horizontal and vertical components of motion separately.*

Initial horizontal velocity $u_x = 4$, initial vertical velocity $u_y = 6$.

Horizontally the ball is moving with constant velocity.    $v_x = u_x = 4$

Vertically the ball is moving with constant acceleration $9.8\,\mathrm{m\,s^{-2}}$ downwards.

*List the known values and the unknowns.*    $u_y = 6,\ a = -9.8,\ t = 1,\ v_y = ?$

*Use $v = u + at$ to find $v_y$.*    $v_y = 6 - 9.8 \times 1 = -3.8$

*The horizontal and vertical components can be combined and written as a vector.*

$$\mathbf{v} = 4\mathbf{i} - 3.8\mathbf{j}$$

*Sketch the vector.*

*Use Pythagoras to find the magnitude.*    $v = \sqrt{4^2 + 3.8^2} = \sqrt{30.44} = 5.52$ to 2 d.p.

*Use trigonometry to find the direction.*    $\tan\theta = \dfrac{3.8}{4} = 0.95 \Rightarrow \theta = 43.5°$ to 1 d.p.

After 1 second the ball is travelling at $5.5\,\mathrm{m\,s^{-1}}$ at $43.5°$ below the horizontal.

---

## Example 2

A stone is thrown over a cliff with an initial velocity of $12\,\mathrm{m\,s^{-1}}$ horizontally.
The stone hits the water after 5 seconds.
Find the height of the cliff above the water and the speed of the stone as it hits the water.

### Solution

*Consider the horizontal and vertical components of the motion separately.*

Horizontally the stone is moving with constant velocity. $\qquad v_x = u_x = 12$

Vertically the stone is moving with constant acceleration $9.8\,\mathrm{m\,s^{-2}}$ downwards.

Vertically: $\qquad\qquad\qquad\qquad\qquad u_y = 0, \ a = -9.8, \ t = 5, \ y = ?, \ v_y = ?$

*The height of the cliff is the magnitude of y when $t = 5$.*

Use $s = ut + \frac{1}{2}at^2$ to find y. $\qquad\qquad y = 0 - \frac{1}{2} \times 9.8 \times 5^2 = -122.5$

The height of the cliff is $122.5\,\mathrm{m}$.

Use $v = u + at$ to find $v_y$. $\qquad\qquad\qquad v_y = 0 - 9.8 \times 5 = -49$

The velocity of the stone when it hits the water is $\mathbf{v} = 12\mathbf{i} - 49\mathbf{j}$.

Find the magnitude of the velocity. $\qquad\qquad v = \sqrt{12^2 + 49^2} = 50.447\ldots$

The stone hits the water at a speed of $50.4\,\mathrm{m\,s^{-1}}$ to 1 d.p.

## Example 3

A ball is thrown with initial velocity $(8\mathbf{i} + 11\mathbf{j})\,\mathrm{m\,s^{-1}}$, where $\mathbf{i}$ and $\mathbf{j}$ are horizontal and vertical unit vectors.
Find the displacement and velocity of the ball after 2 seconds.

### Solution

*The only force acting on the ball is its weight, so it is moving as a projectile with an acceleration of $9.8\,\mathrm{m\,s^{-2}}$ vertically downwards.*
*Consider the horizontal and vertical components of the motion separately.*
*The initial horizontal component of velocity is $8\,\mathrm{m\,s^{-1}}$ and the initial vertical component of velocity is $11\,\mathrm{m\,s^{-1}}$.*

Consider the horizontal motion. $\qquad\qquad v_x = u_x = 8$

*Find x when $t = 2$.* $\qquad\qquad\qquad\qquad x = 2 \times 8 = 16$

Consider the vertical motion. $\qquad\qquad u_y = 11, \ a = -9.8, \ t = 2, \ y = ?, \ v_y = ?$

Use $s = ut + \frac{1}{2}at^2$ to find y. $\qquad\qquad y = 11 \times 2 - \frac{1}{2} \times 9.8 \times 2^2 = 2.4$

Use $v = u + at$ to find $v_y$. $\qquad\qquad\qquad v_y = 11 - 9.8 \times 2 = -8.6$

*Combine the horizontal and vertical components to find the displacement and velocity vectors.*

After 2 seconds the displacement is $(16\mathbf{i} + 2.4\mathbf{j})\,\mathrm{m}$ and the velocity is $(8\mathbf{i} - 8.6\mathbf{j})\,\mathrm{m\,s^{-1}}$.

**Exercise A** (answers p 119)

Take **i** and **j** as the horizontal and vertical unit vectors throughout this exercise.

**1** An object is projected with an initial velocity of $12\,\text{m s}^{-1}$ horizontally.
  **(a)** Show that its velocity after 2 seconds is $(12\mathbf{i} - 19.6\mathbf{j})\,\text{m s}^{-1}$.
  **(b)** Find its velocity after 4 seconds.

**2** An object is projected with initial velocity $(10\mathbf{i} + 20\mathbf{j})\,\text{m s}^{-1}$.
  **(a)** By considering the horizontal and vertical components of the motion separately, find the object's displacement when $t = 0, 1, 2, 3$ and $4$.
  **(b)** Plot these displacements on graph paper and join them to show the path of the object.
  **(c)** Find the velocity of the object when $t = 2$. Draw this vector on your graph.
  **(d)** Find the velocity of the object when $t = 4$. Draw this vector on your graph.

**3** A ball is thrown with initial velocity $(4\mathbf{i} + 7\mathbf{j})\,\text{m s}^{-1}$.
  **(a)** Find its velocity after 2 seconds.
  **(b)** Find its displacement after 2 seconds.

**4** A football is kicked with an initial velocity of $(6\mathbf{i} + 12\mathbf{j})\,\text{m s}^{-1}$.
  **(a)** What is the initial speed of the ball?
  **(b)** What angle does the initial velocity make with the horizontal?
  **(c)** What is the speed of the ball after 2 seconds?
  **(d)** What angle does the velocity make with the horizontal after 2 seconds?

**5** A stone is thrown off a cliff with initial velocity $(4\mathbf{i} + 3\mathbf{j})\,\text{m s}^{-1}$.
  The stone hits the water after 4 seconds.
  **(a)** Find the height of the cliff above the water.
  **(b)** How far from the base of the cliff does the stone hit the water?

**6** An arrow is fired from a bow with an initial velocity of $(40\mathbf{i} + 7.5\mathbf{j})\,\text{m s}^{-1}$.
  It hits the target after 1.5 seconds.
  **(a)** What is the horizontal distance from the bow to the target?
  **(b)** Given that the arrow is fired from a height of 1 metre above ground level, at what height does the arrow hit the target?

**\*7** A ball is thrown with initial velocity $(5\mathbf{i} + 6\mathbf{j})\,\text{m s}^{-1}$.
  **(a)** Write an expression for the velocity of the ball at time $t$.
  **(b)** When is the speed of the ball least?
  **(c)** What is the speed at this time?

## B Projectile problems (answers p 120)

Consider a particle projected from the origin with velocity $10\,\text{m s}^{-1}$ at an angle of $40°$ to the horizontal.

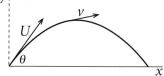

The initial velocity can be resolved into horizontal and vertical components; the horizontal and vertical components of the motion can be considered separately.

There is no force acting horizontally, so the horizontal component of the velocity remains constant.

Vertically, the weight of the particle causes an acceleration of $9.8\,\text{m s}^{-2}$ downwards.

At time $t$, the velocity of the particle can be found using $v = u + at$ in the horizontal and vertical directions.

Horizontally, $v_x = 10\cos 40°$

Vertically, $v_y = 10\sin 40° - 9.8t$

At time $t$, the displacement of the particle can be found using $s = ut + \tfrac{1}{2}at^2$ in the horizontal and vertical directions.

Horizontally, $x = 10t\cos 40°$

Vertically, $y = 10t\sin 40° - 4.9t^2$

---

**K** At time $t$, a particle projected from the origin with initial velocity $U$ at an angle of $\theta$ to the horizontal will be at the point where

$x = Ut\cos\theta$ and $y = Ut\sin\theta - \tfrac{1}{2}gt^2$

The velocity components are

$v_x = U\cos\theta$ and $v_y = U\sin\theta - gt$

---

These equations can be used to solve problems involving projectiles.

Consider a particle projected from point $O$ with initial velocity $15\,\text{m s}^{-1}$ at an angle of $30°$ to the horizontal.

The diagram shows the parabolic path of the projectile.

The **range** of the projectile is the horizontal distance travelled by the projectile from $O$ to $A$.

The **time of flight** of the projectile is the time taken to travel from $O$ to $A$, the time that the projectile is in the air.

At points $O$ and $A$, $y = 0$.

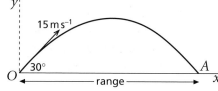

**B1** **(a)** Write down the horizontal and vertical components of the initial velocity.

**(b)** Write an equation for the height of the particle, $y$, at time $t$.

**(c)** Use this equation to find the time of flight of the projectile.

**(d)** Write an equation for the horizontal distance $x$ travelled by the particle at time $t$.

**(e)** By substituting the value of the time of flight into the equation found in part (d) find the range of the projectile.

The path of the projectile is symmetrical, so the projectile reaches its **maximum height** at the mid-point of the path.

When the projectile is at its maximum height the vertical component of its velocity is zero.

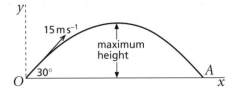

**B2** **(a)** Write an equation for the $y$-component of the velocity of the particle at time $t$.

**(b)** Use this equation to find the time when the particle is at its maximum height.

**(c)** How does this time relate to the time of flight of the particle?

**(d)** By substituting the time found in part (b) into the equation for the height of the particle, find the maximum height of the projectile.

**D** **B3** **(a)** What horizontal distance has the particle travelled when it is at its maximum height?

**(b)** What is the direction of the velocity when the projectile is at its maximum height?

The path of the projectile is in the shape of a parabola. The equation of the path of the projectile can be found by eliminating $t$ from the equations $x = 15t\cos 30°$ and $y = 15t\sin 30° - \frac{1}{2}gt^2$.

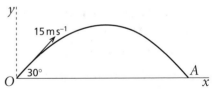

**B4** **(a)** Rearrange the equation for $x$ to find an equation for $t$ in terms of $x$.

**(b)** Substitute the expression for $t$ found in (a) into the equation for $y$ to show that $y = x\tan 30° - \dfrac{gx^2}{450}(1 + \tan^2 30°)$.

(Note that $1 + \tan^2 x = \sec^2 x$.)

**(c)** Find the height of the particle above ground level when it has travelled 3 metres horizontally.

**(d)** By forming and solving a quadratic equation find the two possible values of $x$ when the particle is 2 metres above ground level.

**B5** A particle is projected from ground level with initial velocity $10\,\text{m s}^{-1}$ at an angle of $20°$ to the horizontal.

**(a)** Find the time of flight of the projectile.

**(b)** Find its range.

**(c)** Find its maximum height.

## Example 4

A particle is projected from ground level with initial velocity $(6\mathbf{i} + 5\mathbf{j})\,\text{m s}^{-1}$.
Find the time of flight and range of the particle.

### Solution

*Consider the horizontal and vertical components of the motion separately.*

Initially $u_x = 6$, $u_y = 5$.

*Use $s = ut + \tfrac{1}{2}at^2$ for vertical motion.*
$$y = 5t - \tfrac{1}{2}gt^2$$

The particle hits the ground when $y = 0$.
$$0 = 5t - 4.9t^2$$
$$\Rightarrow \quad 0 = t(5 - 4.9t)$$
$$\Rightarrow \quad t = 0 \text{ and } 1.020\ldots$$

Initially $t = 0$, so the time of flight is $1.02\,\text{s}$ (to 3 s.f.).

*Use $s = ut + \tfrac{1}{2}at^2$ for horizontal motion.* $\quad x = 6t + 0 = 6 \times 1.02 = 6.12$

The range of the particle is $6.12\,\text{m}$ (to 3 s.f.).

---

## Example 5

A hockey ball is hit from ground level with an initial speed of $12\,\text{m s}^{-1}$ at $40°$ to the horizontal.
For how long is the ball more than 2 metres above the ground?

### Solution

*Draw a sketch showing the known values.*

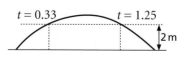

*Use $s = ut + \tfrac{1}{2}at^2$ for vertical motion.*
$$y = Ut\sin\theta - \tfrac{1}{2}gt^2$$
$$2 = 12 \times t \times \sin 40° - \tfrac{1}{2} \times 9.8 \times t^2$$
$$\Rightarrow \quad 2 = 7.713t - 4.9t^2$$

*Rearrange.*
$$4.9t^2 - 7.713t + 2 = 0$$

*Solve using the quadratic formula.*
$$t = \frac{7.713 \pm \sqrt{7.713^2 - 4 \times 4.9 \times 2}}{2 \times 4.9}$$
$$\Rightarrow t = 0.33 \text{ or } 1.25 \text{ to 2 d.p.}$$

*These are the two times when the ball is at a height of 2 metres.*
*The difference between these is the time above that height.*

Time above $2\,\text{m} = 1.25 - 0.33$
$$= 0.92\,\text{s to 2 d.p.}$$

## Example 6

A ball is kicked from ground level at a speed of $20\,\mathrm{m\,s^{-1}}$.
When it is at its maximum height it just passes over a fence 1.6 m high.
Find the angle of projection.

### Solution

*Draw a sketch showing the known values.*

*Use $v = u + at$ for vertical motion.*

$v_y = U\sin\theta - gt$

At maximum height, $v_y = 0$

so $20\sin\theta - gt = 0$

*Rearrange to express t in terms of $\theta$.*
*Leave g in the expression.*

$t = \dfrac{20\sin\theta}{g}$

*Use $s = ut + \frac{1}{2}at^2$ for vertical motion.*

$$y = Ut\sin\theta - \tfrac{1}{2}gt^2$$

$$1.6 = 20 \times \frac{20\sin\theta}{g} \times \sin\theta - \tfrac{1}{2}g \times \frac{400\sin^2\theta}{g^2}$$

$$\Rightarrow \quad 1.6 = \frac{200\sin^2\theta}{g}$$

$$\Rightarrow \sin^2\theta = \frac{1.6g}{200}$$

*Substitute the value of g at this stage.*

$$\sin\theta = \pm\sqrt{\frac{1.6g}{200}} = \pm0.28$$

*We know that $\theta$ is less than 90°.*

$\theta = 16°$ to the nearest degree

*Alternatively you could use $v^2 = u^2 + 2as$ for the vertical motion.*

---

## Exercise B (answers p 120)

**1** A ball is thrown from ground level with initial speed $20\,\mathrm{m\,s^{-1}}$ at an angle of 40°
to the horizontal.

   **(a)** Find the time of flight of the ball (the length of time the ball is in the air).

   **(b)** Find the range of the ball.

**2** A cricket ball is hit from ground level with initial velocity $(4\mathbf{i} + 10\mathbf{j})\,\mathrm{m\,s^{-1}}$.

   **(a)** Find the time of flight.

   **(b)** Find the range of the cricket ball.

**3** A ball is kicked from ground level with initial speed $16\,\mathrm{m\,s^{-1}}$ at an angle of 25°
to the horizontal.
Find the maximum height of the ball.

**4** A hockey ball is hit with an initial velocity of $14\,\mathrm{m\,s^{-1}}$ at an angle $\theta$ to the horizontal where $\sin\theta = 0.6$ as shown in the diagram.

(a) Find the maximum height of the ball.

(b) Find the range of the ball.

**5** Ann throws a ball to Julian with initial velocity $(7\mathbf{i} + 5\mathbf{j})\,\mathrm{m\,s^{-1}}$ and Julian catches it at the same height.

(a) For how long is the ball in the air?

(b) How far apart are Ann and Julian?

**6** A particle is projected from the origin with initial speed $V\,\mathrm{m\,s^{-1}}$ at an angle $\alpha$ to the horizontal.

(a) Show that the time of flight of the particle is given by $t = \dfrac{2V\sin\alpha}{g}$.

(b) Show that the range of the particle is given by $R = \dfrac{2V^2\sin\alpha\cos\alpha}{g}$.

**7** A golf ball is hit so that it leaves the ground with an initial velocity of magnitude $15\,\mathrm{m\,s^{-1}}$, at an angle $\alpha$ to the horizontal, where $\tan\alpha = \frac{3}{4}$, as shown in the diagram.

(a) How high does the ball go?

(b) Given that the ground is horizontal, how far does the ball travel before its first bounce?

**8** A ball is projected at an initial speed of $15\,\mathrm{m\,s^{-1}}$ and just passes over a wall 1.8 m high when it is at its maximum height.
Find the angle of projection of the ball.

**9** Azmat throws a ball to Susan who is 80 m away and who catches it at the same height as it was thrown from.
The ball is in the air for 5 seconds.
Find the initial speed of the ball and the angle at which it was thrown.

**10** A ball is kicked from a point 5 m horizontally away from a wall 1 m high.
The ball just passes over the wall 1 second after it is kicked.

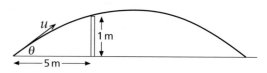

Find the initial speed of the ball and the angle at which it was kicked.

**11** An arrow is fired at a target. It hits the target after 2.5 seconds at the same level as it was fired from.
Given that the arrow was fired at an initial speed of $50\,\mathrm{m\,s^{-1}}$, find the angle of projection and the range of the arrow.

**12** Alison kicks a ball with a velocity of $10\,\mathrm{m\,s^{-1}}$ at an angle $\alpha$ to the horizontal where $\sin\alpha = 0.7$. The ball moves freely under gravity and passes over a wall 2 metres high when it is at its maximum height.

   (a) Find the time for the ball to reach its maximum height.

   (b) Find the vertical distance between the ball and the top of the wall at this time.

   (c) Find the length of time for which the ball is above the height of the wall.

**13** A stone is catapulted from ground level at an angle of $35°$ to the horizontal. Given that the stone hits the ground $25\,\mathrm{m}$ from its point of projection, find its speed of release and the time it is in the air.

**14** A particle is projected from the origin with initial speed $u$ at an angle $\theta$ to the horizontal and moves freely under gravity. When it has moved a horizontal distance $x$, its height above the point of projection is $y$.

   Show that $y = x\tan\theta - \dfrac{gx^2}{2u^2}(1 + \tan^2\theta)$.

## C Release from a given height

Consider a particle projected with velocity $12\,\mathrm{m\,s^{-1}}$ at an angle of $50°$ to the horizontal from a height $4\,\mathrm{m}$ above ground level.

At time $t$, the particle is at the point $(x, y)$.

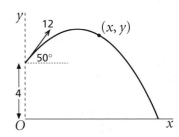

The horizontal component of the displacement of the particle is unaffected by the height of release.

$$x = 12t\cos 50°$$

The vertical component of the displacement is $4\,\mathrm{m}$ when the motion starts, causing the path of the projectile to be displaced vertically by $4\,\mathrm{m}$.

$$y = 12t\sin 50° - \tfrac{1}{2}gt^2 + 4$$

At time $t$, a projectile released at $U\,\mathrm{m\,s^{-1}}$ at $\theta$ to the horizontal from height $h\,\mathrm{m}$ above the ground is at the point where

$$x = Ut\cos\theta \quad\text{and}\quad y = Ut\sin\theta - \tfrac{1}{2}gt^2 + h$$

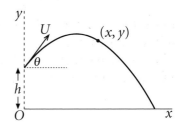

## Example 7

A ball is thrown with an initial speed of $10\,\mathrm{m\,s^{-1}}$ at an angle of $30°$ to the horizontal from a height of $1.5\,\mathrm{m}$ above ground level.
Find its maximum height above the ground and the time when it hits the ground.

### Solution

*Draw a sketch showing the known values.*

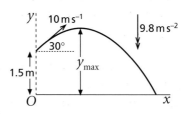

*Use $v = u + at$ for vertical motion.*

$v_y = U\sin\theta - gt$

At the maximum height $v_y = 0$,

so $10\sin 30° - gt = 0$

$\Rightarrow t = \dfrac{10\sin 30°}{g}$

*Use $s = ut + \frac{1}{2}at^2$ for vertical motion.*

Taking the height of release into account,

$y = Ut\sin\theta - \frac{1}{2}gt^2 + h$

$y = 10 \times \dfrac{10\sin 30°}{g} \times \sin 30° - \frac{1}{2}g \times \dfrac{100\sin^2 30°}{g^2} + 1.5$

$\Rightarrow y = \dfrac{50\sin^2 30°}{g} + 1.5 = 2.8$ (to 1 d.p.)

*Alternatively you could use $v^2 = u^2 + 2as$ to find the maximum height.*

*Consider when the ball hits the ground.*

The ball hits the ground when $y = 0$,

so $10t\sin 30° - \frac{1}{2}\times 9.8t^2 + 1.5 = 0$

*Rearrange.*

$4.9t^2 - 5t - 1.5 = 0$

*Solve using the quadratic formula.*

$t = \dfrac{5 \pm \sqrt{5^2 + 4 \times 4.9 \times 1.5}}{2 \times 4.9}$

$\Rightarrow t = -0.242$ or $1.263$

*The time is positive, so take the positive root.* $t = 1.3$ (to 1 d.p.)

The maximum height of the ball is $2.8\,\mathrm{m}$ and it hits the ground after $1.3\,\mathrm{s}$.

---

### Exercise C (answers p 121)

**1** A javelin is thrown from a height of $1.75\,\mathrm{m}$ at an angle of $45°$ to the horizontal with a speed of $25\,\mathrm{m\,s^{-1}}$.

(a) Find the time when the javelin is at its greatest height.

(b) What is the greatest height of the javelin above the ground?

**2** A discus is projected at an angle of 40° with a speed of 21 m s$^{-1}$ and from a height above the ground of 2 m as shown in the diagram.

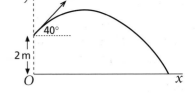

(a) Find an expression for the velocity of the discus at time $t$.

(b) Find an expression for the position vector with respect to $O$ of the discus at time $t$.

(c) What is the length of the throw?

**3** A coin is thrown into a wishing well at a velocity of $(0.5\mathbf{i} + \mathbf{j})$ m s$^{-1}$ where $\mathbf{i}$ and $\mathbf{j}$ are horizontal and upwards vertical unit vectors.
It is 10 m from the top of the well to the water.
If the coin was thrown from the top of the well, find the time taken for it to hit the water.

**4** Tim is standing 12 m away from the net on a tennis court. The net is 1 m high. He hits the tennis ball horizontally with speed $U$ m s$^{-1}$ from a height of 1.75 m.

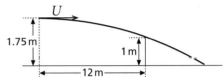

(a) Given that the ball just clears the top of the net, find the time taken for the ball to reach the net.

(b) Hence find the value of $U$.

(c) How far beyond the net does the ball land?

**5** A small relief plane is flying horizontally at 30 m s$^{-1}$. Its height is 210 m.
A package, released from the plane, just clears some trees which are 30 m high.

(a) At what horizontal distance from the trees is the package released?

(b) How far beyond the trees does the package land?

**6** A particle is projected with initial velocity $(2U\mathbf{i} + U\mathbf{j})$ m s$^{-1}$ from a height $h$ m above ground level.
Find an expression, in terms of $U$, $g$ and $h$, for the maximum height reached by the particle.

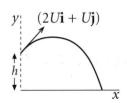

**7** Two children throw stones into the sea.
Jill throws her stone at an angle of 60° to the horizontal and speed 10 m s$^{-1}$, while Jack throws his stone at a 40° angle and can only manage an initial speed of 5 m s$^{-1}$.
The stones are thrown simultaneously and both are released at a height 1.4 m above sea level.

(a) What is the maximum height of Jill's stone?

(b) Which stone lands in the water first?

(c) Whose stone lands further away, and how much further is it?

**\*8** A fairground game involves catapulting an object towards a target
on the ground 20 m away.
The object is released at a height of 1 m above ground level.
Assume that the ground is level and that the object moves as a projectile.
Given that the catapult is angled at 45° to the horizontal and the object hits
the target, find the speed at which the object leaves the catapult.

---

## Key points

- Projectile motion takes place in a vertical plane in the shape of a parabola.
  The only force acting is the weight of the particle. (p 8)

- At time $t$, the horizontal and vertical components of position of a particle
  projected at an initial velocity $U \, \text{m s}^{-1}$ at an angle of $\theta$ to the horizontal
  are given by
  $$x = Ut\cos\theta \quad \text{and} \quad y = Ut\sin\theta - \tfrac{1}{2}gt^2$$ (p 12)

- At time $t$, the horizontal and vertical components of velocity of a particle
  projected at an initial velocity $U \, \text{m s}^{-1}$ at an angle of $\theta$ to the horizontal
  are given by
  $$v_x = U\cos\theta \quad \text{and} \quad v_y = U\sin\theta - gt$$ (p 12)

- The range of a projectile is the horizontal
  distance from $O$ to $A$.
  The time of flight is the time taken
  to travel from $O$ to $A$.
  The maximum height of the projectile occurs
  at the mid-point of the path of the projectile
  when the vertical component of the velocity is zero. (pp 12–13)

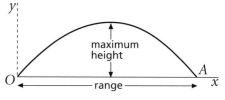

- At time $t$, a projectile released from height $h$ above the ground is at
  the point where
  $$x = Ut\cos\theta \quad \text{and} \quad y = Ut\sin\theta - \tfrac{1}{2}gt^2 + h$$ (p 17)

---

## Mixed questions (answers p 121)

**1 (a)** A stone is projected vertically upwards from ground level with initial speed $12 \, \text{m s}^{-1}$.

  **(i)** Find the maximum height reached by the stone.

  **(ii)** Find the time the stone is in the air.

**(b)** The same stone is projected from ground level with initial speed $12 \, \text{m s}^{-1}$
at an angle of 60° above the horizontal.

  **(i)** Find the maximum height reached by the stone.

  **(ii)** Find the time the stone is in the air.

**(c)** Explain why your answers to (a) and (b) are not the same.

**2** A ball is hit from the top of a vertical cliff and moves freely under gravity to land in the sea.
The ball is hit from a height of 35 m above the level of the sea and it moves off with an initial velocity of 20 m s⁻¹ horizontally as shown in the diagram.

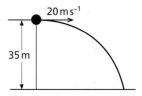

(a) Find the time between the ball being hit and it reaching the sea.

(b) Find the horizontal distance between the foot of the cliff and the point where the stone reaches the sea.

(c) Find the speed of the stone as it reaches the sea.

**3** An athlete puts a shot with initial velocity 8 m s⁻¹ at an angle of 35° to the horizontal.

(a) Find the range of the shot on horizontal ground, assuming that it is thrown from ground level.

(b) The shot is actually released at a height of 1.5 metres. Find the range of the shot taking into account the height of release.

(c) What modelling assumptions have been made in answering this question?

**4** (a) A particle is projected from the origin with initial speed $V$ m s⁻¹ at an angle $\alpha$ to the horizontal.
Show that the maximum height of the particle is $\dfrac{V^2 \sin^2 \alpha}{2g}$.

(b) A ball is hit from ground level at an angle $\alpha$ to the horizontal, where $\tan \alpha = \frac{3}{4}$.
The ball reaches a maximum height of 8 m above ground level.
Find the initial speed of the ball.

**5** David takes a free kick in a football match.
He kicks the ball with velocity $(10\mathbf{i} + 11\mathbf{j})$ m s⁻¹ from a point 20 m from the goal, where $\mathbf{i}$ and $\mathbf{j}$ are horizontal and vertical unit vectors.
The height of the goal is 2.44 m.

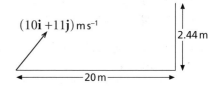

(a) How long does the ball take to travel 20 m horizontally?

(b) Assuming that the goalkeeper cannot reach the ball, does David score a goal?

(c) Find the magnitude and direction of the velocity of the ball after it has travelled 20 m horizontally.

**6** A particle is projected from point $O$ with initial velocity $(a\mathbf{i} + b\mathbf{j})$ m s⁻¹.
It hits the ground again $R$ m from $O$ after $T$ seconds.

(a) Find $a$ and $b$ in terms of $R$, $T$ and $g$.

(b) Find, in terms of $T$ and $g$, an expression for the maximum height above ground level of the particle.

**7** A stone is catapulted from a point $A$, 1.5 m above ground level, with a speed $20\,\text{m s}^{-1}$ at an angle of elevation of $60°$ as shown in the diagram.
At $B$, the stone is moving horizontally and it passes over a tree which is 5 m tall.
The motion of the stone can be modelled as that of a particle moving freely under gravity.

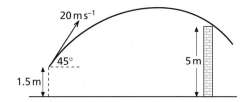

(a) Find the time taken for the stone to reach $B$.

(b) Find the height, $h$ m, of the stone above the tree at $B$.

**8** A ball is thrown with initial velocity $U\,\text{m s}^{-1}$ so that its range is equal to its maximum height.
What is its angle of projection?

**9** A ball is thrown from a height of 1.5 m above horizontal ground with an initial speed of $20\,\text{m s}^{-1}$ at an angle of elevation of $45°$.
The ball just passes over a vertical wall of height 5 m as shown in the diagram.

(a) Find the maximum height of the ball above the ground.

(b) Find the time taken for the ball to reach the wall.

(c) Find the horizontal distance from the initial position of the ball to the wall.

(d) Find the speed of the ball at the instant when it passes over the wall.

(e) Find the direction of motion of the ball at the instant when it passes over the wall.

**10** A particle is projected from a point $O$ on a horizontal plane with velocity $(2U\mathbf{i} + 5U\mathbf{j})$.
The particle strikes the plane at $A$, as shown in the diagram.

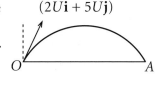

(a) Show that the time taken for the particle to travel from $O$ to $A$ is $\dfrac{10U}{g}$.

(b) Find, in terms of $g$ and $U$, the distance $OA$.

(c) Find, in terms of $U$, the initial speed of the ball.

(d) (i) Find, in terms of $g$ and $U$, the two times during the flight when the particle is moving with speed $\sqrt{5}U$.

　　(ii) Find the height of the particle above the horizontal plane at these times.

**1** A hockey ball is hit at ground level so that it moves with an initial speed of $18\,\text{m s}^{-1}$ at an angle of $30°$ above the horizontal. The motion of the ball can be modelled as that of a particle moving freely under gravity.

   **(a)** Find, to three significant figures, the greatest height above the ground reached by the ball.

   **(b)** When the ball has travelled a distance of $25\,\text{m}$ horizontally, it hits a wall. Find, to three significant figures, the height above ground at which the ball hits the wall.

   **(c)** State one physical factor that could be taken into account in any refinement of the model which would make it more realistic.

**2** A particle $P$ is projected with velocity $(4u\mathbf{i} + 2u\mathbf{j})\,\text{m s}^{-1}$ from a point $O$ on horizontal ground, where $\mathbf{i}$ and $\mathbf{j}$ are horizontal and vertical unit vectors respectively. The particle $P$ hits the ground at point $A$, a distance of $245\,\text{m}$ from $O$.

   **(a)** Show that $u = 12.25$.

   **(b)** Find the time of flight from $O$ to $A$.

   **(c)** Find the speed of the particle at $A$.

   **(d)** Find the height of the particle above the ground when it has moved a horizontal distance of $140\,\text{m}$.

**3** A ball is projected from a point $A$ with an initial speed of $15\,\text{m s}^{-1}$ at an angle $\alpha$ to the horizontal, where $\tan\alpha = \frac{4}{3}$. The point $A$ is $5\,\text{m}$ vertically above $O$, which is on horizontal ground as shown in the diagram. The ball hits the ground at point $B$.

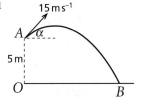

   **(a)** Find the time taken for the ball to move from $A$ to $B$.

   **(b)** Find the horizontal distance $OB$.

   **(c)** Find the speed of the ball immediately before it hits the ground.

**4** A ball is thrown from a point $4\,\text{m}$ above horizontal ground. The ball is projected at an angle $\alpha$ above the horizontal, where $\tan\alpha = \frac{3}{4}$. The ball hits the ground at a point which is a horizontal distance $8\,\text{m}$ from its point of projection, as shown. The initial speed of the ball is $u\,\text{m s}^{-1}$ and the time of flight is $T$ seconds.

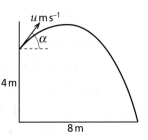

   **(a)** Prove that $uT = 10$.

   **(b)** Find the value of $u$.

As the ball hits the ground, its direction of motion makes an angle $\phi$ with the horizontal.

   **(c)** Find $\tan\phi$.

Edexcel

# 2 Variable acceleration

In this chapter you will learn how to
- work with position, velocity and acceleration vectors given as functions of time
- use Newton's second law of motion to find a force or an acceleration in one or two dimensions

## A Motion in one dimension

A small object moves along a straight line. $O$ is a fixed point on the line.

Suppose the displacement, $x$ m, of the object from $O$ at time $t$ s is given by

$$x = t + 0.1t^3$$

The position of the object at $t = 0, 1, 2, 3, 4$ is shown below.

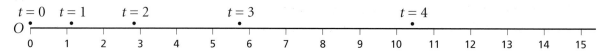

The velocity, $v$ m s$^{-1}$, of the object is the rate of change of displacement with respect to time.

$$v = \frac{dx}{dt} = 1 + 0.3t^2$$

For example, when $t = 3$, $v = 1 + 0.3 \times 3^2 = 3.7$.

The velocity of the object at $t = 0, 1, 2, 3, 4$ is shown below.

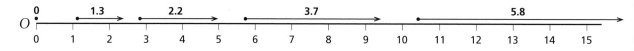

The acceleration, $a$ m s$^{-2}$, of the object is the rate of change of velocity with respect to time.

$$a = \frac{dv}{dt} = 0.6t$$

The acceleration of the object at $t = 0, 1, 2, 3, 4$ is shown below.

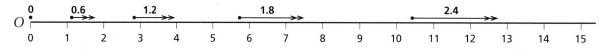

Notice that the acceleration $a$ varies in this example. So you cannot make use of the constant acceleration equations $v = u + at$ and so on. This will be the case throughout this chapter.

The velocity $v$ at time $t$ is obtained by differentiating the displacement $x$: $\quad v = \dfrac{\mathrm{d}x}{\mathrm{d}t}$

The acceleration $a$ at time $t$ is obtained by differentiating $v$: $\quad a = \dfrac{\mathrm{d}v}{\mathrm{d}t}$

So $a$ is the second derivative of $x$ with respect to $t$: $\quad a = \dfrac{\mathrm{d}^2 x}{\mathrm{d}t^2}$

The reverse of differentiation is integration.

If $a$ is given as a function of $t$, by integration we get $v$: $\quad v = \int a \, \mathrm{d}t$

By integrating $v$ we get $x$: $\quad x = \int v \, \mathrm{d}t$

Each time we integrate, a constant term has to be added. To find the value of this constant we need some extra information, as in example 1 below.

## Calculus requirements

For the work in this chapter, you need to be familiar with the calculus (differentiation and integration) covered in Core 1 and Core 2. The results you will need most frequently are as follows.

$$\frac{\mathrm{d}}{\mathrm{d}t}\left(t^n\right) = n t^{n-1} \qquad \int t^n \, \mathrm{d}t = \frac{1}{n+1} t^{n+1} + c$$

---

### Example 1

The velocity $v\,\mathrm{m\,s^{-1}}$ at time $t\,\mathrm{s}$ of an object moving on a straight line is given by the equation $v = 2t^3 - 5t^{\frac{3}{2}}$.

At time $t = 0$ the displacement of the object from the origin is $3\,\mathrm{m}$.

Find an expression for

(a) the acceleration, $a\,\mathrm{m\,s^{-2}}$, of the object in terms of $t$

(b) the displacement, $x\,\mathrm{m}$, of the object in terms of $t$

### Solution

(a) $a = \dfrac{\mathrm{d}v}{\mathrm{d}t} = 6t^2 - \frac{15}{2} t^{\frac{1}{2}}$

(b) $x = \int v \, \mathrm{d}t = \int \left(2t^3 - 5t^{\frac{3}{2}}\right) \mathrm{d}t = \frac{1}{2} t^4 - 2t^{\frac{5}{2}} + c$ where $c$ is a constant

We are told that the displacement $x = 3$ when $t = 0$, so $3 = 0 + 0 + c$, from which $c = 3$.

So $x = \frac{1}{2} t^4 - 2t^{\frac{5}{2}} + 3$

---

### Exercise A (answers p 122)

In each of these questions, an object is assumed to be moving on a straight line. At time $t$ seconds, the displacement of the object from a fixed point $O$ on the line is $x$ metres, its velocity is $v\,\mathrm{m\,s^{-1}}$ and its acceleration is $a\,\mathrm{m\,s^{-2}}$, where $x$, $v$ and $a$ are functions of $t$.

**1** Find $v$ and $a$ in terms of $t$ given that

(a) $x = 3t^4 - t^2$        (b) $x = t^3 + 4t^2 - 6$        (c) $x = t + t^{-1}$

**2** You are given that $v = 0.5t + 1.5t^2$.

   **(a)** Find an expression for $x$ in terms of $t$, including a constant of integration.

   **(b)** Given that $x = 1$ when $t = 0$,

       **(i)** find the value of the constant and hence express $x$ in terms of $t$

       **(ii)** find the value of $x$ when $t = 2$

**3** In each of the following cases, find an expression in terms of $t$ for

       **(i)** the acceleration $a$

       **(ii)** the displacement $x$, given that $x = 0$ when $t = 0$

       **(iii)** the value of $x$ when $t = 3$

   **(a)** $v = 2t^3 - 6t$         **(b)** $v = t^4 - 3t^2$         **(c)** $v = t^3 - 2t^{\frac{1}{2}}$

**4** The acceleration, $a\,\mathrm{m\,s^{-2}}$, of an object moving on a straight line is given by
$$a = 3 + 2\sqrt{t} \quad (t \geq 0)$$
At time $t = 0$ the object passes through the origin $x = 0$ with velocity $4\,\mathrm{m\,s^{-1}}$.

   **(a)** Find an expression in terms of $t$ for

       **(i)** the velocity of the object

       **(ii)** the position of the object

   **(b)** Find the speed of the object and its distance from the origin when $t = 2$.

**5** The velocity, $v\,\mathrm{m\,s^{-1}}$, of an object moving on a straight line is given by
$$v = 6t^2 - 3t$$
The object is at the origin when $t = 1$.

   **(a)** Find the times when the object is instantaneously at rest.

   **(b)** Find the distance moved by the object between these times.

**6** The acceleration, $a\,\mathrm{m\,s^{-2}}$, of an object moving on a straight line is given by
$$a = -\tfrac{3}{4}t^2$$
At time $t = 0$ the object passes through the origin with velocity $16\,\mathrm{m\,s^{-1}}$.

   **(a)** Show that the object comes to rest when $t = 4$.

   **(b)** Find the distance of the object from the origin when it comes to rest.

**7** The velocity, $v\,\mathrm{m\,s^{-1}}$, of an object moving on a straight line is given by
$$v = pt^2 + qt$$
where $p$ and $q$ are constants.

   When $t = 2$, $v = 4$ and $a = -3$.

   **(a)** Find the values of $p$ and $q$.

   **(b)** Given that $x = 5$ when $t = 2$, find the value of $x$ when $t = 4$.

## B Motion in two dimensions 1 (answers p 122)

### Position vector

In two dimensions the position vector, **r**, of a point is expressed as the sum of two components $x$ and $y$ in the directions of two perpendicular unit vectors **i** and **j**.

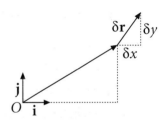

$$\mathbf{r} = x\mathbf{i} + y\mathbf{j}$$

For a moving object, each component $x$, $y$ is a function of $t$, for example

$$\mathbf{r} = 0.1t^3\mathbf{i} + (6t - t^2)\mathbf{j}$$

We can find the position vector of the object for each value of $t$.

When $t = 0$, $\mathbf{r} = 0\mathbf{i} + 0\mathbf{j}$, so the object starts at the origin.

**B1** Verify that, when $t = 1$, $\mathbf{r} = 0.1\mathbf{i} + 5\mathbf{j}$, and find **r** when $t = 2, 3, 4, 5$.

**B2** Plot on a grid the five positions for $t = 0, 1, 2, 3, 4$ and label them '$t = 0$', '$t = 1$' and so on.
Draw a smooth curve through the points to show the path of the moving object.

### Velocity vector

Suppose that in a short time interval $\delta t$, the change in the position vector is $\delta\mathbf{r} = \delta x\mathbf{i} + \delta y\mathbf{j}$, as shown in this diagram.

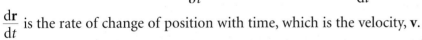

Dividing by $\delta t$, we have $\dfrac{\delta\mathbf{r}}{\delta t} = \dfrac{\delta x}{\delta t}\mathbf{i} + \dfrac{\delta y}{\delta t}\mathbf{j}$.

As $\delta t$ gets smaller and smaller, $\dfrac{\delta\mathbf{r}}{\delta t}$ gets closer and closer to $\dfrac{d\mathbf{r}}{dt}$.

$\dfrac{d\mathbf{r}}{dt}$ is the rate of change of position with time, which is the velocity, **v**.

Similarly $\dfrac{\delta x}{\delta t}$ and $\dfrac{\delta y}{\delta t}$ get closer and closer to $\dfrac{dx}{dt}$ and $\dfrac{dy}{dt}$.

So $\mathbf{v} = \dfrac{dx}{dt}\mathbf{i} + \dfrac{dy}{dt}\mathbf{j}$.

This means that **v** is obtained from **r** by differentiating each component separately.

For example, if $\mathbf{r} = 0.1t^3\mathbf{i} + (6t - t^2)\mathbf{j}$

then $\mathbf{v} = \dfrac{d\mathbf{r}}{dt} = 0.3t^2\mathbf{i} + (6 - 2t)\mathbf{j}$

**B3** Verify that, when $t = 0$, $\mathbf{v} = 6\mathbf{j}$, and find **v** when $t = 1, 2, 3, 4, 5$.

## Acceleration vector

The acceleration **a** is the rate of change of velocity, or $\frac{d\mathbf{v}}{dt}$.

This is obtained by differentiating each component of **v** separately:

$$\mathbf{v} = 0.3t^2\mathbf{i} + (6 - 2t)\mathbf{j}$$

$$\mathbf{a} = \frac{d\mathbf{v}}{dt} = 0.6t\mathbf{i} - 2\mathbf{j}$$

**B4** Find **a** when $t = 0, 1, 2, 3, 4, 5$.

## Position, velocity and acceleration vectors

The diagram below shows the path of the object, together with the velocity and acceleration vectors at each of the points where $t = 0, 1, 2, 3, 4, 5$.

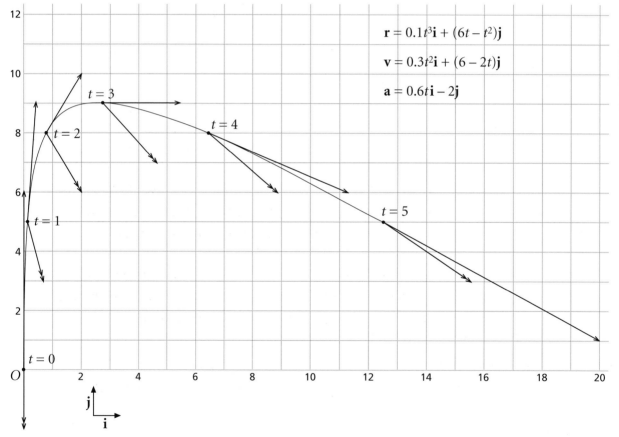

Notice that

- the velocity is always in the direction of the tangent to the path of the object
- the acceleration is always directed towards the 'inside' of the curve of the path

The direction in which an object is moving at an instant is the direction of its velocity.

If the component of velocity in the **i**-direction is 0, then at that instant the object is moving in the **j**-direction, and vice versa.

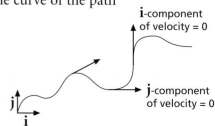

The diagram below shows the path of an object whose position is given by

$$\mathbf{r} = 0.5t^2\mathbf{i} + (5t - 0.2t^3)\mathbf{j}$$

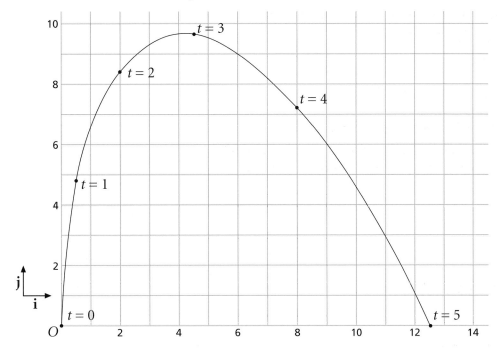

**B5** (a) Verify that the positions at $t = 0, 1, 2, 3, 4, 5$ shown in the diagram are correct.

(b) By differentiating $\mathbf{r}$ with respect to $t$, find an expression for the velocity $\mathbf{v}$.

(c) Find the value of $\mathbf{v}$ when $t = 0, 1, 2, 3, 4, 5$, and check from the diagram that the results you get are reasonable.

(d) Find, to 2 d.p., the value of $t$ when the velocity of the object is in the $\mathbf{i}$-direction.

(e) By differentiating $\mathbf{v}$ with respect to $t$, find an expression for the acceleration $\mathbf{a}$.

(f) Find the value of $\mathbf{a}$ when $t = 0, 1, 2, 3, 4, 5$, and check from the diagram that the results you get are reasonable.

**B6** Find expressions for $\mathbf{v}$ and $\mathbf{a}$ for each of the following paths.

(a) $\mathbf{r} = 5t^2\mathbf{i} + 4t\mathbf{j}$      (b) $\mathbf{r} = (2t^2 - 3t)\mathbf{i} + 4t^3\mathbf{j}$      (c) $\mathbf{r} = (t^3 - 2t)\mathbf{i} - t^4\mathbf{j}$

### Dot notation

Differentiation with respect to time can be represented using dot notation.

$\mathbf{v} = \dfrac{d\mathbf{r}}{dt}$ can also be written as $\dot{\mathbf{r}}$.

$\mathbf{a} = \dfrac{d\mathbf{v}}{dt} = \dfrac{d^2\mathbf{r}}{dt^2}$ can also be written as $\ddot{\mathbf{r}}$.

**B7** If $\mathbf{r} = 6t^{\frac{1}{2}}\mathbf{i} + (4t - 8t^3)\mathbf{j}$, find

(a) $\dot{\mathbf{r}}$                         (b) $\ddot{\mathbf{r}}$

The magnitude of **r** is denoted by $|\mathbf{r}|$ or $r$.
Similarly for $|\mathbf{v}|$ and $|\mathbf{a}|$.

The magnitude of a vector is found by using Pythagoras's theorem. The angle the vector makes with the **i**-direction can be found using trigonometry.

$|\mathbf{r}|$ is the distance from the origin.

$|\mathbf{v}|$ is the speed.

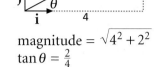

magnitude $= \sqrt{4^2 + 2^2}$

$\tan \theta = \frac{2}{4}$

**B8** The velocity, $\mathbf{v}\,\mathrm{m\,s^{-1}}$, of an object at time $t$ s is given by

$$\mathbf{v} = (3t + 2)\mathbf{i} + (t^2 - 1)\mathbf{j}$$

(a) Find **v** when $t = 2$.

(b) Find the speed of the object when $t = 2$.

(c) Find the angle that the velocity makes with the **i**-direction when $t = 2$.

(d) Find the acceleration $\mathbf{a}\,\mathrm{m\,s^{-2}}$ at time $t$.

(e) Find the magnitude of the acceleration when $t = 2$.

(f) Find the angle that the acceleration makes with the **i**-direction when $t = 2$.

**K**  If $\mathbf{r} = \mathrm{f}(t)\mathbf{i} + \mathrm{g}(t)\mathbf{j}$,

then $\mathbf{v} = \dfrac{\mathrm{d}\mathbf{r}}{\mathrm{d}t} = \dot{\mathbf{r}} = \mathrm{f}'(t)\mathbf{i} + \mathrm{g}'(t)\mathbf{j}$

and $\mathbf{a} = \dfrac{\mathrm{d}\mathbf{v}}{\mathrm{d}t} = \ddot{\mathbf{r}} = \mathrm{f}''(t)\mathbf{i} + \mathrm{g}''(t)\mathbf{j}$

---

### Example 2

The position vector, $\mathbf{r}\,\mathrm{m}$, of a particle at time $t$ s is given by $\mathbf{r} = (5t^2 - 4t)\mathbf{i} + (20 - 3t^2)\mathbf{j}$.

(a) Find an expression for the velocity $\mathbf{v}\,\mathrm{m\,s^{-1}}$ of the particle at time $t$.

(b) Find the value of $t$ for which the particle is moving in the direction of **j**.

(c) Show that the acceleration of the particle is constant and find its magnitude.

### Solution

(a) $\mathbf{v} = \dfrac{\mathrm{d}\mathbf{r}}{\mathrm{d}t} = (10t - 4)\mathbf{i} - 6t\mathbf{j}$

(b) If the particle is moving in the direction of **j**, the **i**-component of its velocity is 0.

$10t - 4 = 0 \implies t = 0.4$

(c) $\mathbf{a} = \dfrac{\mathrm{d}\mathbf{v}}{\mathrm{d}t} = 10\mathbf{i} - 6\mathbf{j}$, which is constant.

$|\mathbf{a}| = \sqrt{10^2 + 6^2} = 11.7$ to 3 s.f.

---

**Example 3**

The position vector $\mathbf{r}$ km, at time $t$ hours, of a boat relative to a point $O$ on the edge of a lake is given by

$$\mathbf{r} = (t^3 - 5t^2 + 3t)\mathbf{i} + (t^3 - 8t^2 + 5t)\mathbf{j}$$

where $\mathbf{i}$ and $\mathbf{j}$ are unit vectors in the directions east and north respectively. Find the value of $t$ for which the boat is moving south-east.

**Solution**

The direction of the boat is the direction of its velocity $\mathbf{v}$.

$$\mathbf{v} = \frac{d\mathbf{r}}{dt} = (3t^2 - 10t + 3)\mathbf{i} + (3t^2 - 16t + 5)\mathbf{j}$$

South-east is the direction of the vector $\mathbf{i} - \mathbf{j}$. (See diagram.)

When $\mathbf{v}$ is in the direction south-east, $\mathbf{v}$ must be a multiple of $\mathbf{i} - \mathbf{j}$.
So $\mathbf{v}$ must be of the form $A(\mathbf{i} - \mathbf{j}) = A\mathbf{i} - A\mathbf{j}$.
In other words, ($\mathbf{j}$-component of $\mathbf{v}$) $= -$($\mathbf{i}$-component of $\mathbf{v}$).

So $3t^2 - 16t + 5 = -3t^2 + 10t - 3 \Rightarrow 6t^2 - 26t + 8 = 0 \Rightarrow 3t^2 - 13t + 4 = 0$
$\Rightarrow (3t - 1)(t - 4) = 0 \Rightarrow t = \frac{1}{3}, t = 4$

When $t = \frac{1}{3}$, $\mathbf{v} = 0\mathbf{i} + 0\mathbf{j} = 0$          When $t = 4$, $\mathbf{v} = 11\mathbf{i} - 11\mathbf{j}$

The boat is instantaneously at rest when $t = \frac{1}{3}$, so the boat is moving south-east when $t = 4$.

---

**Exercise B** (answers p 123)

Give answers to three significant figures where appropriate.

**1** The position vector, $\mathbf{r}$ m, of a particle at time $t$ s is given by
$$\mathbf{r} = (5t - t^2)\mathbf{i} + t^3\mathbf{j}$$
(a) Find an expression for the velocity of the particle at time $t$.
(b) Find the speed of the particle when $t = 2$.
(c) Find an expression for the acceleration of the particle at time $t$.
(d) Find the magnitude of the acceleration when $t = 2$.

**2** The velocity, $\mathbf{v}$ m s$^{-1}$, of a particle at time $t$ s is given by
$$\mathbf{v} = (t + t^3)\mathbf{i} - 4t^2\mathbf{j}$$
(a) Find an expression for the acceleration of the particle at time $t$.
(b) Find the magnitude of the acceleration when $t = 3$.

**3** The position vector, $\mathbf{r}$ m, of a particle at time $t$ s is given by
$$\mathbf{r} = 16t^2\mathbf{i} + (t^3 - 48t)\mathbf{j} \quad (t \geq 0)$$
(a) Find an expression for the velocity of the particle at time $t$.
(b) Find the time at which the particle is moving in the $\mathbf{i}$-direction.
(c) Find the time at which the particle is moving in the direction of the vector $\mathbf{i} - \mathbf{j}$.

**4** The position vector, **r** m, of a particle at time $t$ s is given by
$$\mathbf{r} = (t^3 - 7t^2 + 8)\mathbf{i} + (t^2 - 6t)\mathbf{j}$$

(a) Find an expression for the velocity of the particle at time $t$.

(b) Find the value of $t$ when the particle is moving in the direction of **i**.

(c) Find the speed of the particle at this time.

(d) Show that there are two values of $t$ for which the particle is moving in the direction of **j** and find these values.

(e) Find the speed of the particle at each of these times.

**5** The position vector, **r** cm, of a point moving on a screen is given by
$$\mathbf{r} = \left(\tfrac{1}{3}t^3 - 4t\right)\mathbf{i} + \left(6t^2 - t^3\right)\mathbf{j}$$
where **i** is a horizontal unit vector and **j** is a vertical unit vector.

(a) Find an expression for the velocity of the moving point at time $t$.

(b) Show that when $t = 2$ the velocity of the point is vertical.

(c) Find the values of $t$ for which the velocity is horizontal.

**6** The position vector, **r** m, of a particle at time $t$ s is given by
$$\mathbf{r} = 2t^3\mathbf{i} + (t^2 + 4t)\mathbf{j} \quad (t \geq 0)$$

(a) Find an expression for the velocity of the particle at time $t$.

(b) (i) Find the time at which the particle is moving in the direction of $\mathbf{i} + \mathbf{j}$.

(ii) Find the magnitude of the acceleration at this time.

**7** The unit vectors **i** and **j** are directed east and north respectively.
The position vector, **r** m, of a boat at time $t$ s is given by
$$\mathbf{r} = 0.2t^2\mathbf{i} + (2t - 0.1t^2)\mathbf{j}$$

(a) Find an expression for the velocity of the boat at time $t$.

(b) Find the speed of the boat when $t = 4$.

(c) (i) Show that the acceleration is constant.

(ii) Find the magnitude of the acceleration.

(d) (i) Find the time when the boat is travelling due east.

(ii) Find the speed of the boat at this time.

(iii) Find the distance of the boat from its starting point at this time.

**8** The position vector, **r** m, of a particle at time $t$ s is given by
$$\mathbf{r} = t^{\frac{3}{2}}\mathbf{i} + 4t^{\frac{1}{2}}\mathbf{j}$$

(a) Find the distance of the particle from the origin at time $t = 1$.

(b) Find the speed of the particle at time $t = 1$.

(c) Find the magnitude of the acceleration of the particle at time $t = 1$.

## C Motion in two dimensions 2 (answers p 124)

Because $\mathbf{v} = \dfrac{d\mathbf{r}}{dt}$, it follows that $\mathbf{r} = \int \mathbf{v}\,dt$.

For example, suppose $\mathbf{v} = t^2\mathbf{i} + t^4\mathbf{j}$.

Then $\mathbf{r} = \int \mathbf{v}\,dt = \int (t^2\mathbf{i} + t^4\mathbf{j})\,dt$

$\qquad\qquad = \left(\int t^2\,dt\right)\mathbf{i} + \left(\int t^4\,dt\right)\mathbf{j}$      separating into components

$\qquad\qquad = \left(\tfrac{1}{3}t^3 + c_1\right)\mathbf{i} + \left(\tfrac{1}{5}t^5 + c_2\right)\mathbf{j}$      integrating each component and including a constant of integration for each

$\qquad\qquad = \tfrac{1}{3}t^3\mathbf{i} + \tfrac{1}{5}t^5\mathbf{j} + (c_1\mathbf{i} + c_2\mathbf{j})$      collecting the constants of integration

The two constants of integration can be written as a single constant vector $\mathbf{c}$:

$\qquad \mathbf{r} = \tfrac{1}{3}t^3\mathbf{i} + \tfrac{1}{5}t^5\mathbf{j} + \mathbf{c}$

All that has happened here is that each component of $\mathbf{v}$ has been integrated and a constant of integration has been added. But as we are working in two dimensions, the constant of integration is a vector $\mathbf{c}$.

To find the value of $\mathbf{c}$, we need more information.

For example, suppose that $\mathbf{r} = 2\mathbf{i}$ when $t = 0$.

Then $\tfrac{1}{3}0^3\mathbf{i} + \tfrac{1}{5}0^5\mathbf{j} + \mathbf{c} = 2\mathbf{i}$

$\Rightarrow \qquad\qquad\qquad \mathbf{c} = 2\mathbf{i}$

So $\mathbf{r} = \tfrac{1}{3}t^3\mathbf{i} + \tfrac{1}{5}t^5\mathbf{j} + 2\mathbf{i}$

$\qquad = \left(\tfrac{1}{3}t^3 + 2\right)\mathbf{i} + \tfrac{1}{5}t^5\mathbf{j}$    (collecting terms in $\mathbf{i}$ and $\mathbf{j}$)

**C1** Given that
$$\mathbf{v} = 6t^2\mathbf{i} + (4t - 3)\mathbf{j}$$
and that $\mathbf{r} = \mathbf{i} + \mathbf{j}$ when $t = 0$, find $\mathbf{r}$ in terms of $t$.

**C2** Given that
$$\mathbf{v} = t^{\frac{1}{2}}\mathbf{i} + t^{-\frac{1}{2}}\mathbf{j}$$
and that $\mathbf{r} = \mathbf{0}$ $(= 0\mathbf{i} + 0\mathbf{j})$ when $t = 0$, find $\mathbf{r}$ in terms of $t$.

The process of finding $\mathbf{v}$ from $\mathbf{a}$ by integration is similar: $\mathbf{v} = \int \mathbf{a}\,dt$.

**C3** Given that
$$\mathbf{a} = 3(t^2 - 4)\mathbf{i} + (t + 2)\mathbf{j}$$
and that $\mathbf{v} = 2\mathbf{i} - \mathbf{j}$ when $t = 0$, find $\mathbf{v}$ in terms of $t$.

**K**    $\mathbf{v} = \int \mathbf{a}\,dt$     $\mathbf{r} = \int \mathbf{v}\,dt$      Include a constant of integration $\mathbf{c}$.

## Example 4

The acceleration, $a\,m\,s^{-2}$, of a particle at time $t$ s is given by $\mathbf{a} = (t^2 - 2t)\mathbf{i} + 3\mathbf{j}$.
The particle passes throught the origin $\mathbf{r} = \mathbf{0}$ with velocity $\mathbf{v} = 4\mathbf{i}$ when $t = 0$.

Find expressions for the velocity $\mathbf{v}$ and the position vector $\mathbf{r}$ of the particle in terms of $t$.

### Solution

$\mathbf{v} = \int \mathbf{a}\,dt = \left(\frac{1}{3}t^3 - t^2\right)\mathbf{i} + 3t\mathbf{j} + \mathbf{c}$

When $t = 0$, $\mathbf{v} = 4\mathbf{i}$. So $0\mathbf{i} + 0\mathbf{j} + \mathbf{c} = 4\mathbf{i} \implies \mathbf{c} = 4\mathbf{i}$

So $\mathbf{v} = \left(\frac{1}{3}t^3 - t^2 + 4\right)\mathbf{i} + 3t\mathbf{j}$

$\mathbf{r} = \int \mathbf{v}\,dt = \left(\frac{1}{12}t^4 - \frac{1}{3}t^3 + 4t\right)\mathbf{i} + \frac{3}{2}t^2\mathbf{j} + \mathbf{c}$

When $t = 0$, $\mathbf{r} = \mathbf{0}$. So $\mathbf{c} = \mathbf{0}$

So $\mathbf{r} = \left(\frac{1}{12}t^4 - \frac{1}{3}t^3 + 4t\right)\mathbf{i} + \frac{3}{2}t^2\mathbf{j}$

---

## Exercise C (answers p 124)

**1** The velocity, $\mathbf{v}\,m\,s^{-1}$, of a particle at time $t$ s is given by $\mathbf{v} = (8t - 6t^2)\mathbf{i} + (4t + 3t^2)\mathbf{j}$.
Given that $\mathbf{r} = \mathbf{0}$ when $t = 0$, find an expression for $\mathbf{r}$ in terms of $t$.

**2** The acceleration, $\mathbf{a}\,m\,s^{-2}$, of a particle at time $t$ s is given by $\mathbf{a} = (2 + 5t)\mathbf{i} + (4t + t^2)\mathbf{j}$.
Given that the velocity $\mathbf{v} = 2\mathbf{i}$ when $t = 0$, find an expression for $\mathbf{v}$ in terms of $t$.

**3** The acceleration, $\mathbf{a}\,m\,s^{-2}$, of a particle at time $t$ s is given by $\mathbf{a} = (t - 1)\mathbf{i} + (t^3 - t)\mathbf{j}$.
At time $t = 0$, the particle passes through the origin with velocity $5\mathbf{j}\,m\,s^{-1}$.

Find an expression for

(a) $\mathbf{v}$ in terms of $t$             (b) $\mathbf{r}$ in terms of $t$

**4** In each case below, find expressions for $\mathbf{v}$ and for $\mathbf{r}$ in terms of $t$, given the velocity and the position of the particle at time $t = 0$.
Give each answer in the form $a\mathbf{i} + b\mathbf{j}$.

(a) $\mathbf{a} = (9t^2 + 2)\mathbf{i} + (12t^2 - 1)\mathbf{j}$        $\mathbf{v} = \mathbf{i} + \mathbf{j}$ and $\mathbf{r} = \mathbf{0}$ when $t = 0$

(b) $\mathbf{a} = (t^3 - 2)\mathbf{i} + 2t^2\mathbf{j}$            $\mathbf{v} = 4\mathbf{j}$ and $\mathbf{r} = \mathbf{i} + \mathbf{j}$ when $t = 0$

(c) $\mathbf{a} = \sqrt{t}\,\mathbf{i} - 4\mathbf{j}$                 $\mathbf{v} = \mathbf{0}$ and $\mathbf{r} = \mathbf{0}$ when $t = 0$

**5** The velocity, $\mathbf{v}\,m\,s^{-1}$, of a particle at time $t$ s is given by $\mathbf{v} = (3t - t^2)\mathbf{i} + 8t^3\mathbf{j}$.
At time $t = 0$, the particle passes through the origin.

(a) Find the values of $t$ for which the particle is moving in the direction of $\mathbf{j}$.

(b) Find an expression for the acceleration of the particle at time $t$.

(c) Find an expression for the position of the particle at time $t$.

**6** The velocity, $\mathbf{v}\,m\,s^{-1}$, of a particle at time $t$ s is given by $\mathbf{v} = 4t\mathbf{i} + (2t - 3t^2)\mathbf{j}$.
At time $t = 0$, the particle passes through the point with position vector $\mathbf{r} = 2\mathbf{i} + 4\mathbf{j}$.
Find the distance of the particle from the origin when $t = 5$.

## D Using Newton's laws in one dimension (answers p 124)

Newton's second law of motion, in the form $F = ma$, applies to the motion of a particle in a straight line.

If the resultant force $F$ newtons acting on a particle varies with time, so does the acceleration $a$ (and vice versa).

For example, suppose the resultant force $F$ newtons acting on a particle of mass 5 kg is given by

$$F = 4t - 3t^2$$

Substituting for $F$ and $m$ in $F = ma$, we get $4t - 3t^2 = 5a$

$$\Rightarrow \quad a = 0.8t - 0.6t^2$$

Once an expression for $a$ has been found, it can be integrated to get an expression for $v$, and so on.

If, on the other hand, an expression for $a$ is given, using $F = ma$ gives an expression for $F$.

**D1** The displacement $x$ m at time $t$ s of a particle of mass 2.5 kg moving on a straight line is given by

$$x = 3t^2 - 2t^3$$

(a) By differentiation, find an expression for the velocity $v \, \text{m s}^{-1}$ at time $t$.

(b) Find an expression for the acceleration $a \, \text{m s}^{-1}$ at time $t$.

(c) Use Newton's second law to find an expression for the resultant force, $F$ newtons, acting on the particle at time $t$.

(d) Find the magnitude of the resultant force when $t = 2$.

(e) Find the time at which the force is instantaneously zero.

**D2** A particle of mass 0.4 kg moves in a straight line. At time $t$ s a force $F = 6\sqrt{t} - 2$ newtons acts on the particle and is the only force acting.

(a) Find an expression for the acceleration, $a \, \text{m s}^{-2}$, of the particle at time $t$.

(b) Find the value of $t$ for which the acceleration is zero.

The particle is instantaneously at rest at the origin at time $t = 0$.

(c) Find an expression for the velocity of the particle at time $t$.

(d) Find an expression for the displacement of the particle from the origin at time $t$.

(e) Show that there is a value of $t$ other than $t = 0$ for which the particle is instantaneously at rest, and find this value.

(f) Find the force acting on the particle at each of the times when it is instantaneously at rest.

K  Newton's second law $F = ma$ applies when $F$ and $a$ are functions of time.

If $F$ is given as a function of $t$, then an expression for $a$ in terms of $t$ can be derived, and vice versa.

## Example 5

A particle of mass 0.5 kg moves on a straight line. At time $t$ s a force $F = 6t - t^2$ newtons acts on the particle. At time $t = 0$ the particle is instantaneously at rest at the origin.

(a) Find an expression for the acceleration of the particle at time $t$.

(b) Find an expression for the velocity of the particle at time $t$.

(c) The particle is instantaneously at rest when $t = 0$.
When is it next instantaneously at rest?

## Solution

(a) Use N2L (Newton's 2nd law). $\qquad F = ma$

$$6t - t^2 = 0.5a$$

$$\Rightarrow a = 12t - 2t^2$$

(b) Integrate $a$ to get $v$. $\qquad v = 6t^2 - \frac{2}{3}t^3 + c$

When $t = 0$, $v = 0$, so $c = 0$. $\qquad v = 6t^2 - \frac{2}{3}t^3$

(c) When $v = 0$, $6t^2 - \frac{2}{3}t^3 = 0 \Rightarrow t^2\left(6 - \frac{2}{3}t\right) = 0 \Rightarrow t = 0$ or $t = 9$

The particle is next instantaneously at rest when $t = 9$.

---

## Exercise D (answers p 125)

**1** A particle of mass 0.5 kg moves on a straight line. At time $t$ s a force $F = t^2 - 3t$ newtons acts on the particle. At time $t = 0$ the particle is instantaneously at rest at the origin.

(a) Find an expression for the acceleration of the particle at time $t$.

(b) Find an expression for the velocity of the particle at time $t$.

(c) The particle is instantaneously at rest when $t = 0$. When is it next instantaneously at rest?

(d) Find an expression for the displacement of the particle at time $t$.

(e) Find the time at which the particle returns to the origin.

(f) Find the velocity of the particle as it passes through the origin at this time.

**2** The velocity $v$ m s$^{-1}$ at time $t$ s of a particle of mass 0.5 kg moving on a straight line is given by $v = 10t - 4t^2$.

(a) Find an expression for the acceleration of the particle at time $t$.

(b) Find an expression for the resultant force acting on the particle at time $t$.

(c) Find the time at which the force is instantaneously zero.

(d) (i) Find the times at which the particle is instantaneously at rest.

(ii) Find the resultant force on the particle at these times.

**3** A particle of mass 0.2 kg moves on a straight line. A force of $(6 - kt)$ newtons, where $k$ is a positive constant, acts at time $t$ s on the particle.

(a) Find an expression for the acceleration, $a$ m s$^{-2}$, of the particle at time $t$.

At time $t = 0$, the particle is instantaneously at rest at the origin $x = 0$.

(b) Find an expression for the velocity, $v$ m s$^{-1}$, of the particle at time $t$.

(c) Find an expression for the displacement, $x$ m, of the particle at time $t$.

(d) Given that the particle passes the origin at time $t = 4$, find

    (i) the value of $k$

    (ii) the velocity with which the particle passes the origin at time $t = 4$

**4** A particle of mass 0.05 kg moves on a straight line. A force of $1.5\sqrt{t}$ newtons acts at time $t$ s on the particle, where $t \geq 0$.

(a) Find an expression for the acceleration of the particle at time $t$.

At time $t = 0$, the particle is at the origin $x = 0$ and moving with velocity 2 m s$^{-1}$.

(b) Find an expression for the velocity of the particle at time $t$.

(c) Find the time when the particle is moving with speed 69.5 m s$^{-1}$.

(d) Find an expression for the displacement $x$ m at time $t$.

(e) Find the distance of the particle from the origin when the speed is 69.5 m s$^{-1}$.

**5** The velocity $v$ m s$^{-1}$ at time $t$ s of a particle of mass 1.5 kg moving on a straight line is given by

$$v = 4t^2 - 3t$$

Find an expression for the resultant force on the particle at time $t$.

**6** A small sphere of mass 0.05 kg rolls along a straight horizontal groove. Its displacement $x$ m from the origin at time $t$ seconds is given by

$$x = 20t - 3t^2 - \tfrac{1}{2}t^3$$

Find an expression for the magnitude of the horizontal force on the sphere at time $t$.

## E Using Newton's laws in two dimensions (answers p 125)

Newton's second law of motion in vector form is $\mathbf{F} = m\mathbf{a}$.
This equation may be used either to find $\mathbf{F}$ from $\mathbf{a}$ or to find $\mathbf{a}$ from $\mathbf{F}$.
If $\mathbf{a}$ is a function of time then so is $\mathbf{F}$ (and vice versa).

**E1** The velocity $\mathbf{v}$ m s$^{-1}$ at time $t$ s of a particle of mass 3 kg is given by

$$\mathbf{v} = (5t^2 - 2t)\mathbf{i} + 2t^3\mathbf{j}$$

(a) Find the acceleration $\mathbf{a}$ m s$^{-2}$ in terms of $t$.

(b) Use Newton's second law to show that the resultant force $\mathbf{F}$ newtons acting on the particle at time $t$ s is given by

$$\mathbf{F} = 6(5t - 1)\mathbf{i} + 18t^2\mathbf{j}$$

(c) Show that at time $t = 1$ the magnitude of the force is 30 newtons.

**E2** A particle of mass 2.5 kg is at the origin at time $t = 0$ and moving with velocity $(3\mathbf{i} - 2\mathbf{j})\,\mathrm{m\,s}^{-1}$. It is acted on by a force $\mathbf{F}$ newtons, where $\mathbf{F} = 15t^2\mathbf{i}$.

(a) Use Newton's second law to find an expression for the acceleration, $\mathbf{a}\,\mathrm{m\,s}^{-2}$, of the particle in terms of $t$.

(b) By integration find an expression for the velocity, $\mathbf{v}\,\mathrm{m\,s}^{-1}$, of the particle in terms of $t$, including a constant of integration.

(c) Use the information about the velocity when $t = 0$ to show that
$$\mathbf{v} = (2t^3 + 3)\mathbf{i} - 2\mathbf{j}$$

(d) By integrating again and using the information about the position of the particle when $t = 0$, find $\mathbf{r}$ in terms of $t$.

(e) Find the distance of the particle from the origin when $t = 2$, correct to three significant figures.

> **K** In two dimensions, Newton's second law of motion is $\mathbf{F} = m\mathbf{a}$.
>
> If $\mathbf{F}$ is a function of time $t$ then so is $\mathbf{a}$ (and vice versa).

---

## Example 6

A particle of mass 4 kg is acted on by a force $\mathbf{F}$ newtons at time $t$ seconds, where
$$\mathbf{F} = 4t\mathbf{i} - 6t^2\mathbf{j}$$
No other force acts on the particle.

(a) Find an expression for the acceleration of the particle.

(b) At time $t = 0$, the velocity of the particle is $6\mathbf{i}\,\mathrm{m\,s}^{-1}$. Find an expression for the velocity $\mathbf{v}\,\mathrm{m\,s}^{-1}$ at time $t$.

(c) The particle is initially at the origin. Find an expression for the position vector, $\mathbf{r}$ metres, of the particle at time $t$.

## Solution

(a) Use N2L. $\mathbf{F} = m\mathbf{a}$
$$4t\mathbf{i} - 6t^2\mathbf{j} = 4\mathbf{a}, \text{ so } \mathbf{a} = t\mathbf{i} - \tfrac{3}{2}t^2\mathbf{j}$$

(b) Integrate $\mathbf{a}$. $\mathbf{v} = \tfrac{1}{2}t^2\mathbf{i} - \tfrac{1}{2}t^3\mathbf{j} + \mathbf{c}$

When $t = 0$, $\mathbf{v} = 6\mathbf{i}$

So $6\mathbf{i} = 0\mathbf{i} - 0\mathbf{j} + \mathbf{c} \Rightarrow \mathbf{c} = 6\mathbf{i}$

So $\mathbf{v} = \tfrac{1}{2}t^2\mathbf{i} - \tfrac{1}{2}t^3\mathbf{j} + 6\mathbf{i}$
$$= \left(\tfrac{1}{2}t^2 + 6\right)\mathbf{i} - \tfrac{1}{2}t^3\mathbf{j}$$

(c) Integrate $\mathbf{v}$. $\mathbf{r} = \left(\tfrac{1}{6}t^3 + 6t\right)\mathbf{i} - \tfrac{1}{8}t^4\mathbf{j} + \mathbf{c}$

When $t = 0$, $\mathbf{r} = \mathbf{0}$

So $\mathbf{0} = 0\mathbf{i} - 0\mathbf{j} + \mathbf{c} \Rightarrow \mathbf{c} = \mathbf{0}$

So $\mathbf{r} = \left(\tfrac{1}{6}t^3 + 6t\right)\mathbf{i} - \tfrac{1}{8}t^4\mathbf{j}$

---

**Exercise E** (answers p 125)

1 The acceleration, $\mathbf{a}\,\mathrm{m\,s^{-2}}$, of a particle at time $t\,\mathrm{s}$ is given by $\mathbf{a} = (4 - 5t)\mathbf{i} + (t - t^2)\mathbf{j}$. The mass of the particle is $0.4\,\mathrm{kg}$. Find an expression for the resultant force on the particle at time $t$.

2 The velocity, $\mathbf{v}\,\mathrm{m\,s^{-1}}$, of a particle at time $t\,\mathrm{s}$ is given by $\mathbf{v} = (10t - t^2)\mathbf{i} + (7t + 3)\mathbf{j}$. The mass of the particle is $0.2\,\mathrm{kg}$. Find an expression for

(a) the acceleration of the particle at time $t$

(b) the resultant force on the particle at time $t$

3 The resultant force $\mathbf{F}$ newtons acting on a particle of mass $0.5\,\mathrm{kg}$ at time $t\,\mathrm{s}$ is given by
$$\mathbf{F} = (t^2 - 2)\mathbf{i} + (2t + 3)\mathbf{j}$$

(a) Find an expression for the acceleration of the particle at time $t$.

(b) Given that the velocity of the particle at time $t = 0$ is $4\mathbf{i}\,\mathrm{m\,s^{-1}}$, find an expression for the velocity at time $t$.

4 The position vector, $\mathbf{r}\,\mathrm{m}$, of a particle of mass $2\,\mathrm{kg}$ at time $t\,\mathrm{s}$ is given by
$$\mathbf{r} = t^3\mathbf{i} + (t^2 - 2t)\mathbf{j}$$

(a) Find an expression for the velocity $\mathbf{v}\,\mathrm{m\,s^{-1}}$ at time $t$.

(b) Find an expression for the acceleration $\mathbf{a}\,\mathrm{m\,s^{-2}}$ at time $t$.

(c) Find an expression for the resultant force $\mathbf{F}$ newtons acting on the particle at time $t$.

(d) Find the magnitude of the force when $t = 2$.

5 A particle of mass $0.5\,\mathrm{kg}$ is moving under the action of a single force $\mathbf{F}$ newtons that varies with time. The velocity $\mathbf{v}\,\mathrm{m\,s^{-1}}$ of the particle at time $t\,\mathrm{s}$ is given by
$$\mathbf{v} = t^2\mathbf{i} + (4t - 3t^2)\mathbf{j}$$
Find the magnitude of $\mathbf{F}$ when $t = 5$.

6 The position vector $\mathbf{r}\,\mathrm{m}$ of a particle of mass $1.5\,\mathrm{kg}$ at time $t\,\mathrm{s}$ is given by
$$\mathbf{r} = (t^2 - 2t)\mathbf{i} + t^3\mathbf{j}$$
Find an expression for the resultant force $\mathbf{F}$ newtons acting on the particle at time $t$.

---

**Key points**

• If $x = \mathrm{f}(t)$ then $v = \dfrac{\mathrm{d}x}{\mathrm{d}t} = \mathrm{f}'(t)$ and $a = \dfrac{\mathrm{d}v}{\mathrm{d}t} = \mathrm{f}''(t)$  (p 25)

• If $\mathbf{r} = \mathrm{f}(t)\mathbf{i} + \mathrm{g}(t)\mathbf{j}$ then

$\mathbf{v} = \dfrac{\mathrm{d}\mathbf{r}}{\mathrm{d}t} = \dot{\mathbf{r}} = \mathrm{f}'(t)\mathbf{i} + \mathrm{g}'(t)\mathbf{j}$ $\qquad$ $\mathbf{a} = \dfrac{\mathrm{d}\mathbf{v}}{\mathrm{d}t} = \ddot{\mathbf{r}} = \mathrm{f}''(t)\mathbf{i} + \mathrm{g}''(t)\mathbf{j}$  (p 30)

• $\mathbf{v} = \int \mathbf{a}\,\mathrm{d}t \quad \mathbf{r} = \int \mathbf{v}\,\mathrm{d}t \qquad$ Include a constant of integration, whose value can be found from information given.  (p 33)

2 Variable acceleration | **39**

## Mixed questions (answers p 125)

**1** The position vector, $\mathbf{r}$ m, of a particle at time $t$ s is given by

$$\mathbf{r} = (4t^2 - 2)\mathbf{i} + (t^3 - t^2)\mathbf{j}$$

(a) Find the time at which the particle is moving in the $\mathbf{i}$-direction.

(b) Find the speed of the particle when $t = 2$.

(c) Find the time at which the acceleration of the particle is in the $\mathbf{i}$-direction.

(d) Find the magnitude of the acceleration when $t = 0$.

**2** The acceleration, $a$ m s$^{-2}$, of a particle moving on a straight line is given by

$$a = 4 - 3t^2 \quad (t \geq 0)$$

The particle is at rest at the origin when $t = 0$.

(a) Find the value of $t$ for which the particle is again instantaneously at rest.

(b) Find the distance between the positions of the particle at $t = 2$ and $t = 4$.

**3** A particle of mass 2 kg is moving under the action of a single force $\mathbf{F}$ newtons. At time $t$ seconds, the position vector, $\mathbf{r}$ metres, of the particle is given by

$$\mathbf{r} = 4t^{\frac{1}{2}}\mathbf{i} + \tfrac{1}{2}t^2\mathbf{j}$$

(a) Find an expression for $\mathbf{F}$ in terms of $t$.

(b) Find the magnitude of $\mathbf{F}$ when $t = 4$.

**4** A particle $P$ moves on a straight line so that, at time $t$ seconds, its velocity $v$ m s$^{-1}$ is given by

$$v = 12t - 3t^2 \quad 0 \leq t \leq 2$$
$$v = 12 \qquad\qquad t > 2$$

The particle is at rest at the origin when $t = 0$.

(a) Find an expression for the acceleration of the particle when

   (i) $0 \leq t \leq 2$           (ii) $t > 0$

(b) Find the displacement of the particle from the origin when $t = 2$.

(c) Find the displacement of the particle from the origin when $t = 10$.

**5** The speed, $\mathbf{v}$ m s$^{-1}$, of a particle of mass 2 kg at time $t$ s is given by

$$\mathbf{v} = (t^3 + 3t)\mathbf{i} + (1 - 4t)\mathbf{j}$$

The particle passes through the point with position vector $(2\mathbf{i} + \mathbf{j})$ m when $t = 0$.

(a) Find an expression for the displacement of the particle at time $t$.

(b) Find an expression for the resultant force on the particle at time $t$.

(c) Find, to three significant figures, the magnitude and direction of the force acting on the particle when $t = 2$.

**6** At time $t$ seconds, a particle $P$ has position vector $\mathbf{r}$ m relative to a fixed origin $O$ where

$$\mathbf{r} = (t^3 - 6t^2)\mathbf{i} + 5t^2\mathbf{j}$$

(a) Find the velocity of $P$ at time $t$.

(b) Find the acceleration of $P$ at time $t$.

(c) (i) Show that the magnitude of the acceleration is a minimum when $t = 2$.

   (ii) Find the magnitude of the acceleration at this time.

## Test yourself (answers p 126)

**1** At time $t$ s, the position vector $\mathbf{r}$ m of a particle relative to a fixed origin $O$ is given by

$$\mathbf{r} = (4t^2 + 3)\mathbf{i} + (5t - t^2)\mathbf{j}$$

(a) Find an expression for the velocity of the particle at time $t$.

(b) Show that the acceleration of the particle is constant and find its magnitude.

**2** The acceleration, $\mathbf{a}$ m s$^{-2}$, of a particle at time $t$ s is given by

$$\mathbf{a} = 3t\mathbf{i} - \mathbf{j}$$

At time $t = 0$ the particle passes through the origin with velocity $(\mathbf{i} + 2\mathbf{j})$ m s$^{-1}$.

(a) Find an expression for the velocity of the particle at time $t$.

(b) Find an expression for the displacement of the particle at time $t$.

**3** The acceleration, $a$ m s$^{-2}$, of an object moving on a straight line is given by

$$a = 6t - 9$$

At time $t = 0$, the object passes through the origin $x = 0$ with velocity $6$ m s$^{-1}$.

(a) Find an expression for the velocity in terms of $t$.

(b) Find the distance between the two points where the object is instantaneously at rest.

**4** The position vector, $\mathbf{r}$ m, of a particle at time $t$ s is given by

$$\mathbf{r} = (4t^2 - 6t)\mathbf{i} + 2t^2\mathbf{j} \quad (t \geq 0)$$

(a) Find the velocity of the particle at time $t$.

(b) Find the time when the particle is moving parallel to the vector $\mathbf{i} + \mathbf{j}$.

**5** A particle $P$ of mass $0.3$ kg is moving under the action of a single force $\mathbf{F}$ newtons. At time $t$ seconds the velocity of $P$, $\mathbf{v}$ m s$^{-1}$, is given by

$$\mathbf{v} = 3t^2\mathbf{i} + (6t - 4)\mathbf{j}$$

(a) Calculate, to three significant figures, the magnitude of $\mathbf{F}$ when $t = 2$.

When $t = 0$, $P$ is at the point $A$. The position vector of $A$ with respect to a fixed origin $O$ is $(3\mathbf{i} - 4\mathbf{j})$ m. When $t = 4$, $P$ is at the point $B$.

(b) Find the position vector of $B$.

Edexcel

# 3 Centre of mass

In this chapter you will learn how to find
- the centre of mass of a system of particles
- the centre of mass of a plane lamina and a composite body
- the equilibrium position of a body

## A Centre of mass of a system of particles (answers p 126)

In Mechanics 1 we saw that the point on a body at which its mass can be considered to be concentrated is called the centre of mass of the body.

Consider a light rod of length 2 m with a particle of mass 1 kg attached at each end.

Remember that, if an object is modelled as light, its mass can be ignored.

The mass of the system of rod and particles can be considered to be concentrated at its centre of mass.

The resultant of the weights of the particles

- has a magnitude equal to the sum of the two separate weights

- acts through the centre of mass of the system

The system of rod and particles can be supported at the halfway point, which is the centre of mass, and it will remain in equilibrium.

If the system is in equilibrium, the resultant force is zero and the total moment about any point is zero.

The force diagram for the rod and particles is shown.

The forces are in equilibrium vertically, so  $2g = R$.

Take moments about the support. $\qquad g \times 1 + R \times 0 - g \times 1 = 0$

The total moment about the support is zero, so the system is in equilibrium.

If one of the 1 kg particles is replaced by a 2 kg particle, the centre of mass of the system will no longer be in the centre of the rod. The support will need to be moved for the system to remain in equilibrium.

**A1** (a) By resolving the forces vertically, find the magnitude of the reaction at the support.

(b) By taking moments about the support, find the distance, $x$ m, of the centre of mass of the system from $A$.

The system of rod and particles can be replaced by an equivalent single particle of the same total mass acting at the centre of mass of the system.

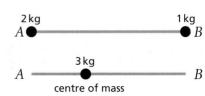

**A2** **(a)** Find the total moment about $A$ of the weights of the two particles.

   **(b)** Find the total moment about $A$ of the weight of the equivalent particle acting at the centre of mass.

**A3** **(a)** Find the total moment about $B$ of the weights of the two particles.

   **(b)** Find the total moment about $B$ of the weight of the equivalent particle acting at the centre of mass.

**A4** **(a)** Find the total moment about the mid-point of the rod of the weights of the two particles.

   **(b)** Find the total moment about the mid-point of the rod of the weight of the equivalent particle acting at the centre of mass.

In fact, the total moment of the forces for the system of rod and particles about **any** point is equal to the moment of the force on the equivalent particle at the centre of mass of the system.

 When calculating moments about a given point, a set of particles can be replaced by a single particle of the same total mass concentrated at the centre of mass.

Consider a system of particles arranged in a horizontal straight line as shown.

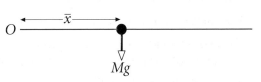

This is the force diagram for the system.

The total moment about $O$ is $m_1gx_1 + m_2gx_2 + m_3gx_3$.

The system of particles can be replaced with a single particle of the same total mass positioned at the centre of mass of the system with force diagram as shown, where $\bar{x}$ is the distance of the centre of mass from $O$ and $M$ is the total mass of the individual particles.

The total moment about $O$ is $Mg\bar{x}$.

The two systems are equivalent, so the total moment is equal to the sum of the individual moments.

$$Mg\bar{x} = m_1gx_1 + m_2gx_2 + m_3gx_3$$
$$\Rightarrow \quad M\bar{x} = m_1x_1 + m_2x_2 + m_3x_3$$
$$\Rightarrow \quad M\bar{x} = \Sigma mx$$

This method can be applied to any number of particles where $\Sigma mx$ is the sum of all the individual products, mass × distance from $O$.

K The centre of mass of a system of particles arranged in a straight line can be found using

total mass × distance of centre of mass from $O$
= the sum of all the products mass × distance from $O$

that is,

$$M\bar{x} = \sum mx$$

where $M$ is the total mass and $\bar{x}$ is the distance of the centre of mass from $O$.

### Example 1

Four particles of masses 4 kg, 4 kg, 2 kg and 5 kg are positioned in a straight line as shown. Find the distance of the centre of mass from $O$.

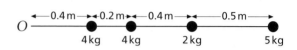

### Solution

Use $M\bar{x} = \sum mx$.

$$(4 + 4 + 2 + 5)\bar{x} = 4 \times 0.4 + 4 \times 0.6 + 2 \times 1.0 + 5 \times 1.5$$

$$\Rightarrow \qquad 15\bar{x} = 13.5$$

$$\Rightarrow \qquad \bar{x} = 0.9$$

The centre of mass is 0.9 m from $O$.

### Exercise A (answers p 126)

**1** Find the distance from $O$ of the centre of mass of each system of particles.

(a)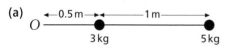

(b)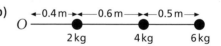

(c)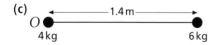

(d)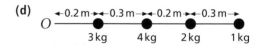

**2** A light rod $AB$ has particles attached as shown.

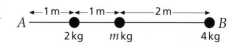

(a) Find the distance of the centre of mass from $A$.

(b) The 2 kg particle is removed.
Find the new position of the centre of mass.

**3** A light rod $AB$ of length 2 m has a particle of mass 10 kg attached at $A$ and a particle of mass $m$ kg attached at $B$.
Given that the centre of mass is 1.5 m from $A$, find the value of $m$.

**4** Particles of masses 2 kg, $m$ kg and 4 kg are attached to a light rod $AB$ as shown.
The centre of mass is 2.5 m from $A$.
Find the value of $m$.

5 A light rod $XY$ of length 6 m has a particle of mass 5 kg attached at $X$
and a particle of mass 6 kg attached at $Y$.
A particle of mass 4 kg is attached to the rod so that the centre of mass
of the system of rod and particles is at the mid-point of the rod.
Find the distance of the 4 kg mass from $X$.

6 A light rod $PQ$ of length 5 m has particles of mass $p$ kg and $2p$ kg attached.
The centre of mass of the system of rod and particles is 3 m from $P$.
If the $p$ kg particle is 0.5 m from $P$, find the distance of the $2p$ kg particle from $P$.

## B A system of particles in a plane

Consider a system of particles arranged with respect
to the origin $O$ as shown.

With the $y$-axis vertical, the total moment of the particles
about $O$ is

$$m_1 g x_1 + m_2 g x_2 + m_3 g x_3$$

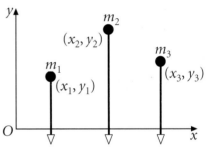

The system can be replaced by a single particle of mass $M$,
where $M = (m_1 + m_2 + m_3)$, acting at the centre of mass of the system $(\bar{x}, \bar{y})$.
The moment of this particle about $O$ is

$$M g \bar{x}$$

The two systems are equivalent, so the total moment is equal to the sum of
the individual moments.

$$M g \bar{x} = m_1 g x_1 + m_2 g x_2 + m_3 g x_3$$
$$\Rightarrow \quad M \bar{x} = m_1 x_1 + m_2 x_2 + m_3 x_3$$
$$\Rightarrow \quad M \bar{x} = \Sigma m x$$

If the system is now turned over, so that the $x$-axis is vertical,
the total moment about $O$ is

$$m_1 g y_1 + m_2 g y_2 + m_3 g y_3$$

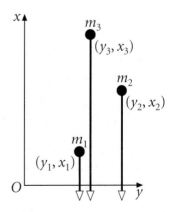

The moment of the equivalent single particle about $O$ is

$$M g \bar{y}$$

So $\quad M g \bar{y} = m_1 g y_1 + m_2 g y_2 + m_3 g y_3$
$$\Rightarrow \quad M \bar{y} = m_1 y_1 + m_2 y_2 + m_3 y_3$$
$$\Rightarrow \quad M \bar{y} = \Sigma m y$$

The coordinates $(\bar{x}, \bar{y})$ of the centre of mass of a system of particles
in a plane are given by

$$M \bar{x} = \Sigma m x, \quad M \bar{y} = \Sigma m y$$

## Example 2

A light rectangular framework has particles attached to the corners as shown.

Find the coordinates of its centre of mass with respect to the position of the 2 kg mass.

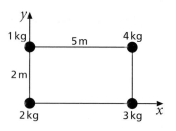

## Solution

*The framework is light, so its weight can be ignored.*

Use $M\bar{x} = \Sigma mx$.

$$(2 + 3 + 4 + 1)\bar{x} = 2 \times 0 + 3 \times 5 + 4 \times 5 + 1 \times 0$$
$$\Rightarrow \qquad 10\bar{x} = 35$$
$$\Rightarrow \qquad \bar{x} = 3.5$$

Use $M\bar{y} = \Sigma my$.

$$(2 + 3 + 4 + 1)\bar{y} = 2 \times 0 + 3 \times 0 + 4 \times 2 + 1 \times 2$$
$$\Rightarrow \qquad 10\bar{y} = 10$$
$$\Rightarrow \qquad \bar{y} = 1$$

The coordinates of the centre of mass are (3.5, 1).

## Exercise B (answers p 126)

**1** Find the coordinates of the centre of mass of each system of particles.

(a)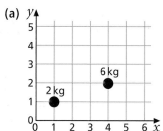

(b)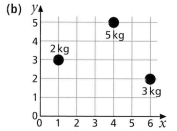

(c)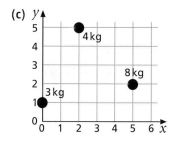

(d)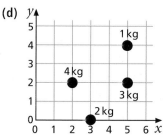

**2** A light rectangular framework has particles attached to the corners as shown.
Find the coordinates of the centre of mass with respect to the axes shown.

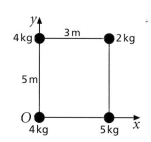

**3** A light rectangular framework $ABCD$ has particles attached as shown.

    **(a)** Find the distance of the centre of mass from $AD$.

    **(b)** Find the distance of the centre of mass from $AB$.

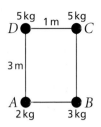

**4** Particles are attached to the corners of a light square framework $ABCD$, of side 3 m, as shown.

    **(a)** Find the coordinates of the centre of mass of the framework with respect to the axes shown.

    **(b)** A particle of mass $3p$ is attached to the mid-point of $AB$. Find the centre of mass of the new system.

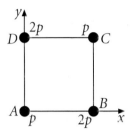

**5** A light framework $ABC$ with particles of mass 3 kg, $m$ kg and 5 kg attached as shown has centre of mass at the point with coordinates $(\bar{x}, \bar{y})$.

    **(a)** Given that $\bar{x} = 2$, find the value of $m$.

    **(b)** Find the $y$-coordinate of the centre of mass.

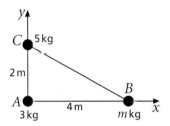

**6** A light rectangular framework $PQRS$ has particles attached as shown.

    **(a)** Find the distance of the centre of mass from $PQ$.

    **(b)** Find the distance of the centre of mass from $PS$.

    **(c)** The 2 kg particle is removed. Find the position of the new centre of mass.

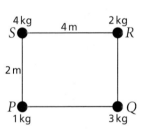

**7** A light framework $ABCD$ has particles of mass $p$ kg, 1 kg, $q$ kg and 2 kg attached as shown.
The centre of mass of the framework has coordinates $(1, 2)$ with respect to the axes shown.
Find the values of $p$ and $q$.

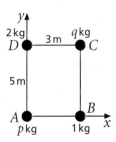

## C Centre of mass by symmetry (answers p 127)

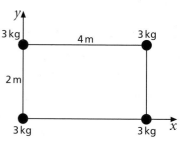

**C1** A system of particles is attached to a light rectangular framework as shown.

(a) Calculate the coordinates of the centre of mass of the system.

(b) Use the symmetry of the system to explain your answer to (a).

**K** If a system of particles has a line of symmetry, the centre of mass lies on this line.

A lamina can be modelled as a plane area with mass but negligible thickness.
If the lamina is uniform, its mass is distributed evenly throughout its area.

**C2** State the position of the centres of mass of the following uniform laminae.

(a) A circular disc of radius 1 m     (b) A square lamina of side 2 m

(c) A rectangular lamina of length 3 m and width 2 m

**K** If a uniform lamina has a line of symmetry, the centre of mass lies on this line.
If the lamina has more than one line of symmetry, the centre of mass lies on their point of intersection.

## Exercise C (answers p 127)

**1** Find, using symmetry or otherwise, the coordinates of the centre of mass of each of the following systems of particles.

(a)
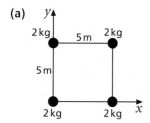

(b)
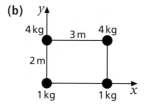

**2** Write down the coordinates of the centre of mass of each uniform lamina.

(a)
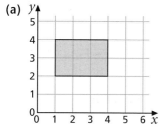

(b)
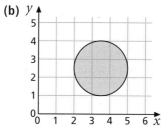

(c)
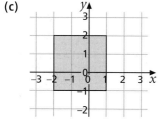

(d)
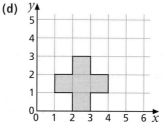

## D Centre of mass of special shapes (answers p 127)

Consider the uniform triangular lamina shown.

It is a scalene triangle with no lines of symmetry,
so the centre of mass cannot be found using symmetry.

If $M$ is the mid-point of side $BC$, then the line joining
vertex $A$ to point $M$ is the **median** through $A$.
The median divides triangle $ABC$ into two triangles
with equal bases and the same height, and hence
with equal area.

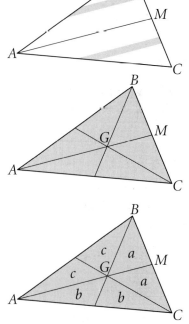

Imagine the lamina is split into thin strips of equal width,
parallel to $AM$.
These strips pair off: strips the same distance from $AM$,
but on different sides of it, have the same area.
So the centre of mass must lie on the line $AM$.

This applies for each of the medians.
Thus the centre of mass, $G$, of the triangular lamina
lies at the point of intersection of its medians.

In triangle $ABC$, the areas marked $a$ are equal;
they have equal bases and the same height.

This is also true for the areas marked $b$ and $c$.

But $2a + c = 2b + c$ (each half of $\triangle ABC$).

So $a = b$.

So the area of $\triangle CAG$ is twice the area of $\triangle CGM$.
Since these triangles have the same height from vertex $C$,
base $AG = 2 \times$ base $GM$.

So $AG = \frac{2}{3}AM$ and similarly for the other medians.

The centre of mass of a uniform triangular lamina is at the point of intersection
of the medians, $\frac{2}{3}$ of the distance along a median from the vertex.

This result is given in the formula booklet provided in the examination and
may be quoted without proof.

**D1** $PQR$ is a uniform isosceles triangular lamina, where $PR = 6$ m
and $PQ = QR = 8$ m.

(a) Use Pythagoras's theorem to find, to three significant figures,
the length of the median from vertex $Q$.

(b) Find, to three significant figures, the distance of
the centre of mass of the triangle from the side $PR$.

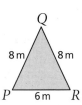

**K** The centre of mass, $G$, of a uniform circular arc of radius $r$ and angle at the centre $2\alpha$ lies on the line of symmetry at a distance of $\dfrac{r \sin \alpha}{\alpha}$ from the centre.

The centre of mass, $G$, of a uniform sector of a circle of radius $r$ and angle at the centre $2\alpha$ lies on the line of symmetry at a distance of $\dfrac{2r \sin \alpha}{3\alpha}$ from the centre.

$\alpha$ must be in radians.

The proof of these results is beyond the scope of this book.
The results are given in the formula booklet provided in the examination and may be quoted without proof.

---

### Example 3

$ABC$ is a uniform triangular lamina.
Find the coordinates of its centre of mass.

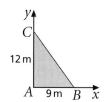

### Solution

The centre of mass, $G$, of triangle $ABC$ lies at the point of intersection of the medians, $AR$, $BP$ and $CQ$.

$R$ is the midpoint of $BC$, which has coordinates $\left(4\tfrac{1}{2}, 6\right)$.

$G$ lies on $AR$ such that $AG = \tfrac{2}{3}AR$.

So the coordinates of $G$ are $\left(\tfrac{2}{3} \times 4\tfrac{1}{2}, \tfrac{2}{3} \times 6\right) = (3, 4)$.

The centre of mass of $ABC$ is at the point $G\,(3, 4)$.

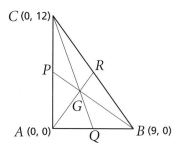

---

### Example 4

A uniform wire is bent into the shape of a semicircle of radius $5\,\text{m}$.
Find the position of the centre of mass of the wire.

### Solution

*Angles must be measured in radians.*
*The angle in a semicircle is $\pi$, so $\alpha = \dfrac{\pi}{2}$.*

The centre of mass is $\dfrac{r \sin \alpha}{\alpha}$ from the centre.

$$\frac{r \sin \alpha}{\alpha} = \frac{5 \sin \dfrac{\pi}{2}}{\dfrac{\pi}{2}} = 3.183$$

The centre of mass is on the line of symmetry of the semicircle $3.18\,\text{m}$ (to 3 s.f.) from the centre of the circle.

---

**Exercise D** (answers p 127)

1 The centre of mass, *G*, of a uniform semicircular lamina of radius 10 m lies on the axis of symmetry, *OA*, of the semicircle.
Find the distance *OG*.

2 *ABC* is a uniform triangular lamina, where *AB* = *BC* = 15 m and *AC* = 10 m.
Find the distance of the centre of mass from *AC*.

3 Find the coordinates of the centre of mass of each uniform lamina.

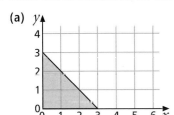

(a)
(b)

4 A uniform wire is bent into the shape of the arc of a circle *AB*, with *O* the centre of the circle, as shown.
Find the distance of the centre of mass from *O*.

5 A uniform lamina is in the shape of the sector of a circle *OPQ* as shown.
Find the distance of the centre of mass from *O*.

6 (a) *OAB* is a uniform lamina in the shape of the quadrant of a circle of radius 8 m.
Find the coordinates of the centre of mass of the lamina.

(b) A semicircular lamina is formed by joining the lamina *OAB* to an identical lamina *OBC* as shown.

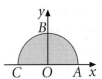

(i) Find the coordinates of the centre of mass of the lamina *OBC*.

(ii) Explain why the centre of mass of the semicircular lamina must lie on the line joining the centres of mass of *OAB* and *OBC*.

(iii) By symmetry, the centre of mass of the semicircular lamina must also lie on the line *OB*.
State the coordinates of the centre of mass of the semicircular lamina.

(iv) Use the formula for the centre of mass of a sector to confirm the answer found in (iii).

## E Centre of mass of a composite body (answers p 127)

Consider the uniform L-shaped lamina shown.
Its centre of mass cannot be found by symmetry.
However, several different methods can be used
to find the centre of mass of a composite body.
They are demonstrated in the following questions.

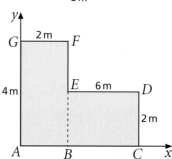

The lamina can be divided into two rectangles
whose centres of mass can be found.

**E1** Find the coordinates of the centre of mass
of rectangle

    **(a)** *ABFG*               **(b)** *BCDE*

The lamina is uniform, so its mass is distributed evenly throughout its area.
Suppose its mass per unit area is $a \, \mathrm{kg\,m^{-2}}$.

**E2** Write down an expression for the mass of rectangle

    **(a)** *ABFG*               **(b)** *BCDE*

Each rectangle can be replaced by a particle of the same mass positioned
at the centre of mass of the rectangle.
The centre of mass of the composite lamina can then be found by replacing
the lamina by these two particles and finding their centre of mass.

**E3** Find the coordinates of the centre of mass of the composite lamina.

When using the above approach, you may find it helpful to complete a table
like this to summarise the known values for the lamina and its components.

| | Area | Mass | Distance of centre of mass from *AG* | Distance of centre of mass from *AC* |
|---|---|---|---|---|
| Rectangle *ABFG* | $8\,\mathrm{m^2}$ | $8a\,\mathrm{kg}$ | 1 m | 2 m |
| Rectangle *BCDE* | $12\,\mathrm{m^2}$ | $12a\,\mathrm{kg}$ | 5 m | 1 m |
| Lamina | $20\,\mathrm{m^2}$ | $20a\,\mathrm{kg}$ | $\bar{x}$ m | $\bar{y}$ m |

In the expressions for the coordinates of the centre of mass of the composite lamina,
the mass per unit area, *a*, cancelled out and hence was not required.
The mass of a uniform lamina is proportional to its area, so areas can be used
instead of masses in the calculations, and the mass column in the table is not required.

**E4** *ABCDE* is a uniform lamina.
It can be divided into a rectangle and a triangle.

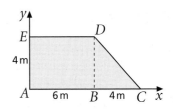

(a) Complete this table showing the areas and centres of mass of the rectangle, triangle and lamina.

| | Area | Distance of centre of mass from *AE* | Distance of centre of mass from *AC* |
|---|---|---|---|
| Rectangle *ABDE* | $24\,\text{m}^2$ | | |
| Triangle *BCD* | $8\,\text{m}^2$ | | |
| Lamina | $32\,\text{m}^2$ | $\bar{x}\,\text{m}$ | $\bar{y}\,\text{m}$ |

(b) Find the coordinates of the centre of mass of the lamina.

Now consider the uniform lamina shown.
It can be thought of as a large rectangle *ABCD*
with a small rectangle *EFGH* removed.

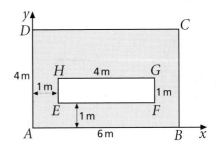

**E5** (a) Complete this table showing the areas and centres of mass of the rectangles and lamina.
Let the coordinates of the centre of mass of the lamina be $(x_L, y_L)$.

| | Area | Distance of centre of mass from *AD* | Distance of centre of mass from *AB* |
|---|---|---|---|
| Rectangle *ABCD* | $24\,\text{m}^2$ | | |
| Rectangle *EFGH* before removal | $4\,\text{m}^2$ | | |
| Lamina | $20\,\text{m}^2$ | $x_L\,\text{m}$ | $y_L\,\text{m}$ |

(b) Now consider rectangle *ABCD* to be a composite body consisting of the lamina and rectangle *EFGH*. The centre of mass of *ABCD* is at $(\bar{x}, \bar{y})$.

(i) Use values from the table and $M\bar{x} = \Sigma mx$ to show that $72 = 12 + 20x_L$.

(ii) Use values from the table and $M\bar{y} = \Sigma my$ to show that $48 = 6 + 20y_L$.

(iii) Hence find the coordinates of the centre of mass of the lamina.

**K** The centre of mass of a composite body can be found by replacing each component part by a particle positioned at its centre of mass, then finding the centre of mass of this system of particles.
The mass of each component of a uniform lamina is proportional to its area.

## Example 5

A uniform lamina $ABCD$ of mass $4p$ kg has a particle of mass $p$ kg attached at point $X$ as shown.
Find the coordinates of the centre of mass of the composite body.

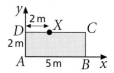

### Solution

*Tabulate the mass and position of the centre of mass of each component.*
*By symmetry, the centre of mass of the rectangle is at its centre.*

|  | Mass | Distance of centre of mass from $AD$ | Distance of centre of mass from $AB$ |
|---|---|---|---|
| Rectangle $ABCD$ | $4p$ kg | 2.5 m | 1 m |
| Particle | $p$ kg | 2 m | 2 m |
| Composite body | $5p$ kg | $\bar{x}$ m | $\bar{y}$ m |

*Find the centre of mass of the composite body.*

$M\bar{x} = \sum mx \Rightarrow 5p\bar{x} = 4p \times 2.5 + p \times 2 = 12p \Rightarrow \bar{x} = 2.4$

$M\bar{y} = \sum my \Rightarrow 5p\bar{y} = 4p \times 1 + p \times 2 = 6p \Rightarrow \bar{y} = 1.2$

The centre of mass of the composite body is at $(2.4, 1.2)$.

## Example 6

The diagram shows a uniform lamina which has an isosceles triangle cut out.
Find the coordinates of the centre of mass of the lamina.

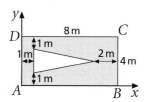

### Solution

*The lamina consists of a rectangle with a triangle cut out.*
*Tabulate the areas and centres of mass of the rectangle, triangle and lamina.*
*By symmetry, the centre of mass of the rectangle is at its centre and the centre of mass of the triangle is on its line of symmetry $\frac{1}{3}$ of the distance along the median from the base.*

|  | Area | Distance of centre of mass from $AD$ | Distance of centre of mass from $AB$ |
|---|---|---|---|
| Rectangle $ABCD$ | $32$ m$^2$ | 4 m | 2 m |
| Cut-out triangle | $5$ m$^2$ | $2\frac{2}{3}$ m | 2 m |
| Lamina | $27$ m$^2$ | $x_L$ m | $y_L$ m |

The distance of centre of mass of rectangle $ABCD$ from $AD$ is given by

$$32 \times 4 = 5 \times 2\frac{2}{3} + 27 \times x_L$$

$$\Rightarrow \quad 128 = 13\frac{1}{3} + 27x_L \qquad \Rightarrow \quad x_L = 4.25 \text{ (to 3 s.f.)}$$

The lamina has a line of symmetry through the mid-point of $AD$, so $y_L = 2$.

The centre of mass of the lamina is at $(4.25, 2)$.

**Exercise E** (answers p 128)

**1** The uniform lamina shown consists of two rectangles.

(a) Write down the coordinates of the centre of mass of the rectangle *ABCG*.

(b) Write down the coordinates of the centre of mass of the rectangle *CDEF*.

(c) Find the coordinates of the centre of mass of the lamina.

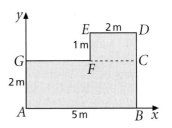

**2** Find the coordinates of the centre of mass of each of the following uniform laminae.

(a)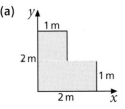

(b)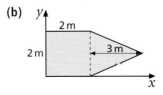

(c)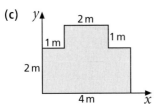

(d)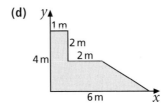

**3** The diagram shows a uniform lamina *ABCDEF*.

(a) Explain why the centre of mass of the lamina must lie on the line that goes through *A* and *D*.

(b) Find the coordinates of the centre of mass of the lamina.

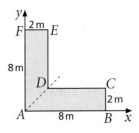

**4** A uniform wire is bent to form the triangle shown.

(a) Complete this table showing the lengths and centres of mass for the components of the triangle.

| | Length | Distance of centre of mass from *AC* | Distance of centre of mass from *AB* |
|---|---|---|---|
| Side *AB* | 0.3 m | 0.15 m | 0 m |
| Side *BC* | 0.5 m | | |
| Side *AC* | 0.4 m | | |
| Triangle *ABC* | | $\bar{x}$ m | $\bar{y}$ m |

(b) Find the distance of the centre of mass of the triangle from *AC*.

(c) Find the distance of the centre of mass of the triangle from *AB*.

**5** A letter C is formed by bending a uniform wire into the shape shown.

(a) Find the distance of the centre of mass from $QR$.

(b) Find the distance of the centre of mass from $QP$.

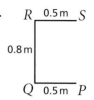

**6** A uniform triangular lamina $ABC$ has a rectangle cut out as shown.

(a) Find the coordinates of the centre of mass of the triangle.

(b) Find the coordinates of the centre of mass of the rectangle.

(c) Find, to 2 d.p., the coordinates of the centre of mass of the lamina.

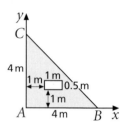

**7** Find the coordinates of the centre of mass of each of the following laminae.

(a)

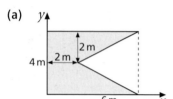

(b)

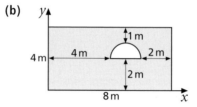

**8** A pendulum consists of a disc of mass 0.2 kg and radius 5 cm attached to a uniform rod, $AB$, of mass 0.1 kg and length 0.9 m. The centre of the disc is fixed at $B$.
Find the distance of the centre of mass of the pendulum from $A$.

**9** A uniform wire of mass 1.5 kg is bent to form a rectangle. It has particles attached as shown.

(a) Show that the distance of the centre of mass of the composite body is 1.8 m from $AB$.

(b) Find the distance of the centre of mass from $AD$.

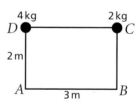

**10** A shop sign is made from a uniform rod $AB$ of mass 0.5 kg and length 1.2 m with a uniform plate of mass 1.5 kg attached as shown.

(a) Find the distance of the centre of mass of the sign from $AB$.

(b) Find the distance of the centre of mass of the sign from $BC$.

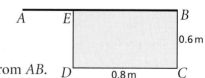

**11** An earring is made from a uniform metal disc of radius 1.5 cm with a semicircle of radius 0.5 cm removed as shown.
Find the distance of the centre of mass from $A$.

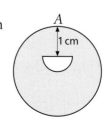

## F Equilibrium (answers p 128)

**D**

**F1 (a)** A uniform rectangular lamina *ABCD* is suspended
by a string attached at *A*.
It is held in position with the longer side *AB*
horizontal, as shown.
If released, do you think it would stay in this position?
Why not?

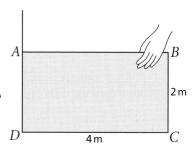

**(b)** The lamina is now turned and held in
the position shown.
Will it stay in this position if released?
Why not?

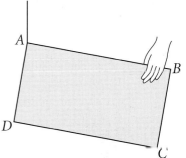

**(c)** Sketch the position you think it would stay in when released, explaining
your reason.

**(d)** Use trigonometry to find the angle between *AB* and the vertical
when the released lamina is in equilibrium.

**F2 (a)** Find the distance of the centre of mass of the uniform
rectangular lamina *PQRS* from the side

    **(i)** *PQ*               **(ii)** *PS*

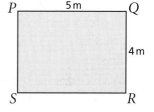

**(b)** The lamina is suspended from *P* and hangs in equilibrium.

    **(i)** Sketch the position of the lamina, showing the
position of the centre of mass.

    **(ii)** Use trigonometry to find the angle between *PQ* and the vertical.

**(c)** The lamina is now suspended from *S* and hangs in equilibrium.

    **(i)** Sketch the position of the lamina, showing the position of the centre of mass.

    **(ii)** Find the angle between *SP* and the vertical.

**F3** The uniform rectangular lamina *KLMN* is suspended
from *K* and hangs in equilibrium.
Find the angle between *KL* and the vertical.

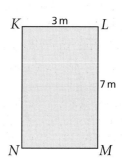

**K** A body freely suspended from one point will hang in equilibrium with its centre of mass vertically below the point of suspension.

**F4** **(a)** Show that the centre of mass of the lamina *ABCDEFG* is 2.25 m from *AG*.

**(b)** Show that the centre of mass of the lamina *ABCDEFG* is 1.75 m from *AB*.

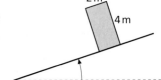

**(c)** The lamina is now freely suspended from *A* and hangs in equilibrium.

**(i)** Sketch the suspended lamina, showing the position of the centre of mass.

**(ii)** Show that the angle between *AB* and the vertical is 38° to the nearest degree.

**D** **F5** A uniform rectangular lamina rests on a rough plane which is initially horizontal and is then gradually tilted so that its angle to the horizontal increases.

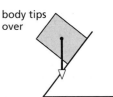

**(a)** What condition must be met to ensure that the lamina does not slip down the plane?

**(b)** What condition must be met to ensure that the lamina does not tip over?

**(c)** Given that the lamina does not slip, find the angle the plane makes with the horizontal when the lamina tips over.

**K** A body can rest in equilibrium on a plane only if the centre of mass of the body is vertically above a point of contact with the plane.

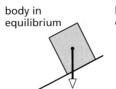
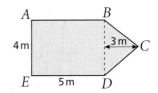

---

### Example 7

The uniform lamina shown consists of a rectangle and an isosceles triangle. It is freely suspended from *A*.

Find, to the nearest degree, the angle *AB* makes with the vertical.

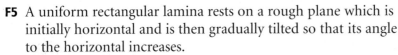

### Solution

*First find the centre of mass of the composite lamina.*

*By symmetry, the centre of mass of the lamina is 2 m from AB.*

*Tabulate the area and distance of the centre of mass from AE for each component.*

|  | Area | Distance of centre of mass from *AE* |
|---|---|---|
| Rectangle *ABDE* | 20 m² | 2.5 m |
| Triangle *BCD* | 6 m² | 6 m |
| Lamina | 26 m² | $\bar{x}$ m |

Hence $26\bar{x} = 20 \times 2.5 + 6 \times 6 \Rightarrow \bar{x} = 3.31$ to 3 s.f.

*Now sketch the lamina with the centre of mass marked.*
*Draw a line through A and the centre of mass to indicate*
*the vertical and the angle to be found.*
*You do not need to reorientate the diagram.*
*Use trigonometry to find the angle.*

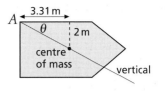

$\tan\theta = \frac{2}{3.31}$

So $\theta = 31°$ to the nearest degree

$AB$ makes an angle of $31°$ with the vertical.

---

## Example 8

A uniform rectangular lamina $ABCD$ of mass $2\,\text{kg}$ has
a particle of mass $p\,\text{kg}$ attached at the mid-point of $AD$.

(a) Find, in terms of $p$, the position of the centre of mass.

(b) The lamina is freely suspended from $A$.
Given that it hangs in equilibrium with $AB$ at an angle
of $45°$ to the vertical, find the value of $p$.

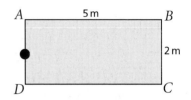

## Solution

(a) *Tabulate the mass and position of the centre of mass for each component.*

|  | Mass | Distance of centre of mass from $AD$ | Distance of centre of mass from $DC$ |
|---|---|---|---|
| Rectangle $ABCD$ | $2\,\text{kg}$ | $2.5\,\text{m}$ | $1\,\text{m}$ |
| Particle | $p\,\text{kg}$ | $0\,\text{m}$ | $1\,\text{m}$ |
| Composite body | $(p+2)\,\text{kg}$ | $\bar{x}\,\text{m}$ | $\bar{y}\,\text{m}$ |

*Find the centre of mass of the composite body.*
Using $M\bar{x} = \sum mx$, $(p+2)\bar{x} = 2 \times 2.5 + p \times 0 \Rightarrow \bar{x} = \dfrac{5}{p+2}$

The composite body has a line of symmetry through the mid-point of $AD$, so $\bar{y} = 1$.
The centre of mass is $\dfrac{5}{p+2}\,\text{m}$ from $AD$ and $1\,\text{m}$ from $AB$.

(b) *The centre of mass is shown on the diagram.*
*When the lamina is suspended, the line through A*
*and the centre of mass is vertical, so this line is drawn*
*and is labelled as vertical.*

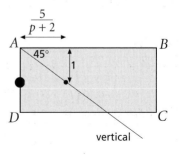

$\tan 45° = \dfrac{1}{\dfrac{5}{p+2}}$

$\Rightarrow \quad \dfrac{5}{p+2} = 1$

$\Rightarrow \quad p = 3$

## Exercise F (answers p 129)

**1** A uniform wire is bent to form a rectangular framework
*PQRS* as shown, where *G* is the point of intersection of
the diagonals of the rectangle.

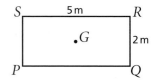

  **(a)** Explain why the centre of mass of the framework
  is at point *G*.

  **(b)** The framework is suspended from *Q* and hangs in equilibrium.
  Show that the angle *QR* makes with the vertical is 68° to the nearest degree.

**2** *ABCD* is a uniform rectangular lamina as shown.

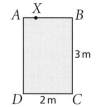

  **(a)** State the distance of the centre of mass from

    **(i)** *AB*          **(ii)** *AD*

  **(b)** The lamina is suspended from *A* and hangs in equilibrium.
  Find the angle that *AB* makes with the vertical.

  **(c)** The lamina is now suspended from point *X*, where *AX* = 0.5 m.
  Find the angle that *XB* makes with the vertical.

**3** *ABCD* is a uniform lamina as shown.

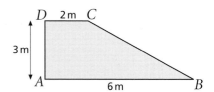

  **(a)** Show that the distance of the centre of mass
  from *AB* is 1.25 m.

  **(b)** Find the distance of the centre of mass from *AD*.

  **(c)** The lamina is freely suspended from *B*.
  Find the angle that *AB* makes with the vertical.

**4** *PQRS* is a uniform rectangular lamina with
an isosceles triangle cut out as shown.

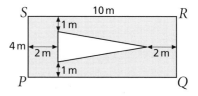

  **(a)** Find the distance of the centre of mass from

    **(i)** *PQ*          **(ii)** *PS*

  **(b)** The lamina is freely suspended from *S*.
  Find the angle that *SP* makes with the vertical.

**5** A mobile is made from a light rectangular framework
with particles attached to the corners as shown.

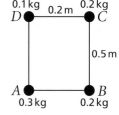

  **(a)** Find the distance of the centre of mass of the mobile from

    **(i)** *AB*          **(ii)** *AD*

  **(b)** The mobile is freely suspended from the mid-point of *AD*.
  Find the angle that *AD* makes with the vertical.

**6** A uniform wire of length 5 m and mass 2 kg is bent
into the shape shown.
A particle of mass *p* kg is attached to the wire 0.8 m from *A*.
The framework is freely suspended from *B* and hangs
with *AB* horizontal.
Find the value of *p*.

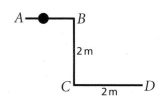

**7** A uniform lamina consisting of a rectangle and semicircle rests
on a rough plane inclined at an angle $\theta$ to the horizontal as shown.
Given that the lamina does not slip, find, to the nearest degree,
the maximum value of $\theta$ for the lamina to remain in equilibrium.

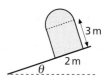

---

## Key points

- The total moment of the weights of a system of particles about a given point
  is equal to the moment of the weight of a single particle of the same total mass
  acting at the centre of mass of the system.                                    (p 43)

- The centre of mass of a system of particles arranged in a straight line can be
  found using

      total mass × distance of centre of mass from $O$
           = the sum of all the products mass × distance from $O$
  that is,

  $M\bar{x} = \Sigma mx$, where $M$ is the total mass and $\bar{x}$ is the distance of the centre
  of mass from $O$.                                                              (pp 43–44)

- The coordinates $(\bar{x}, \bar{y})$ of the centre of mass of a system of particles in a plane
  are given by

  $M\bar{x} = \Sigma mx, \quad M\bar{y} = \Sigma my$                              (p 45)

- If a system of particles or a uniform lamina has a line of symmetry,
  the centre of mass lies on this line.
  If it has more than one line of symmetry, the centre of mass lies on their point of
  intersection.                                                                  (p 48)

- The centre of mass of a uniform triangular lamina is at the point of intersection
  of the medians, $\frac{2}{3}$ of the distance along a median from the vertex.   (p 49)

- The centre of mass of a uniform circular arc of radius $r$ and angle
  at the centre $2\alpha$ lies at a distance of $\dfrac{r \sin \alpha}{\alpha}$ from the centre.  (p 50)

- The centre of mass of a uniform sector of a circle of radius $r$ and angle
  at the centre $2\alpha$ lies at a distance of $\dfrac{2r \sin \alpha}{3\alpha}$ from the centre.  (p 50)

- The centre of mass of a composite body can be found by replacing each component
  part by a particle positioned at its centre of mass, then finding the centre of mass
  of this system of particles.
  The mass of each component of a uniform lamina is proportional to its area.      (p 53)

- A body freely suspended from one point will hang in equilibrium with
  its centre of mass vertically below the point of suspension.
  A body can rest in equilibrium on a plane only if the centre of mass
  of the body is vertically above a point of contact with the plane.              (p 58)

## Mixed questions (answers p 129)

**1** An earring consists of a circle of radius 1 cm and a quadrant of a circle of radius 3 cm cut from a uniform metal plate and joined together as shown.
Find the distance of the centre of mass of the earring from $A$.

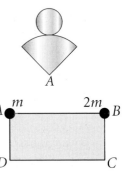

**2** A uniform rectangular plate $ABCD$ has mass $3m$. The sides $AB$ and $AD$ have length $4a$ and $a$ respectively. Particles of mass $m$ and $2m$ are attached to the plate at $A$ and $B$ as shown.

(a) Show that the distance of the centre of mass of the system from $AB$ is $\frac{1}{4}a$.

(b) Find the distance of the centre of mass of the system from $AD$.

(c) The corner $C$ of the plate is freely hinged to a fixed point and the plate hangs in equilibrium.
Find, to the nearest degree, the angle that $CD$ makes with the vertical.

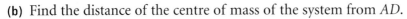

**3** The uniform lamina $ABCD$ consists of a rectangle and triangle as shown.

(a) Find the distance of the centre of mass from $AB$.

(b) Find the distance of the centre of mass from $AD$.

(c) The lamina has mass $M$. It rests in a vertical plane with $AB$ on a horizontal surface. A particle of mass $m$ is attached to the lamina at $C$, and the lamina is about to tip. Find $m$ in terms of $M$.

**4** A light rectangular framework has particles attached as shown.

(a) The framework is freely suspended from $X$ and hangs with $AB$ horizontal. Find the distance $AX$.

(b) It is now suspended from $Y$ and hangs with $AD$ at an angle of $10°$ to the horizontal, with $A$ higher than $D$. Find the distance $AY$.

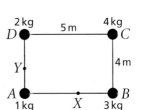

**5** A uniform rectangular lamina $ABCD$ has a circle of radius 0.5 m cut out as shown.
The lamina is suspended from $A$ and hangs in equilibrium. Find, to the nearest degree, the angle that $AD$ makes with the vertical.

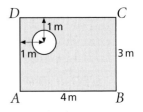

**\*6** A uniform wire is bent into the shape shown, where $BC$ is the arc of a circle, centre $A$.

(a) Find the distance of the centre of mass from $A$.

(b) The wire is suspended from $C$ and hangs in equilibrium. Find, to the nearest degree, the angle that $CA$ makes with the vertical.

**1** Three particles of masses 1 kg, 3 kg and $m$ kg are placed in the $x$–$y$ plane at the points $(2, 3)$, $(4, 1)$ and $(8, 6)$ respectively. The centre of mass of this system of particles is at the point $(\bar{x}, 3)$. All distances are measured in metres.

(a) Show that $m = 2$.

(b) Find the value of $\bar{x}$.

**2** A uniform lamina is formed by taking a square plate of side 20 cm and removing the quadrant with radius 10 cm from the square as shown.

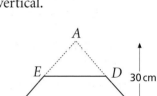

(a) Find the distance of the centre of mass from $AE$.

(b) Find the distance of the centre of mass from $AB$.

(c) The lamina is freely suspended from $B$ and hangs at rest. Find, to the nearest degree, the angle between $BC$ and the vertical.

**3** A uniform plane lamina is in the shape of an isosceles triangle $ABC$, where $AB = AC$.
The mid-point of $BC$ is $M$, $AM = 30$ cm and $BM = 40$ cm.
The mid-points of $AC$ and $AB$ are $D$ and $E$ respectively.
The triangular portion $ADE$ is removed leaving a uniform plane lamina $BCDE$ as shown.

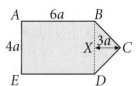

(a) Show that the centre of mass of the lamina $BCDE$ is $6\frac{2}{3}$ cm from $BC$.

The lamina $BCDE$ is freely suspended from $D$ and hangs in equilibrium.

(b) Find, in degrees to one decimal place, the angle which $DE$ makes with the vertical.

Edexcel

**4** A uniform lamina $ABCDE$ consists of a rectangle and an isosceles triangle, where $AB = ED = 6a$ and $AE = BD = 4a$.
The point $X$ is the mid-point of $BD$ and $XC = 3a$.

(a) Explain why the distance of the centre of mass of the lamina from $AB$ is $2a$.

(b) Find the distance of the centre of mass of the lamina from $AE$.

(c) The mass of the lamina is $m$. A particle of mass $km$ is attached to the lamina at the mid-point of $AE$. The lamina is freely suspended from the mid-point of $AB$ and hangs in equilibrium with $AB$ horizontal. Find the value of $k$.

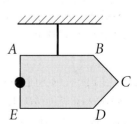

# 4 Work, energy and power

In this chapter you will
- learn what is meant by the work done by a force
- learn about kinetic energy and gravitational potential energy
- use the work–energy principle and the principle of conservation of energy
- learn what is meant by power

---

**Key points from Mechanics 1**

- If a force of $F$ newtons, acting on an object of mass $m$ kg, causes an acceleration $a$ m s$^{-2}$, then $F = ma$. (Newton's second law)

- If an object is moving with constant velocity, then its acceleration is zero. So the resultant force on the object is zero.

- If an object is moving on a rough surface, the friction force $F$ is equal to $\mu R$, where $\mu$ is the coefficient of friction and $R$ is the normal reaction.

- The constant acceleration equations for motion in one dimension are

$$v = u + at \qquad\qquad s = ut + \tfrac{1}{2}at^2$$
$$s = \tfrac{1}{2}(u + v)t \qquad\quad s = vt - \tfrac{1}{2}at^2$$
$$v^2 = u^2 + 2as$$

---

## A Work (answers p 130)

In Mechanics 1 we found that when a force was applied to an object for a period of time it caused a change in momentum of the object. Now we will look at the link between the force applied and the distance moved by the object.

 **A1** Imagine a packing case at rest on rough horizontal ground. If you apply a force, $F$ N, to push the packing case along you will do work.

Now you use the same force, $F$ N, to push the case along for twice the distance. What effect will this have on the work you do?

When a force moves an object a given distance, the force does **work**. The further the object is moved, the greater the work done by the force.

 When a constant force $F$ N applied to an object moves it a distance $s$ m in the direction of the force, the work done is defined as the product of the force and the distance.

Work done $= Fs$

The unit of work is the joule (J). This is named after James Prescott Joule (1818–89), an English physicist who established that the various forms of energy are equivalent. 1 joule is the work done when a force of 1 newton acts through a distance of 1 metre.

**A2** A truck is pushed along a smooth track by a force of 40 N.
Calculate the work done in moving the truck 10 m.

**A3 (a)** A packing case is resting on smooth horizontal ground.
It is pulled a distance $d$ m by a horizontal force $F$ N.
State the work done in moving the case.

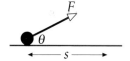

    **(b)** The force is now inclined at 30° to the horizontal.
The case is again pulled a distance $d$ m.

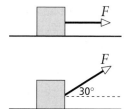

       **(i)** Draw a force diagram for the packing case.

       **(ii)** What force is causing the motion of the case?

       **(iii)** State the work done in moving the case.

When a force is applied at an angle to the direction of motion, only the component of the force acting in the direction of motion does work. The component of force that is perpendicular to the direction of motion does no work, as there is no motion in that direction.

> The work done by a constant force moving an object in a straight line, acting at an angle $\theta$ to the direction of motion, is given by
>
>     Work done $= Fs\cos\theta$
>
> A force acting perpendicular to the direction of motion does no work.

**A4** A particle of weight 8 N is pulled 10 m along a smooth horizontal surface by a force of 25 N inclined at an angle of 40° to the horizontal.

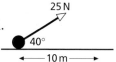

    **(a)** State the work done by the weight of the particle.

    **(b)** Find, to 3 s.f., the work done by the 25 N force.

Consider a car driving along a horizontal road. The car's engine provides a driving force, also known as a **tractive force**, which causes the car to move forwards. The car's motion may also be subject to resistance forces.

**A5** A car moves along a horizontal road at a constant velocity.
The driving force of the car's engine is 2500 N.
Find the work done by the car's engine in moving 50 m.

---

### Example 1

A particle is pulled 5 m along smooth horizontal ground by a force of 80 N.
Calculate the work done by the force when it is

**(a)** horizontal                **(b)** inclined at 25° to the horizontal

### Solution

**(a)** Work done $= Fs = 80 \times 5 = 400$ J

**(b)** Work done $= Fs\cos\theta = 80 \times 5 \times \cos 25° = 363$ J to 3 s.f.

---

**Exercise A** (answers p 130)

**1** An object of mass 2 kg is pushed across a horizontal surface by a horizontal force of magnitude 15 N.
Find the work done by the force in moving the object 8 m.

**2** A car travels at constant speed along a straight horizontal road for 50 m.
The driving force of the car's engine is 3000 N.
Find the work done by the car's engine.

**3 (a)** A particle is pulled along a horizontal surface by a force of 3.5 N inclined at 20° to the horizontal.
Find the work done by the force in moving the particle 10 m.

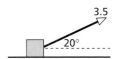

**(b)** The angle of the force is increased to 40°.

   **(i)** Explain why the force will now do less work in moving the particle.

   **(ii)** Find the work done in moving the particle 10 m.

**4** A box is pushed for 15 m along horizontal ground by a constant force.
The work done by the force is 5250 J.
Find the magnitude of the force.

**5** A box of mass 18 kg is raised 12 m vertically at constant speed.
Find the work done by the force raising the box.

**6 (a)** A sledge is pulled along smooth ground by a force of 90 N inclined at 30° to the horizontal.
Find the work done by the force in moving the sledge 6 m.

**(b)** If the sledge had been moved 6 m with the force horizontal, how much more work would have been done?

**7** A truck is pulled along a smooth horizontal track by a force of 150 N inclined at 60° to the horizontal.
Given that the work done by the force is 375 J, find the distance moved by the truck.

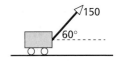

## B  Kinetic energy (answers p 130)

**B1** A van of mass 2000 kg starts from rest and travels with constant acceleration.
After travelling a distance of 100 m its velocity is 20 m s$^{-1}$.
Any resistance to motion can be ignored.

   **(a)** Use one of the constant acceleration equations to find the acceleration of the van.

   **(b)** Use Newton's second law of motion to find the driving force of the van's engine.

   **(c)** Find the work done by the van's engine during this motion.

During the motion of the van, the van's engine has done work which has caused an increase in the van's energy.
The energy possessed by a body due to its motion is called **kinetic energy**.

**B2** A body of mass $m$ kg is initially at rest. It is acted on by a constant force $F$ N. After it has travelled a distance $s$ m, its velocity is $v$ m s$^{-1}$.

(a) Use the constant acceleration equations to show that the acceleration of the body is given by $a = \dfrac{v^2}{2s}$.

(b) Substitute this expression for $a$ into $F = ma$, and hence show that $Fs = \frac{1}{2}mv^2$.

The expression on the left side of the equation above, $Fs$, is the work done by the force, measured in joules. The expression on the right side of the equation represents the kinetic energy of the body, which is also measured in joules.

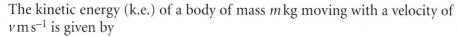

The kinetic energy (k.e.) of a body of mass $m$ kg moving with a velocity of $v$ m s$^{-1}$ is given by

$$\text{k.e.} = \tfrac{1}{2}mv^2$$

The unit of energy is the joule.

**B3** A car of mass 2500 kg travels with constant acceleration over a distance of 200 m. Its velocity increases from 15 m s$^{-1}$ to 30 m s$^{-1}$.
Any resistance to motion can be ignored.

(a) (i) Find the acceleration of the car.

(ii) Use Newton's second law of motion to find the driving force of the car's engine and hence the work done by the car's engine during this motion.

(b) (i) Find the kinetic energy of the car at the start of the motion.

(ii) Find the kinetic energy of the car at the end of the motion.

(iii) Find the change in the car's kinetic energy during this motion.

**B4** A body of mass $m$ kg moves with constant acceleration, increasing its velocity from $u$ m s$^{-1}$ to $v$ m s$^{-1}$ over a distance of $s$ m.

(a) Show that the acceleration of the body is given by $a = \dfrac{v^2 - u^2}{2s}$.

(b) Substitute this expression for $a$ into $F = ma$, and hence show that $Fs = \frac{1}{2}mv^2 - \frac{1}{2}mu^2$.

The work done by a force acting on a body is equal to the change in kinetic energy of the body.

$$Fs = \tfrac{1}{2}mv^2 - \tfrac{1}{2}mu^2$$

**B5** A truck of mass 10 kg is moving at a speed of 18 m s$^{-1}$.
It comes to rest after travelling 40 m.

Find the kinetic energy lost by the truck in coming to rest.

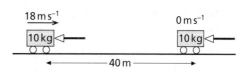

When the speed of an object is reduced, it loses kinetic energy and the amount of work done by the force that brings the object to rest is negative.
This force is a resisting force which acts in the opposite direction to the direction of motion.

**K** A force acting in the direction opposite to the direction of motion does a negative amount of work.

**B6** Find the magnitude of the resisting force acting on the truck in B5.

**B7** A box of mass 40 kg is resting on rough horizontal ground. It is pulled by a horizontal force of 150 N. A constant resisting force of 80 N acts on the box.

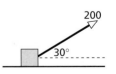

The box moves from rest a distance of 5 m.

(a) Use Newton's second law and the constant acceleration equations to find the final velocity of the box.

(b) Hence find the gain in kinetic energy of the box.

(c) Find the work done by the 150 N force.

(d) Find the work done by the resisting force.

(e) (i) State the resultant force causing the motion of the box.

(ii) Find the work done by the resultant force. Comment on your result.

When an object is acted upon by a number of forces, the change in kinetic energy of the object is equal to the work done by the resultant force acting on the object. If the resultant force acts in the direction of motion, the object will gain kinetic energy. If the resultant force opposes the direction of motion, the object will lose kinetic energy.

---

### Example 2

A particle of mass 5 kg is acted upon by a horizontal force. The initial speed of the particle is $1 \, \mathrm{m\,s^{-1}}$ and the force does 200 J of work. Find the final speed of the particle.

### Solution

Work done = change in kinetic energy = $\frac{1}{2}mv^2 - \frac{1}{2}mu^2$

$$200 = \frac{1}{2} \times 5v^2 - \frac{1}{2} \times 5 \times 1^2 = 2.5v^2 - 2.5$$

$\Rightarrow \quad 2.5v^2 = 202.5$

$\Rightarrow \qquad v^2 = 81$

$\Rightarrow \qquad v = 9$

The final speed of the particle is $9 \, \mathrm{m\,s^{-1}}$.

---

### Example 3

A box of mass 25 kg is pulled 50 m along rough horizontal ground by a force of 200 N inclined at 30° to the horizontal. The coefficient of friction between the box and the ground is 0.4.

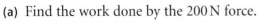
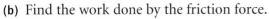

(a) Find the work done by the 200 N force.

(b) Find the work done by the friction force.

(c) If the box started from rest, find its speed after moving 50 m.

## Solution

*Sketch a force diagram for the box.*
*Show the horizontal and vertical components of the 200 N force.*

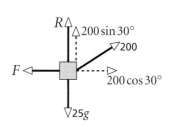

(a) *The motion is horizontal, so use $work = Fs\cos\theta$.*

Work done by 200 N force $= 200 \times 50 \times \cos 30° = 8660\,J$ to 3 s.f.

(b) *The forces are in equilibrium vertically.*

Resolve the forces vertically. $\qquad R + 200\sin 30° = 25 \times 9.8$

$$\Rightarrow \qquad\qquad R = 145\,N$$

The box is moving, so $F = \mu R$. $\quad F = 0.4 \times 145 = 58\,N$

*The friction force acts in the opposite direction to the direction of motion, so the work done by this force is negative.*

Work done by the friction force $= -58 \times 50 = -2900\,J$

(c) *Find the increase in kinetic energy, which is equal to the total work done on the box.*

Increase in k.e. $= 8660 - 2900 = 5760\,J$ to 3 s.f.

Increase in k.e. $= \frac{1}{2}mv^2 - \frac{1}{2}mu^2 \qquad \frac{1}{2} \times 25 \times v^2 - 0 = 5760$

$$\Rightarrow \qquad\qquad v^2 = \frac{2 \times 5760}{25}$$

$$\Rightarrow \qquad\qquad v = 21.5 \text{ to 3 s.f.}$$

After 50 m, the box is moving at $21.5\,m\,s^{-1}$ to 3 s.f.

*An alternative method would be to use Newton's second law to find the acceleration of the box and then use $v^2 = u^2 + 2as$ to find $v$.*

---

## Exercise B (answers p 131)

**1** A car of mass 2000 kg is travelling at $15\,m\,s^{-1}$.
   Find the kinetic energy of the car.

**2** A cyclist on a horizontal road increases her velocity from $5\,m\,s^{-1}$ to $8\,m\,s^{-1}$.
   The total mass of cyclist and bicycle is 90 kg.
   Resistance to motion may be ignored.

   (a) Find the change in kinetic energy.

   (b) State the work done by the cyclist.

**3** A van of mass 3500 kg reduces its speed from $18\,m\,s^{-1}$ to $12\,m\,s^{-1}$.
   Find the van's loss in kinetic energy.

**4** A car of mass 1500 kg is travelling at $40\,m\,s^{-1}$ along a horizontal road.

   (a) What is the kinetic energy of the car?

   (b) The car's brakes are applied and the car comes to rest in 100 m.
      Given that the brakes cause a constant retarding force, find the magnitude
      of this force.

**5** A particle of mass 2 kg is moving at 5 m s$^{-1}$.
A force of 50 N acts on the particle in the direction of motion.
Find the speed of the particle after it has moved a further 4 m.

**6** A van of mass 4000 kg travels along a straight horizontal road. The driving force
of the van's engine is 6500 N and the van is subject to a constant resistance.
The van's speed increases from 10 m s$^{-1}$ to 20 m s$^{-1}$ while travelling 100 m.

(a) Find the increase in the van's kinetic energy.

(b) Find the magnitude of the resistance force.

**7** A sledge of mass 240 kg is pulled on level ground from rest by dogs with
a total forward force of 150 N against resistance of 45 N.
How fast will the sledge be moving after it has moved 56 m?

**8** A sledge of mass 15 kg is pulled from rest along rough horizontal ground by
a horizontal force of 50 N.
The coefficient of friction between the sledge and the ground is 0.3 .

(a) Draw a force diagram for the sledge.

(b) Find the magnitude of the friction force.

(c) The sledge moves 20 m. Find the work done by

(i) the 50 N force          (ii) the friction force

(d) Find the speed of the sledge when it has moved 20 m.

**9** A box of mass 18 kg is pulled from rest along rough horizontal ground
by a force of 85 N inclined at 30° to the horizontal.
The coefficient of friction between the box and the ground is 0.4 .
Find the kinetic energy of the box when it has moved 6 m.

## C Potential energy (answers p 131)

**C1** A ball of mass 0.1 kg is dropped from a height of 2 m above ground level.

(a) What is the initial kinetic energy of the ball?

(b) Describe what happens to the kinetic energy of the ball as it falls.

(c) Use the constant acceleration equations to find the speed of the ball,
and hence its kinetic energy, as it hits the ground.

(d) (i) What force is doing work as the ball falls?

(ii) Find the work done by this force in bringing the ball to ground level.

As the ball drops it gains kinetic energy. This is because the weight of the ball
is doing work as the ball drops.

**C2** A particle of mass $m$ kg is held at height $h$ m above ground level
and released.
Show that the work done by the weight as the particle drops to
the ground is $mgh$ J.

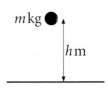

The **gravitational potential energy** of a body is defined as the work that would be done by its weight in moving the body from its current position to a fixed reference position. The reference position is an arbitrary position, often ground level, where the gravitational potential energy is taken to be zero.

A particle of mass $m$ kg at height $h$ m above ground level has gravitational potential energy (p.e.) $mgh$ joules relative to the ground.

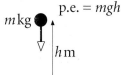

Note that 'gravitational potential energy' is often abbreviated to 'potential energy'.

**C3** A particle of mass $m$ kg is thrown vertically downwards with an initial speed $u$ m s$^{-1}$ from a point $A$ that is $a$ m above the ground. As it passes point $B$, which is $b$ m above the ground, its speed is $v$ m s$^{-1}$.

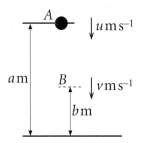

(a) Find an expression for the gain in kinetic energy in terms of $m$, $u$ and $v$.

(b) Find an expression for the loss in potential energy in terms of $m$, $a$ and $b$.

(c) Find an expression for $v^2$ in terms of $u$, $g$, $a$ and $b$, and hence show that the gain in kinetic energy is equal to the loss in potential energy.

The result in C3 can be expressed as        k.e. at $B$ – k.e. at $A$ = p.e. at $A$ – p.e. at $B$

This may be rearranged as        k.e. at $B$ + p.e. at $B$ = k.e. at $A$ + p.e. at $A$

In other words, the total of the potential energy and the kinetic energy of the object is constant so long as the only force acting on the object is its weight. As the kinetic energy of the particle increases, so its potential energy decreases. Conversely, as the kinetic energy decreases, so the potential energy increases. Thus $mgh$ represents potential energy because the particle's weight has the potential to increase the kinetic energy of the particle.

**C4** A ball of mass 0.1 kg is thrown vertically upwards from ground level with initial speed 8 m s$^{-1}$.

(a) What is the initial kinetic energy of the ball?

(b) Describe what happens to the kinetic energy of the ball during its motion.

(c) Show that the speed of the ball when it is $x$ m above ground level is given by $v^2 = 64 - 2gx$.

(d) Describe what happens to the potential energy of the ball during its motion.

(e) What is the potential energy of the ball when it is $x$ m above ground level?

(f) Show that the sum of the kinetic energy and potential energy of the ball is constant.

If a particle of mass $m$ kg is raised vertically by $x$ m, then its potential energy is increased by $mgx$ joules.
If it is lowered vertically by $x$ m, then its potential energy is reduced by $mgx$ joules.

**C5** A box of mass 18 kg is lifted through a height of 2.5 m.
Find its gain in potential energy.

**C6** (a) A particle of mass 5 kg falls 10 m vertically.
Find its loss in potential energy.

(b) Another particle of mass 5 kg slides down a smooth plane inclined
at 25° to the horizontal.
Its final position is 10 m vertically lower than its original position.

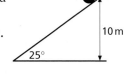

(i) Show that the distance travelled along the plane is $\dfrac{10}{\sin 25°}$ m.

(ii) Show that the work done by the weight, and hence the loss in potential
energy, in moving the particle down the plane, is 490 J.
Comment on this result.

> **K** The change in potential energy of an object is $mgh$ J, where $h$ m is the
> vertical distance between its initial and final positions. This value is not
> affected by the path of the object between these two positions.

---

### Example 4

A boy of mass 28 kg slides down a slide of length 4 m
inclined at 20° to the horizontal.
Calculate his loss in potential energy.

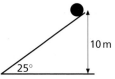

### Solution

*The loss in potential energy is mgh, where h is the vertical distance moved.*

$h = 4 \sin 20°$

Loss in p.e. $= 28 \times 9.8 \times 4 \sin 20° = 375$ J to 3 s.f.

---

### Example 5

A box of mass 15 kg is pulled for 8 m up a plane inclined at 30° to
the horizontal by a force of 50 N acting parallel to the plane.
The coefficient of friction between the box and the plane is 0.4.

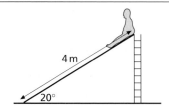

(a) Calculate the work done by the friction force.

(b) Calculate the gain in potential energy.

### Solution

(a) *Sketch a force diagram.*
*The friction force acts in the opposite direction to
the direction of motion, so it does negative work.*

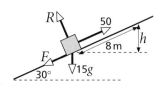

Resolve forces perpendicular to the plane. $R = 15 \times 9.8 \times \cos 30° = 147 \cos 30°$

The box is moving so $F = \mu R$.       $\Rightarrow F = 0.4 \times 147 \cos 30° = 58.8 \cos 30°$

Work done by the friction force $= -Fs = -58.8 \cos 30° \times 8 = -407$ J to 3 s.f.

**(b)** *Calculate the vertical height h moved by the box.*

$$h = 8\sin 30°$$

Gain in p.e. $= mgh = 15 \times 9.8 \times 8\sin 30° = 588\,\text{J}$ to 3 s.f.

---

## Exercise C (answers p 132)

**1** An object of mass 8 kg is 4 m above ground level.
Find its potential energy relative to the ground.

**2** A boy of mass 30 kg sits at the top of a slide of length 5 m inclined at
36° to the horizontal.
Calculate his potential energy relative to the ground.

**3** A lift of mass 1500 kg travels down a vertical distance of 40 m.
Find its loss in potential energy.

**4** A car of mass 1500 kg travels 50 m up a slope inclined at $\theta°$ to the horizontal,
where $\sin\theta = \frac{1}{10}$.
The driving force of the car's engine is 4000 N and the car is subject to
a constant resistance of 500 N.

(a) Find the work done by the car's engine.

(b) Find the work done by the resistance force.

(c) Find the gain in potential energy of the car.

**5** A sledge of mass 20 kg slides down a slope 15 m long inclined at
30° to the horizontal. It is subject to a resistance of 80 N.

(a) Find the loss in potential energy of the sledge.

(b) Find the work done by the resistance force.

**6** A girl of mass 26 kg slides down a slide of length 4 m inclined
at 35° to the horizontal.
The coefficient of friction between the girl and the slide is 0.2 .

(a) Draw a force diagram for the girl.

(b) Find the magnitude of the friction force.

(c) Find the work done by the friction force.

(d) Find the girl's loss in potential energy.

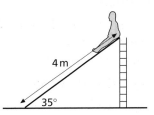

**7** A box of mass 20 kg is pulled 6 m up a plane inclined at
15° to the horizontal by a force of 240 N parallel to the plane.
The coefficient of friction between the box and the plane is 0.35 .

(a) Find the work done by the 240 N force.

(b) Find the work done by the friction force.

(c) Find the gain in potential energy of the box.

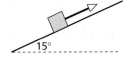

# D Conservation of energy (answers p 132)

**D1** A ball of mass 0.2 kg is thrown vertically upwards with initial speed $8\,\text{m\,s}^{-1}$.

   **(a)** **(i)** Find the maximum height reached by the ball.

       **(ii)** Hence find the ball's gain in potential energy in reaching this height.

   **(b)** **(i)** What is the speed of the ball when it is at its maximum height?

       **(ii)** Find the ball's loss in kinetic energy in reaching this height. Comment on your result.

**D2** A sledge of mass 15 kg slides down a smooth slope inclined at 30° to the horizontal. The slope is 10 m long and the sledge is released from rest at the top.

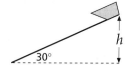

   **(a)** **(i)** Find the change in vertical height, $h$ m, of the sledge during the motion.

       **(ii)** Hence find the loss in potential energy of the sledge during the motion.

   **(b)** **(i)** By resolving forces down the plane and using Newton's second law, show that the acceleration of the sledge down the plane is $4.9\,\text{m\,s}^{-2}$.

       **(ii)** Find the speed of the sledge when it reaches the bottom of the slope.

      **(iii)** Hence find the gain in kinetic energy of the sledge during the motion. Comment on your result.

**D3** A box of mass 15 kg is released from rest on a plane of length 10 m inclined at 25° to the horizontal. A constant resisting force of 50 N acts on the box.

   **(a)** **(i)** Find the change in vertical height, $h$ m, of the box during the motion.

       **(ii)** Hence find the loss in potential energy of the box during the motion.

   **(b)** **(i)** By resolving forces down the plane and using Newton's second law, show that the acceleration of the box down the plane is approximately $0.808\,\text{m\,s}^{-2}$.

       **(ii)** Find the speed of the box when it reaches the bottom of the slope.

      **(iii)** Hence find the gain in kinetic energy of the box during the motion. Comment on your result.

In the first two questions the change in kinetic energy is equal to the change in potential energy. When one is lost, the other is gained. The total mechanical energy of the system is constant. The only external force doing work is gravity.

In the third question the change in kinetic energy is not equal to the change in potential energy. This is because an external force other than gravity, that is the resisting force, is also doing work. The amount of work done by this force is negative and the total mechanical energy of the system is reduced. The normal reaction of the plane on the object is perpendicular to the direction of motion and so does no work.

**K** The sum of the potential energy and the kinetic energy of a system will remain constant if no external force other than gravity does work.

Gain in kinetic energy = loss in potential energy

This is known as the **principle of conservation of mechanical energy**.

Note that if there is a loss in kinetic energy of the system, then there will be a gain in potential energy.

The principle of conservation of mechanical energy applies only if the mechanical energy of a system is not converted to another form of energy, such as light, sound or heat. For example, when a friction force acts on an object, mechanical energy is converted into heat energy.
If no external force other than gravity acts, then mechanical energy is not converted into any other form, and the principle of conservation of mechanical energy applies.

**D4** (a) Find the change in energy of the box in question D3.

(b) Calculate the work done by the resisting force in question D3. Comment on your result.

**K** If an external force other than gravity does work, then the work done by the force is equal to the change in mechanical energy of the system.

Work done by force = gain in potential energy + gain in kinetic energy

This is known as the **work–energy principle**.

The work–energy principle explains why work and energy have the same units.
If the work done by the force is positive, then the total mechanical energy of the system increases.
If the work done by the force is negative, then the total mechanical energy of the system decreases.

We have seen that the work–energy principle is true for situations involving constant acceleration. In fact it can be shown to be true for all situations and can thus be used to solve problems that cannot be solved using the constant acceleration equations.

**D5** A stone of mass 0.2 kg is thrown vertically upwards from the top of a cliff with an initial speed of 5 m s$^{-1}$. The top of the cliff is 30 m above the water.

(a) Use the principle of conservation of mechanical energy to find the maximum height above the top of the cliff reached by the stone.

(b) Use the principle of conservation of mechanical energy to find the speed of the stone when it hits the water.

(c) Explain why you did not need to know the mass of the stone.

(d) What assumptions have been made in applying the principle of conservation of energy to this situation?

**D6** A ball of mass 0.1 kg is projected up a smooth track inclined at 40° to the horizontal. The initial speed of the ball is $10\,\text{m}\,\text{s}^{-1}$.

    **(a)** Draw a force diagram and hence explain why the principle of conservation of mechanical energy can be used in this situation.

    **(b)** Find the initial kinetic energy of the ball.

    **(c)** Assuming that the ball does not reach the end of the track, state the loss in kinetic energy of the ball in reaching its maximum height up the track.

    **(d)** State the increase in potential energy of the ball in reaching its maximum height up the track.

    **(e)** Hence find the maximum distance the ball reaches up the track.

**D7** A box of mass 16 kg slides from rest down a slope of length 2.5 m inclined at 35° to the horizontal. A constant resisting force of 40 N acts on the box.

    **(a)** Draw a force diagram and hence explain why the principle of conservation of mechanical energy cannot be applied in this situation.

    **(b)** Find the work done by the resisting force during the motion.

    **(c)** Find the potential energy lost by the box.

    **(d)** Find the kinetic energy gained by the box.

    **(e)** Hence find the speed of the box when it reaches the bottom of the slope.

---

### Example 6

A ball of mass 0.1 kg is projected at $1\,\text{m}\,\text{s}^{-1}$ from a height of 2.5 m above ground level down a smooth curved track $AB$. Find the speed of the ball when it reaches $B$.

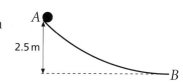

#### Solution

*The normal reaction on the ball is always perpendicular to the direction of motion, so gravity is the only force doing work and the principle of conservation of mechanical energy can be used.*

Gain in kinetic energy = loss in potential energy

$$\tfrac{1}{2}\times 0.1 \times v^2 - \tfrac{1}{2}\times 0.1 \times 1^2 = 0.1 \times 9.8 \times 2.5$$

$$\Rightarrow v^2 = 50 \quad \Rightarrow v = 7.07 \text{ to 3 s.f.}$$

The ball is travelling at $7.07\,\text{m}\,\text{s}^{-1}$ when it reaches $B$.

*Note that the mass of the ball was not required, as it appears in all terms in the equation.*

---

### Example 7

A load of mass 20 kg is pulled from rest up a plane inclined at 25° to the horizontal by a force of 150 N. The coefficient of friction between the load and the plane is 0.3.

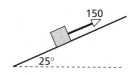

Find the kinetic energy gained by the load, and hence its speed, when it has moved 5 m up the plane.

## Solution

*Draw a force diagram.*
*The principle of conservation of mechanical energy cannot be applied because the 150 N force and the friction force F both do work in addition to the work done by gravity.*
*No work is done by R as it acts perpendicular to the direction of motion.*

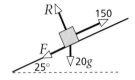

*Find the magnitude of the friction force.*

*Resolve perpendicular to the plane.* $\qquad$ $R = 20g\cos 25°$
*To retain accuracy do not substitute values for g and $\cos 25°$ until the final answer is required.*

*The load is moving, so $F = \mu R$.* $\qquad F = 0.3 \times 20g\cos 25° = 6g\cos 25°$

Work done by 150 N force $= 150 \times 5 = 750$

Work done by friction force $= -6g\cos 25° \times 5 = -30g\cos 25°$

*The height increases, so there is a gain in p.e.* Gain in p.e. $= mgh = 20g \times 5 \sin 25°$
$$= 100g\sin 25°$$

*The load started from rest, so there is a gain in k.e. of $\frac{1}{2}mv^2$, where v is the speed after 5 m.*

Work done = gain in p.e. + gain in k.e. $\qquad 750 - 30g\cos 25° = 100g\sin 25° + \frac{1}{2}mv^2$

$\Rightarrow \qquad\qquad \frac{1}{2}mv^2 = 750 - 30g\cos 25° - 100g\sin 25°$

$\Rightarrow \qquad\qquad \frac{1}{2}mv^2 = 69.4$ to 3 s.f.

$\qquad\qquad\qquad \frac{1}{2} \times 20 \times v^2 = 69.4$

$\Rightarrow \qquad\qquad\qquad v^2 = 6.94 \Rightarrow v = 2.63$ to 3 s.f.

When it has moved 5 m up the plane the kinetic energy gained is 69.4 J and the load is moving at $2.63 \, \text{m s}^{-1}$, both to 3 s.f.

---

## Exercise D (answers p 133)

**1** A stone of mass 0.2 kg is dropped from a height of 3 m above ground level.

(a) Find the potential energy lost by the stone as it reaches the ground.

(b) Use the principle of conservation of energy to find the kinetic energy of the stone, and hence its velocity, as it reaches the ground.

**2** A ball of mass 0.1 kg is hit vertically upwards with initial speed $15 \, \text{m s}^{-1}$.

(a) Find its potential energy with respect to its initial position when it has travelled 3 m.

(b) Find its speed at this point.

(c) (i) What is the potential energy gained by the ball at its highest point?

(ii) Find the maximum height of the ball above its initial position.

**3** A particle of mass 0.1 kg on a string of length 1 m is released from rest when the string makes an angle of 80° with the vertical as shown.
Use the principle of conservation of mechanical energy to find its speed at the lowest point of its path.

**4** A girl of mass 30 kg slides down a helter-skelter.
She starts from rest and has reached a speed of $4\,\mathrm{m\,s^{-1}}$ at the bottom.
The height of the helter-skelter is 10 m.

(a) Find the girl's loss in potential energy.

(b) Find her gain in kinetic energy.

(c) Find the work done by the friction force.

**5** A boy and his bicycle have a total mass of 60 kg.
At the top of a hill he is travelling at $6\,\mathrm{m\,s^{-1}}$ and he applies his brakes as
he cycles down the hill. He is travelling at $10\,\mathrm{m\,s^{-1}}$ at the bottom, having
dropped a vertical distance of 30 m.

(a) Find the loss in potential energy.

(b) Find the gain in kinetic energy.

(c) Find the work done by the brakes.

(d) Comment on the assumptions that you have made.

**6** A stone of mass 0.3 kg is dropped from a height of 5 m above ground level.
The speed of the stone when it reaches the ground is $6\,\mathrm{m\,s^{-1}}$.

(a) Find the total energy lost by the stone during the motion.

(b) Find the magnitude of the resistance force acting on the stone.

**7** A particle of mass 2 kg is projected up a slope inclined at 30° to the horizontal
with an initial speed of $8\,\mathrm{m\,s^{-1}}$. It travels 5 m up the slope before coming to rest.

(a) Find the work done by the friction force.

(b) Find the magnitude of the friction force.

(c) Find the coefficient of friction between the particle and the slope.

## E Power (answers p 133)

**D** **E1** (a) Tim pushes a packing case along horizontal ground with a force of 150 N.
He pushes it 5 m in 10 seconds.
How much work has he done?

(b) Alison pushes the same packing case with a force of 150 N.
She pushes it 5 m in 15 seconds.
How much work has she done?

(c) How could you describe the difference between the two situations?

**Power** is defined as the rate of doing work. This is the rate of generating or using energy.
If a person or engine can do a given amount of work in a shorter time, the energy
is generated in a shorter time and the person or engine is said to be more powerful.

**K** $$\text{Power} = \frac{\text{work done}}{\text{time taken}}$$

The unit of power is the watt (W). This is named after James Watt (1736–1819), the Scottish inventor of the modern steam engine.
1 watt is the power which can produce 1 joule of work in 1 second.

**E2** Find the power of each push in E1.

**E3** A lift of mass 1000 kg travels downwards a distance of 25 m in 40 s at constant speed.

    **(a)** Calculate the work done by the lift's motor.

    **(b)** What is the power of the lift's motor?

Consider a vehicle whose engine is producing a driving force $F$ N and is moving at constant speed $v$ m s$^{-1}$.

The vehicle travels $v$ m in 1 second.

Hence the work done by the driving force in 1 second is $Fv$ J.

The power is the work done per second; hence the power of the vehicle is $Fv$ W.

This formula applies whether or not the driving force is constant.
If the velocity of the vehicle is not constant it can be used to find the power at the instant when the velocity is $v$ m s$^{-1}$.

**(K)**   Power = driving force × velocity  $(P = Fv)$

**E4** **(a)** A car's engine produces a driving force of 950 N. The car is travelling at 18 m s$^{-1}$.
       Find the power output of the car's engine.

    **(b)** The engine of a van is operating at 5 kW. The van is travelling at 15 m s$^{-1}$.
       Find the driving force of the van's engine. (1 kW = 1000 W)

**(D)**  **E5** A car's engine is running at its maximum power.
      The car travels along a horizontal road at constant speed.
      It reaches a hill and its speed decreases.
      How does the driving force change?

The next three questions are about a car of mass 1500 kg travelling on a straight, horizontal road. It is subject to a constant resistance of 1200 N.

**E6** The car is travelling at its maximum speed.

    **(a)** What is the car's acceleration?

    **(b)** Find the driving force of the car's engine.

    **(c)** Given that the maximum power of the car's engine is 45 kW, find the maximum speed of the car.

**E7** The speed of the car is now reduced to 25 m s$^{-1}$. The resistance remains constant at 1200 N.

    **(a)** Given that the engine continues to operate at maximum power, find its driving force.

    **(b)** Use Newton's second law to show that the acceleration of the car is 0.4 m s$^{-2}$ when its speed is 25 m s$^{-1}$.

The car now travels at constant speed up a hill inclined at an angle $\alpha$ to the horizontal, where $\sin \alpha = \frac{1}{15}$.
It is subject to the same constant resistance.

The force diagram for the car is shown.

As the car is travelling up a hill, the engine has to do work against gravity as well as against the resistance force. Hence the driving force of the engine must be greater.

The engine is still operating at its maximum power but the speed of the car is less than when travelling on the horizontal because of the greater driving force.

**E8** (a) By resolving the forces parallel to the plane, find the magnitude of the driving force, $F$ N.

(b) Find the speed of the car travelling up the hill.

In the questions above, the car was subject to a constant resistance force. A resistance force need not be constant. It may vary with the speed at which the car is travelling.

**E9** A van of mass 2500 kg travels along a straight horizontal road subject to a resistance of magnitude $40v$ when travelling at $v$ m s$^{-1}$.
The van has a maximum speed of 35 m s$^{-1}$.

(a) (i) Find the magnitude of the resistance when the van is travelling at its maximum speed.

(ii) Hence show that the maximum power of the van is 49 000 W.

(b) (i) Find the magnitude of the resistance when the van is travelling at 20 m s$^{-1}$.

(ii) If the van's engine is operating at maximum power, find the driving force of the engine when the van is travelling at 20 m s$^{-1}$.

(iii) Use Newton's second law to find the maximum acceleration of the van when it is travelling at 20 m s$^{-1}$.

---

## Example 8

A car of mass 1500 kg has a power output of 40 000 W. When the car is travelling on a horizontal road at 25 m s$^{-1}$ it is subject to a resistance of 550 N.

(a) Find the tractive force of the engine.

(b) Find the acceleration of the car.

### Solution

(a) *The power and speed are known so use $P = Fv$ to calculate the tractive force. Remember that the tractive force is the driving force.*

$$40\,000 = 25F$$

$$\Rightarrow \qquad F = 1600$$

The tractive force is 1600 N.

**(b)** *Draw a force diagram.*
   *(Vertical forces balance out and are not shown.)*

   Apply N2L.
   $$1600 - 550 = 1500a$$
   $$\Rightarrow \quad 1050 = 1500a$$
   $$a = 0.7$$

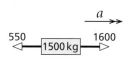

The acceleration is $0.7\,\mathrm{m\,s^{-2}}$.

---

## Example 9

A van of mass 3000 kg is travelling up a slope inclined at an angle $\alpha$ to the horizontal, where $\sin\alpha = 0.1$. A resistance force of magnitude $kv$ acts on the van, where $k$ is a constant and $v\,\mathrm{m\,s^{-1}}$ is the van's speed.
When the van is travelling at a constant speed of $20\,\mathrm{m\,s^{-1}}$ up the slope its engine is operating at its maximum power output of 78 kilowatts.

**(a)** Find the value of $k$.

**(b)** Find the maximum speed of the van on a horizontal road.

## Solution

**(a)** *Draw a force diagram.*

   *Use $P = Fv$ to calculate the driving force.*
   *Remember to use the power in watts.*
   $$78\,000 = 20F$$
   $$\Rightarrow \quad F = 3900$$

   Resolve the forces along the plane.
   $$F = kv + 3000g\sin\alpha$$
   $$\Rightarrow \quad 3900 = 20k + 2940$$
   $$\Rightarrow \quad k = \frac{3900 - 2940}{20}$$
   $$\Rightarrow \quad k = 48$$

**(b)** *Draw a force diagram.*
   *The resistance is $48v$ and the magnitude of the driving force has changed.*

   *The van is at maximum speed, so the acceleration is zero.*

   Resolve the forces horizontally.
   $$F = 48v$$

   At maximum speed, the power output is maximum.
   $$P = Fv$$
   $$78\,000 = 48v^2$$
   $$\Rightarrow \quad v^2 = 1625$$
   $$\Rightarrow \quad v = 40.3 \text{ to 3 s.f.}$$

The maximum speed the van is $40.3\,\mathrm{m\,s^{-1}}$ on a horizontal road.

---

**Exercise E** (answers p 134)

1 A car is travelling on a horizontal road at $27 \, \mathrm{m \, s^{-1}}$.
   Given that the driving force of the car's engine is 2000 N, find its rate of working.

2 A weightlifter lifts a load of 55 kg through a height of 1.8 m in 2 seconds.
   (a) Find the work done by the weightlifter.
   (b) What is the power of this lift, assuming it is constant?

3 A crane lifts a beam of mass 240 kg a height of 15 m at a constant speed of $3 \, \mathrm{m \, s^{-1}}$.
   Find the power of the crane.

4 A van has a maximum power output of 45 kW. When driving on a horizontal
   road it is subject to a constant resistance of magnitude 1500 N.
   Find the maximum speed of the van.

5 A car of mass 1200 kg is subject to a constant resistance of 1250 N when moving
   along a straight horizontal road. The car's engine is working at a rate of 40 000 W.
   Find the acceleration of the car when it is travelling at $24 \, \mathrm{m \, s^{-1}}$.

6 A train of mass 450 tonnes has a maximum speed of $40 \, \mathrm{m \, s^{-1}}$ on the level.
   It is subject to a constant resistance of 140 000 N.
   (a) Find the power of the engine.
   (b) Assuming the same power and resistance, find the maximum speed
       up a slope inclined at $\theta°$ to the horizontal, where $\sin \theta = \frac{1}{120}$.

7 (a) A van of mass 2500 kg is moving along a level road against a constant resistance.
       The engine of the van is working at 60 kW.
       The maximum speed of the van is $32 \, \mathrm{m \, s^{-1}}$.
       Find the magnitude of the resistance.
   (b) The van now moves up a road inclined at an angle $\theta$ to the horizontal,
       where $\sin \theta = \frac{1}{20}$.
       Assuming the same power and resistance, find the deceleration when
       the van is moving at $20 \, \mathrm{m \, s^{-1}}$.

8 A car of mass 1400 kg has a maximum power output of 55 kW.
   The car has a maximum speed of $45 \, \mathrm{m \, s^{-1}}$ when travelling down a hill inclined
   at $\theta°$ to the horizontal, where $\sin \theta = 0.04$.
   Find the magnitude of the resistance force.

9 A car of mass 1600 kg has a maximum power output of 45 000 W.
   The car travels on a horizontal road subject to a resistance of magnitude
   $25v$ N when travelling at $v \, \mathrm{m \, s^{-1}}$.
   (a) (i) If the car is operating at its maximum power, find the driving force
           of the engine when the car is travelling at $18 \, \mathrm{m \, s^{-1}}$.
       (ii) Find the acceleration of the car at this speed.
   (b) Show that the maximum speed of the car is $42.4 \, \mathrm{m \, s^{-1}}$ to 3 s.f.

## Key points

- When a constant force $F$ N applied to an object moves it a distance $s$ m in the direction of the force, the work done is the product of the force and the distance moved.

    Work done $= Fs$

    The unit of work is the joule. (p 64)

- The work done by a constant force moving an object in a straight line, acting at an angle $\theta$ to the direction of motion, is given by

    Work done $= Fs \cos \theta$

    A force acting perpendicular to the direction of motion does no work. A force acting in the direction opposite to the direction of motion does a negative amount of work. (pp 65, 68)

- The kinetic energy (k.e.) of a body of mass $m$ kg moving with a velocity of $v$ m s$^{-1}$ is given by k.e. $= \frac{1}{2} m v^2$.
  The unit of energy is the joule. (p 67)

- The work done by a force acting on a body is equal to the change in kinetic energy of the body.

    $Fs = \frac{1}{2} m v^2 - \frac{1}{2} m u^2$ (p 67)

- The gravitational potential energy (p.e.) of a body is defined as the work that would be done by its weight in moving the body from its current position to an arbitrary fixed reference position, where the p.e. is taken to be zero.

    A particle of mass $m$ kg at height $h$ m above ground level has gravitational potential energy $mgh$ joules relative to the ground.

    The change in potential energy of an object is $mgh$ joules, where $h$ m is the vertical distance between its initial and final positions. The change in potential energy is not affected by the path of the object between these two positions. (pp 71–72)

- The principle of conservation of mechanical energy states that the sum of the potential energy and the kinetic energy of a system will remain constant if no external force other than gravity does work.

    Gain in kinetic energy = loss in potential energy (p 75)

- The work–energy principle states that if an external force other than gravity does work, then the work done by the force is equal to the change in mechanical energy of the system.

    Work done by force = gain in potential energy + gain in kinetic energy (p 75)

- Power $= \dfrac{\text{work done}}{\text{time taken}} = $ driving force $\times$ velocity

    The unit of power is the watt. (pp 78–79)

## Mixed questions (answers p 134)

**1** A ball of mass 0.1 kg moves on a track as shown. It leaves $A$ with a speed of $2\,\text{m s}^{-1}$.

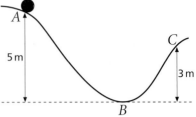

(a) Assuming that the track is smooth, use an energy method to find

   (i) the speed of the ball at $B$

   (ii) the speed of the ball at $C$

(b) Comment on the effect that assuming the track is smooth has had on your answer.

**2** (a) A cyclist and his bicycle have a combined mass of 90 kg. He freewheels down a straight road inclined at an angle $\alpha$ to the horizontal, where $\sin\alpha = \frac{1}{15}$. His initial speed is $4\,\text{m s}^{-1}$ and the resistance to motion is modelled as constant with magnitude 25 N. Find the speed of the cyclist when he has travelled a distance of 50 m.

(b) The cyclist now cycles up the same road at a constant speed of $4\,\text{m s}^{-1}$. The resistance to motion remains unchanged. Find the rate at which the cyclist is working.

**3** In a ski-jump competition, a skier of mass 80 kg moves from rest at a point $A$ on a ski slope. The skier's path is an arc $AB$. The starting point $A$ of the slope is 32.5 m above horizontal ground. The end $B$ of the slope is 8.1 m above the ground. When the skier reaches $B$, she is travelling at $20\,\text{m s}^{-1}$, and moving upwards at an angle $\alpha$ to the horizontal, where $\tan\alpha = \frac{3}{4}$, as shown. The distance along the slope from $A$ to $B$ is 60 m. The resistance to motion while she is on the slope is modelled as a force of constant magnitude $R$ newtons.

(a) By using the work–energy principle, find the value of $R$.

On reaching $B$, the skier then moves through the air and reaches the ground at the point $C$. The motion of the skier in moving from $B$ to $C$ is modelled as that of a particle moving freely under gravity.

(b) Find the time for the skier to move from $B$ to $C$.

(c) Find the horizontal distance from $B$ to $C$.

(d) Find the speed of the skier immediately before she reaches $C$.          Edexcel

**4** A car of mass 1300 kg has a maximum speed of $35\,\text{m s}^{-1}$ when travelling on a horizontal road. The car experiences a resistance force of $kv\,\text{N}$, where $v\,\text{m s}^{-1}$ is the speed of the car and $k$ is a constant.

(a) Given that the maximum power of the car is 49 000 W, find the value of $k$.

(b) Find the maximum possible acceleration of the car when it is travelling at $25\,\text{m s}^{-1}$ on a horizontal road.

## Test yourself (answers p 134)

**1** A bullet of mass 10 g is fired horizontally at a fixed board of depth 3 cm. The bullet hits the board with a speed of $500\,\mathrm{m\,s^{-1}}$ and emerges with a speed of $200\,\mathrm{m\,s^{-1}}$. The board exerts a constant resistance force on the bullet. Find the magnitude of the resistance force.

**2** A ball of mass 0.2 kg is projected up a track inclined at 30° to the horizontal with an initial speed of $6\,\mathrm{m\,s^{-1}}$.

   **(a)** By modelling the track as smooth, use an energy method to find the maximum distance the ball reaches up the slope.

   **(b)** An improved model assumes that the track is rough. Given that the ball reaches a maximum distance of 2.5 m up the track, find the coefficient of friction between the ball and the track.

**3** A car of mass 1500 kg moves at a constant speed of $26\,\mathrm{m\,s^{-1}}$ up a straight road inclined at an angle $\alpha$ to the horizontal, where $\sin\alpha = \frac{1}{25}$. The non-gravitational resistance to the motion of the car is constant and has magnitude 1400 N.

   **(a)** Find the rate of working of the car's engine.

   **(b)** The car now travels along a horizontal road. The car's engine continues to work at the same rate and the resistance to motion is unchanged. Find the maximum speed of the car along the horizontal road.

**4** A car of mass 1000 kg is moving along a straight horizontal road with a constant acceleration of $f\,\mathrm{m\,s^{-2}}$. The resistance to motion is modelled as a constant force of magnitude 1200 N. When the car is travelling at $12\,\mathrm{m\,s^{-1}}$, the power generated by the engine of the car is 24 kW.

   **(a)** Calculate the value of $f$.

   When the car is travelling at $14\,\mathrm{m\,s^{-1}}$, the engine is switched off and the car comes to rest, without braking, in a distance of $d$ metres.

   **(b)** Assuming the same model for resistance, use the work–energy principle to calculate the value of $d$.

   **(c)** Give a reason why the model used for the resistance to motion may not be realistic.

Edexcel

**5** A car of mass 1300 kg is moving down a straight road inclined at an angle $\theta$ to the horizontal, where $\sin\theta = \frac{1}{20}$. The non-gravitational resistance to motion is modelled as a constant force of magnitude $R$ newtons. When the car is moving at a constant speed of $25\,\mathrm{m\,s^{-1}}$, its engine is working at a rate of 20 kW.

   **(a)** Find the value of $R$.

   **(b)** The car now moves up the same road. Given that the car's engine is working at the same rate and the resistance to motion remains the same, find the deceleration of the car when it is moving at $15\,\mathrm{m\,s^{-1}}$.

# 5 Momentum

In this chapter you will
- solve problems involving impulse in two dimensions
- use Newton's law of restitution
- solve problems involving several impacts

## A Momentum and impulse (answers p 134)

The momentum of a moving object is the product mass × velocity.
Because velocity is a vector quantity, so is momentum.

This diagram shows an object of mass 5 kg moving in two
dimensions with a velocity of $(4\mathbf{i} + 2\mathbf{j})\,\text{m s}^{-1}$.

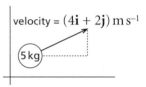

Its momentum, in $\text{kg m s}^{-1}$, is mass × velocity

$$= 5(4\mathbf{i} + 2\mathbf{j}) = 20\mathbf{i} + 10\mathbf{j}$$

**A1** Find the momentum of each of the following objects.

(a) An object of mass 0.5 kg moving with velocity $(2\mathbf{i} + 6\mathbf{j})\,\text{m s}^{-1}$

(b) An object of mass 2 kg moving with velocity $(3\mathbf{i} - 5\mathbf{j})\,\text{m s}^{-1}$

When a force acts on an object for a given time, the product force × time is
called the impulse of the force. Impulse is measured in newton seconds (N s).
Because force is a vector quantity, so is impulse.

For example, a force of $(3\mathbf{i} - 2\mathbf{j})$ newtons acting for 4 seconds has an impulse
of $4(3\mathbf{i} - 2\mathbf{j}) = (12\mathbf{i} - 8\mathbf{j})\,\text{N s}$.

In Mechanics 1, where we studied motion in one dimension, we saw that
Newton's second law of motion can be expressed in the form

impulse = change in momentum

This equation remains true for motion in two or three dimensions, where
the quantities impulse and momentum are vectors.

For example, suppose an object of mass 5 kg is initially
moving with velocity $(2\mathbf{i} + 3\mathbf{j})\,\text{m s}^{-1}$.
Its momentum, in $\text{kg m s}^{-1}$, is $5(2\mathbf{i} + 3\mathbf{j}) = 10\mathbf{i} + 15\mathbf{j}$.

A force then acts on the object for a time with the result
that afterwards it is moving with velocity $(8\mathbf{i} + \mathbf{j})\,\text{m s}^{-1}$.
So its final momentum is $5(8\mathbf{i} + \mathbf{j}) = (40\mathbf{i} + 5\mathbf{j})\,\text{kg m s}^{-1}$.

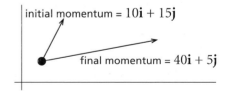

The dotted vector represents the change in momentum:

$$(40\mathbf{i} + 5\mathbf{j}) - (10\mathbf{i} + 15\mathbf{j}) = 30\mathbf{i} - 10\mathbf{j}$$

This is equal to the impulse, in N s.

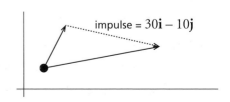

**A2** An object of mass 0.2 kg is initially moving with velocity $(5\mathbf{i} - 2\mathbf{j})\,\text{m s}^{-1}$. A force acts for a time on the object and afterwards it is moving with velocity $(3\mathbf{i} + 4\mathbf{j})\,\text{m s}^{-1}$.

  (a) Find the initial momentum and the final momentum of the object and show these on a diagram.

  (b) Find the impulse of the force, showing it on the diagram.

Because change in momentum is equal to impulse, the same units may be used for both impulse and momentum. It is customary to use the unit N s (newton second) for momentum rather than $\text{kg m s}^{-1}$, although momentum is still found by multiplying mass and velocity.

The equation        impulse = final momentum – initial momentum

may be written as     final momentum = initial momentum + impulse

**A3** A force of $(\mathbf{i} + 2\mathbf{j})\,\text{N}$ acts for 3 seconds on an object that is initially at rest.

  (a) Find the impulse of the force.

  (b) The initial momentum of the object is zero. What is its final momentum?

  (c) Given that the mass of the object is 0.2 kg, find its final velocity.

**A4** An object of mass 0.5 kg is initially moving with velocity $(8\mathbf{i} - 6\mathbf{j})\,\text{m s}^{-1}$. A force of $(2\mathbf{i} + \mathbf{j})\,\text{N}$ acts on the object for 5 seconds.

  (a) Find the initial momentum of the object.

  (b) Find the impulse of the force.

  (c) Find the final momentum of the object.

  (d) Hence find the final velocity of the object.

**K**

Momentum and impulse are vector quantities.

Momentum of an object = mass × velocity

Impulse of a force = force × time

Impulse of force acting on an object = change in momentum of the object

Momentum and impulse are both measured in N s (newton second).

---

### Example 1

A particle of mass 2 kg is moving with velocity $4\mathbf{i}\,\text{m s}^{-1}$ when it is given an impulse of $(2\mathbf{i} - 4\mathbf{j})\,\text{N s}$. Find the final velocity of the particle.

### Solution

Initial momentum = $2 \times 4\mathbf{i} = 8\mathbf{i}\,\text{N s}$

Change in momentum = impulse = $(2\mathbf{i} - 4\mathbf{j})\,\text{N s}$

So final momentum = $8\mathbf{i} + (2\mathbf{i} - 4\mathbf{j}) = (10\mathbf{i} - 4\mathbf{j})\,\text{N s}$

Final velocity = momentum ÷ mass = $(10\mathbf{i} - 4\mathbf{j}) \div 2 = (5\mathbf{i} - 2\mathbf{j})\,\text{m s}^{-1}$

---

## Example 2

An object of mass 2.5 kg is initially moving with velocity $(6\mathbf{i} + \mathbf{j})\,\text{m s}^{-1}$.
A force of $(3\mathbf{i} - 2\mathbf{j})\,\text{N}$ acts on the object for 4 seconds.
Find the final velocity of the object.

### Solution

Initial momentum of object $= 2.5(6\mathbf{i} + \mathbf{j}) = (15\mathbf{i} + 2.5\mathbf{j})\,\text{N s}$

Impulse of force $= 4(3\mathbf{i} - 2\mathbf{j}) = (12\mathbf{i} - 8\mathbf{j})\,\text{N s}$

So change in momentum $= (12\mathbf{i} - 8\mathbf{j})\,\text{N s}$

So final momentum $= (15\mathbf{i} + 2.5\mathbf{j}) + (12\mathbf{i} - 8\mathbf{j}) = (27\mathbf{i} - 5.5\mathbf{j})\,\text{N s}$

Final velocity $=$ final momentum $\div$ mass $= (27\mathbf{i} - 5.5\mathbf{j}) \div 2.5 = (10.8\mathbf{i} - 2.2\mathbf{j})\,\text{m s}^{-1}$

## Example 3

A ball of mass 0.5 kg is moving with velocity $(3\mathbf{i} - 2\mathbf{j})\,\text{m s}^{-1}$ when it is struck by a bat.
Immediately after being struck, the ball has velocity $(8\mathbf{i} + 14\mathbf{j})\,\text{m s}^{-1}$.
Find the magnitude and direction of the impulse exerted by the bat on the ball.

### Solution

Momentum of ball before impact $= 0.5(3\mathbf{i} - 2\mathbf{j}) = (1.5\mathbf{i} - \mathbf{j})\,\text{N s}$

Momentum of ball after impact $= 0.5(8\mathbf{i} + 14\mathbf{j}) = (4\mathbf{i} + 7\mathbf{j})\,\text{N s}$

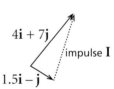

These vectors are shown in the diagram.
The dotted vector shows the impulse **I**.

Impulse **I** $=$ change in momentum $= (4\mathbf{i} + 7\mathbf{j}) - (1.5\mathbf{i} - \mathbf{j})$
$$= (2.5\mathbf{i} + 8\mathbf{j})\,\text{N s}$$

Magnitude of impulse, $I = \sqrt{2.5^2 + 8^2} = 8.38\,\text{N s}$ to 3 s.f.

Direction of impulse, $\theta = \tan^{-1}\frac{8}{2.5} = 72.6°$ to 3 s.f.

The bat exerts an impulse of $8.38\,\text{N s}$ on the ball at an angle of $72.6°$ to the **i**-direction.

## Exercise A

**1** A particle of mass 3 kg is moving with velocity $(2\mathbf{i} - \mathbf{j})\,\text{m s}^{-1}$ when it is
given an impulse of $(3\mathbf{i} + 2\mathbf{j})\,\text{N s}$.
Find the final velocity of the particle.

**2** An object of mass 0.5 kg is initially moving with velocity $(-4\mathbf{i} + \mathbf{j})\,\text{m s}^{-1}$.
A force of $6\mathbf{j}\,\text{N}$ acts on the object for 5 seconds.

   **(a)** Find the impulse of the force.

   **(b)** Find the final velocity of the object.

**3** A ball of mass 2 kg is moving with velocity $4\mathbf{j}\,\text{m s}^{-1}$ when it hits a fixed wall.
It rebounds with velocity $(6\mathbf{i} - 3\mathbf{j})\,\text{m s}^{-1}$.
Find the impulse exerted by the wall on the ball.

**4** An object of mass 1.5 kg is moving with velocity $(-4\mathbf{i} + \mathbf{j})\,\mathrm{m\,s^{-1}}$ when it is given an impulse of $6\mathbf{i}\,\mathrm{N\,s}$.
Find the final speed of the object.

**5** A force of $(2\mathbf{i} - 3\mathbf{j})\,\mathrm{N}$ acts on an object of mass 2.5 kg for 2 seconds.
The velocity of the object immediately after the force is removed is $(8\mathbf{i} - 2\mathbf{j})\,\mathrm{m\,s^{-1}}$.
Find the initial velocity of the object.

**6** An object of mass 3 kg is moving with velocity $5\mathbf{i}\,\mathrm{m\,s^{-1}}$.
A constant force acts on the object for 4 seconds.
The final velocity of the object is $(-3\mathbf{i} + 4\mathbf{j})\,\mathrm{m\,s^{-1}}$.
Find the magnitude of the force.

**7** A ball of mass 0.25 kg is moving with velocity $(3\mathbf{i} - \mathbf{j})\,\mathrm{m\,s^{-1}}$ when it strikes a fixed post. The ball rebounds with velocity $(-2\mathbf{i} + 4\mathbf{j})\,\mathrm{m\,s^{-1}}$.
Find the magnitude and direction of the impulse exerted by the post on the ball.

**8** A ball of mass 0.2 kg is struck by a bat which gives it an impulse of $(4\mathbf{i} + 3\mathbf{j})\,\mathrm{N\,s}$.
Immediately after being struck the velocity of the ball is $(12\mathbf{i} + 10\mathbf{j})\,\mathrm{m\,s^{-1}}$.

(a) Find the speed of the ball immediately after it is struck.

(b) Find the speed of the ball immediately before it is struck.

**9** A particle of mass 0.8 kg is moving with velocity $(2\mathbf{i} - 4\mathbf{j})\,\mathrm{m\,s^{-1}}$ when it receives an impulse of magnitude $8\sqrt{2}\,\mathrm{N\,s}$ in the direction of the vector $\mathbf{i} + \mathbf{j}$.

(a) State the impulse in the form $a\mathbf{i} + b\mathbf{j}$.

(b) Find the velocity of the particle immediately after receiving the impulse.

**10** An object of mass 0.5 kg is moving with velocity $(10\mathbf{i} - 6\mathbf{j})\,\mathrm{m\,s^{-1}}$ when it is given an impulse of $(-2\mathbf{i} + 3\mathbf{j})\,\mathrm{N\,s}$.

(a) Find the final velocity of the object.

(b) Find the angle through which the object is deflected as a result of the impulse.

## B Conservation of momentum (answers p 135)

**B1 (a)** Two particles, $A$ and $B$, are moving on a straight line in the same direction.
If $A$ is moving faster than $B$, then the particles will collide.
Describe what could happen to the motion of the two particles after the collision.

(b) If the two particles were moving towards each other, what could happen to their motion after the collision?

When two objects moving on a straight line collide, the principle of conservation of momentum applies: the total momentum before the collision is equal to the total momentum after the collision.

If an object of mass $m_1$ travelling with velocity $u_1$ collides with an object of mass $m_2$ travelling with velocity $u_2$, and if $v_1$ and $v_2$ are the velocities of the objects immediately after the collision, then

$$m_1 u_1 + m_2 u_2 = m_1 v_1 + m_2 v_2$$

**B2** An object of mass 1 kg moving on a straight line with a speed of $5\,\text{m s}^{-1}$ collides with an object of mass 4 kg moving in the same direction with a speed of $2.5\,\text{m s}^{-1}$.

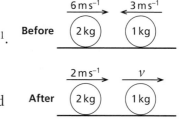

After the collision, the 1 kg object moves in the same direction with a speed of $2\,\text{m s}^{-1}$.

(a) Show that the total momentum of the two objects before the collision is $15\,\text{N s}$.

(b) Find an expression for the total momentum of the two objects after the collision.

(c) Use the principle of conservation of momentum to find the speed of the 4 kg object after the collision.

**B3** An object of mass 2 kg moving on a straight line with a speed of $6\,\text{m s}^{-1}$ collides with an object of mass 1 kg moving in the opposite direction with a speed of $3\,\text{m s}^{-1}$.

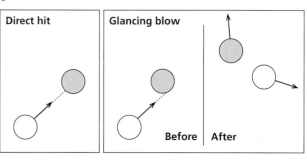

After the collision the 2 kg object moves in the same direction with a speed of $2\,\text{m s}^{-1}$.

Use the principle of conservation of momentum to find the speed of the 1 kg object after the collision.

A collision in two dimensions is more complicated than in one dimension. It is easiest to see this if both objects are thought of as round, like snooker balls.

A snooker ball can give either a direct hit or a 'glancing blow' to another stationary ball. After a direct hit, the second ball moves in the same straight line as the first, so the situation is one-dimensional.

After a glancing blow, the balls move in different directions.

If both balls are moving before they collide, then both may change direction as a result of the collision.

The principle of conservation of momentum applies to motion in two (or three) dimensions. In vector form, the equation is

$$m_1 \mathbf{u}_1 + m_2 \mathbf{u}_2 = m_1 \mathbf{v}_1 + m_2 \mathbf{v}_2$$

When applying conservation of momentum, you do not need to worry about exactly what happens when the objects collide. Only the situations before and after the collision are relevant.

**B4** An object $A$ of mass 3 kg has a velocity of $(4\mathbf{i} + 4\mathbf{j})\,\mathrm{m\,s^{-1}}$.

It collides with an object $B$ of mass 2 kg travelling with velocity $(2\mathbf{i} - 3\mathbf{j})\,\mathrm{m\,s^{-1}}$.

Afterwards, $A$ moves with velocity $(2\mathbf{i} - \mathbf{j})\,\mathrm{m\,s^{-1}}$ and $B$ with velocity $\mathbf{v}_2\,\mathrm{m\,s^{-1}}$ (unknown).

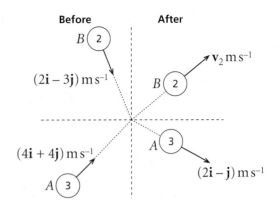

If the known quantities are substituted in the conservation of momentum equation you get

$$3(4\mathbf{i} + 4\mathbf{j}) + 2(2\mathbf{i} - 3\mathbf{j}) = 3(2\mathbf{i} - \mathbf{j}) + 2\mathbf{v}_2$$

By solving this equation, show that $\mathbf{v}_2 = 5\mathbf{i} + 4.5\mathbf{j}$.

**B5** Suppose the situation before the collision is the same as in B4, but that the two objects coalesce and move together with velocity $\mathbf{v}$.

Write down the equation of conservation of momentum in this case.

Solve the equation to find the value of $\mathbf{v}$.

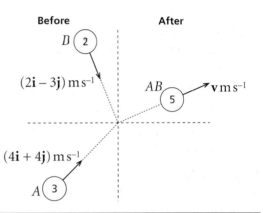

---

## Example 4

An object of mass 8 kg, moving with velocity $(3\mathbf{i} + 2\mathbf{j})\,\mathrm{m\,s^{-1}}$, collides with a stationary object of mass 2 kg.

Immediately after the collision, the velocity of the 2 kg object is $(\mathbf{i} + \mathbf{j})\,\mathrm{m\,s^{-1}}$. Find the velocity after the collision of the 8 kg object.

## Solution

*As usual, sketch the situation before and after the collision.*

From the conservation of momentum,

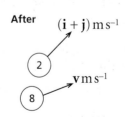

$$8(3\mathbf{i} + 2\mathbf{j}) = 8\mathbf{v} + 2(\mathbf{i} + \mathbf{j})$$
$$\Rightarrow \quad 24\mathbf{i} + 16\mathbf{j} = 8\mathbf{v} + 2\mathbf{i} + 2\mathbf{j}$$
$$\Rightarrow \quad 22\mathbf{i} + 14\mathbf{j} = 8\mathbf{v}$$
$$\Rightarrow \quad \mathbf{v} = 2.75\mathbf{i} + 1.75\mathbf{j}$$

The velocity of the 8 kg object after the collision is $(2.75\mathbf{i} + 1.75\mathbf{j})\,\mathrm{m\,s^{-1}}$.

---

**Exercise B** (answers p 135)

**1** An object of mass $4\,\text{kg}$ moving on a straight line with a speed of $6\,\text{m}\,\text{s}^{-1}$ collides with a stationary object of mass $2\,\text{kg}$.

Immediately after the collision, the $4\,\text{kg}$ object moves forward at $2\,\text{m}\,\text{s}^{-1}$. What are the speed and direction of the $2\,\text{kg}$ object after the collision?

**2** An object of mass $3\,\text{kg}$, moving with velocity $(4\mathbf{i} + 3\mathbf{j})\,\text{m}\,\text{s}^{-1}$, collides with an object of mass $2\,\text{kg}$, moving with a velocity of $(2\mathbf{i} + \mathbf{j})\,\text{m}\,\text{s}^{-1}$.

Immediately after the collision, the velocity of the $3\,\text{kg}$ object is $(3\mathbf{i} + 2\mathbf{j})\,\text{m}\,\text{s}^{-1}$. Find the velocity after the collision of the $2\,\text{kg}$ object.

**3** An object of mass $3\,\text{kg}$ moving on a straight line with a speed of $5\,\text{m}\,\text{s}^{-1}$ collides with an object of mass $2\,\text{kg}$ moving in the same direction with a speed of $2\,\text{m}\,\text{s}^{-1}$.

After the collision, the two objects coalesce.
Find the speed of the combined object after the collision.

**4** An object of mass $4\,\text{kg}$ moving with velocity $(-\mathbf{i} + 3\mathbf{j})\,\text{m}\,\text{s}^{-1}$ collides with an object of mass $3\,\text{kg}$ moving with velocity $(2\mathbf{i} - \mathbf{j})\,\text{m}\,\text{s}^{-1}$.

Immediately after the collision, the $4\,\text{kg}$ object moves with velocity $2\mathbf{i}\,\text{m}\,\text{s}^{-1}$. Find the velocity of the $3\,\text{kg}$ object after the collision.

**5** An object of mass $3\,\text{kg}$ moving on a straight line with a speed of $8\,\text{m}\,\text{s}^{-1}$ collides with an object of mass $4\,\text{kg}$ moving in the opposite direction with a speed of $3\,\text{m}\,\text{s}^{-1}$.

Immediately after the collision, the $3\,\text{kg}$ object moves forward at $2\,\text{m}\,\text{s}^{-1}$.

(a) Find the impulse exerted on the $3\,\text{kg}$ object during the collision.

(b) Find the speed of the $4\,\text{kg}$ object after the collision.

(c) Find the impulse exerted on the $4\,\text{kg}$ object during the collision. Comment on your answer.

**6** A moving particle $A$ collides with another moving particle $B$. The mass of $A$ is $1.5\,\text{kg}$ and its velocities before and after the collision are $(4\mathbf{i} + 2\mathbf{j})\,\text{m}\,\text{s}^{-1}$ and $(2\mathbf{i} - \mathbf{j})\,\text{m}\,\text{s}^{-1}$ respectively.

(a) (i) Find the impulse exerted on $A$ during the collision.

(ii) State the impulse exerted on $B$ during the collision.

(b) The mass of $B$ is $0.5\,\text{kg}$. Immediately after the collision the velocity of $B$ is $(\mathbf{i} + \mathbf{j})\,\text{m}\,\text{s}^{-1}$.
Find the velocity of $B$ immediately before the collision.

**7** A shell of mass $15\,\text{kg}$ is moving with a velocity of $(30\mathbf{i} + 35\mathbf{j})\,\text{m}\,\text{s}^{-1}$ when there is an internal explosion which causes it to split into two parts of masses $5\,\text{kg}$ and $10\,\text{kg}$.

(a) Explain why the principle of conservation of momentum applies here.

(b) Immediately after the explosion the $5\,\text{kg}$ part has a velocity of $20\mathbf{i}\,\text{m}\,\text{s}^{-1}$. Find the velocity of the $10\,\text{kg}$ part immediately after the explosion.

## C Newton's law of restitution (answers p 135)

A ball moving along a smooth horizontal surface collides directly
with a wall and rebounds. As it is a direct impact, the ball rebounds
with a velocity that is perpendicular to the wall.

The speed $u\,\mathrm{m\,s^{-1}}$ at which the ball travels towards the wall is called
the **approach speed**, and the speed $v\,\mathrm{m\,s^{-1}}$ at which it rebounds is called
the **separation speed**.

If there is no loss of mechanical energy in the collision, then we say
the collision is **perfectly elastic**. In this case, the kinetic energy after
the impact, $\frac{1}{2}mv^2$, is equal to that before the impact, $\frac{1}{2}mu^2$, so $v = u$.

In practice a perfectly elastic collision never occurs, because some mechanical
energy is converted to other forms, such as heat or sound, during the collision.
So in practice the speed of separation is less than the speed of approach.

**C1** Two particles $A$ and $B$, each of mass 1 kg, are moving
on a straight line in the same direction as shown.
Particle $A$ catches up with $B$ and they collide.
Immediately after the collision $A$ moves in the same direction
as before with speed $3\,\mathrm{m\,s^{-1}}$.

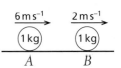

(a) Use the principle of conservation of momentum to show that
the speed of $B$ after the collision is $5\,\mathrm{m\,s^{-1}}$.

(b) (i) Find the kinetic energy lost by $A$ during the collision.

(ii) Find the kinetic energy gained by $B$ during the collision.

(iii) Has energy been conserved during the collision?
If not, state the change in energy during the collision.

(c) Explain why the approach speed of $A$ towards $B$ before the collision is $4\,\mathrm{m\,s^{-1}}$.

(d) What is the separation speed of $B$ from $A$ after the collision?

Experiments show that for a particular pair of objects the ratio of the
separation speed to the approach speed is a constant. This fact was discovered
by Newton and is called 'Newton's law of restitution'.

The constant is called the **coefficient of restitution** and is denoted by $e$.
Newton's law of restitution is usually stated in the following form:

> If two objects moving on the same straight line collide then
>
> separation speed = $e \times$ approach speed
>
> where $e$ is a constant called the **coefficient of restitution** for the objects.

Newton's law of restitution applies for direct collisions between two movable
objects or between a movable object and a fixed object, such as a wall.

**C2** State the value of the coefficient of restitution for the particles in C1.

**C3** (a) State the value of the coefficient of restitution for a perfectly elastic collision.

    (b) (i) What is the separation speed for a collision in which the particles coalesce?

       (ii) State the value of the coefficient of restitution for a collision in which the particles coalesce.

**C4** An object of mass 1 kg is moving on a straight line with a speed of $5\,\text{m s}^{-1}$ towards a stationary object of mass 2 kg.

After the collision the stationary object moves off with a speed of $3\,\text{m s}^{-1}$.

Before   $5\,\text{m s}^{-1}$   1 kg   2 kg
After   $v$   $3\,\text{m s}^{-1}$

    (a) Use the principle of conservation of momentum to find the speed and direction of the 1 kg object after the collision.

    (b) Find the approach speed of the objects.

    (c) Find the separation speed of the objects.

    (d) Find the coefficient of restitution.

**C5** An object of mass 3 kg moving on a straight line with speed $4\,\text{m s}^{-1}$ collides with an object of mass 4 kg moving in the opposite direction with speed $2\,\text{m s}^{-1}$.

Immediately after the collision the 3 kg object moves in the opposite direction at $1\,\text{m s}^{-1}$.

Before   $4\,\text{m s}^{-1}$   $2\,\text{m s}^{-1}$   3 kg   4 kg
After   $1\,\text{m s}^{-1}$   $v$

    (a) Find the speed and direction of the 4 kg object after the collision.

    (b) Find the coefficient of restitution between the two objects.

---

The coefficient of restitution satisfies the inequality $0 \le e \le 1$.

In a perfectly elastic collision $e = 1$ and mechanical energy is conserved.

If the collision is not perfectly elastic some mechanical energy is converted into other forms such as heat or sound.

In an inelastic collision, where the particles coalesce, $e = 0$.

---

If the value of the coefficient of restitution is known, Newton's law of restitution can be used with the principle of conservation of momentum to find the outcome of a collision.

**C6** A particle $A$, of mass 1 kg, is moving on a straight line at $4\,\text{m s}^{-1}$ towards a particle $B$, of mass 3 kg, moving in the same direction at $2\,\text{m s}^{-1}$.

Before   $4\,\text{m s}^{-1}$   $2\,\text{m s}^{-1}$   1 kg   3 kg
After   $v_A$   $v_B$

The particles collide and move off as shown.
The coefficient of restitution between $A$ and $B$ is $0.6$.

    (a) Use the principle of conservation of momentum to show that $v_A + 3v_B = 10$.

    (b) Use Newton's law of restitution to show that $v_B - v_A = 1.2$.

    (c) Solve these equations simultaneously to find $v_A$ and $v_B$.

**C7** Two particles, each of mass 2 kg, are moving towards each other on a straight line as shown.
The coefficient of restitution is 0.8.

(a) Use the principle of conservation of momentum to write an equation connecting $v_A$ and $v_B$.

(b) Use Newton's law of restitution to write another equation connecting $v_A$ and $v_B$.

(c) Solve these equations simultaneously to find $v_A$ and $v_B$.

## Example 5

An object of mass 2 kg which is moving on a straight line with a speed of $5\,\mathrm{m\,s^{-1}}$ collides directly with another object of mass 3 kg moving in the opposite direction with a speed of $2\,\mathrm{m\,s^{-1}}$.
The coefficient of restitution between the objects is 0.75.

(a) Find the speed and direction of each object after the collision.

(b) Find the kinetic energy lost in the collision.

### Solution

(a) *Sketch the situation before and after the collision.*
*The velocities of the objects after the collision have been labelled $v_A$ and $v_B$. We do not know their directions, so they have both been shown as positive. If a value is found to be negative, the object is moving in the opposite direction.*

From the conservation of momentum, $\quad 2 \times 5 - 3 \times 2 = 2v_A + 3v_B$

$$\Rightarrow \quad 2v_A + 3v_B = 4 \quad\quad (1)$$

Approach speed $= 5 + 2 = 7$

Separation speed $= v_B - v_A$

From Newton's law of restitution, $\quad v_B - v_A = 0.75 \times 7 = 5.25 \quad\quad (2)$

Add (1) and $2 \times (2)$. $\quad\quad 5v_B = 14.5$

$$\Rightarrow \quad v_B = 2.9$$

Substitute into (2). $\quad\quad v_A = 2.9 - 5.25 = -2.35$

After the collision the direction of motion of each object is reversed.
The 3 kg object moves at $2.9\,\mathrm{m\,s^{-1}}$ and the 2 kg object moves at $2.35\,\mathrm{m\,s^{-1}}$.

(b) Total k.e. before collision $= \frac{1}{2} \times 2 \times 5^2 + \frac{1}{2} \times 3 \times 2^2 = 31\,\mathrm{J}$

Total k.e. after collision $= \frac{1}{2} \times 2 \times 2.35^2 + \frac{1}{2} \times 3 \times 2.9^2 = 18.1375\,\mathrm{J}$

Loss of k.e. in collision $= 31 - 18.1375 = 12.9\,\mathrm{J}$ to 3 s.f.

**Example 6**

A particle of mass $m$ is moving with speed $u$ on a smooth horizontal table when it collides directly with a particle of mass $2m$ which is at rest on the table. The coefficient of restitution between the particles is $e$. After colliding, the two particles move off in the same direction.

**(a)** Find, in terms of $e$ and $u$, the speeds of the particles after the collision.

**(b)** Show that $e < \frac{1}{2}$.

**Solution**

**(a)** *Sketch the situation before and after the collision.*
*The velocities after the collision have been labelled $v_A$ and $v_B$.*

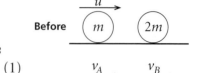

From conservation of momentum, $\qquad mu = mv_A + 2mv_B$

$\Rightarrow \quad v_A + 2v_B = u \qquad\qquad (1)$

Approach speed $= u$

Separation speed $= v_B - v_A$

From Newton's law of restitution, $\quad v_B - v_A = eu \qquad (2)$

Add (1) and (2). $\qquad\qquad\qquad\qquad 3v_B = u + eu$

$\Rightarrow \quad v_B = \frac{1}{3}u(1 + e)$

Substitute into (2). $\qquad\qquad\qquad v_A = \frac{1}{3}u(1 + e) - eu = \frac{1}{3}u(1 - 2e)$

**(b)** The two objects move off in the same direction as each other, so $\quad v_A > 0$.

$\Rightarrow \quad 1 - 2e > 0$

$\Rightarrow \quad e < \frac{1}{2}$

---

**Exercise C** (answers p 135)

**1** A particle $A$ of mass $1\,\mathrm{kg}$ moving on a straight line with a speed of $5\,\mathrm{m\,s^{-1}}$ collides directly with a stationary particle $B$ of mass $2\,\mathrm{kg}$.

Immediately after the collision $A$ moves in the same direction with a speed of $1\,\mathrm{m\,s^{-1}}$.

**(a)** Find the speed of $B$ after the collision.

**(b)** Find the coefficient of restitution between $A$ and $B$.

**2** For each of the following collisions find

    **(i)** the unknown velocity         **(ii)** the coefficient of restitution

**(a)** Before $\quad 8\,\mathrm{m\,s^{-1}} \quad 2\,\mathrm{m\,s^{-1}}$
          $2\,\mathrm{kg}$    $8\,\mathrm{kg}$
    After $\quad\leftarrow 1\,\mathrm{m\,s^{-1}} \quad\rightarrow v$

**(b)** Before $\quad 3\,\mathrm{m\,s^{-1}} \quad \leftarrow 2\,\mathrm{m\,s^{-1}}$
          $5\,\mathrm{kg}$    $2\,\mathrm{kg}$
    After $\quad\rightarrow v \quad\quad 3\,\mathrm{m\,s^{-1}}$

**3** A particle of mass 4 kg moving on a straight line with a speed of $5\,\mathrm{m\,s^{-1}}$ collides directly with a particle of mass 1 kg moving in the same direction with a speed of $2\,\mathrm{m\,s^{-1}}$.
The coefficient of restitution is $0.75$.
Find the speed and direction of each particle after the collision.

**4** A ball of mass 2 kg moving on a straight line with a speed of $3\,\mathrm{m\,s^{-1}}$ collides with a ball of mass 1 kg which is at rest.
The coefficient of restitution between the balls is $0.5$.
(a) Find the speed and direction of each ball after the collision.
(b) Find the magnitude of the impulse given to each ball in the collision.
(c) Find the kinetic energy lost in the collision.

**5** A particle of mass 2 kg moving on a straight line with a speed of $4\,\mathrm{m\,s^{-1}}$ collides with a particle of mass 4 kg moving in the opposite direction with a speed of $1\,\mathrm{m\,s^{-1}}$.
The coefficient of restitution between the particles is $\frac{1}{3}$.
Find the speed and direction of each particle after the collision.

**6** A particle of mass 2 kg moving on a straight line with a speed of $8\,\mathrm{m\,s^{-1}}$ collides directly with a particle of mass 2.5 kg moving in the opposite direction with a speed of $4\,\mathrm{m\,s^{-1}}$.
The 2 kg particle is brought to rest by the collision.
(a) Find the speed of the 2.5 kg particle after the collision.
(b) Find the coefficient of restitution between the particles.
(c) Find the kinetic energy lost in the collision.

**7** A particle of mass $m$ is moving on a straight line with speed $u$ towards an identical particle of mass $m$ moving in the opposite direction with speed $u$.
(a) (i) Given that the coefficient of restitution between the particles is $\frac{1}{2}$, find the speed of each particle after the collision.
  (ii) Find the kinetic energy lost in the collision.
(b) (i) Given that the collision is perfectly elastic, find the speed of each particle after the collision.
  (ii) Find the kinetic energy lost in the collision.
    Explain your answer.

**8** A smooth sphere $A$ of mass $m$ is moving on a horizontal table with speed $v$ when it collides directly with a smooth sphere $B$ of mass $4m$ which is at rest on the table.
The coefficient of restitution between the spheres is $e$.
(a) Show that the speed of $B$ immediately after the collision is $\frac{1}{5}v(1 + e)$.
(b) Find the speed of $A$ immediately after the collision.

**9** A particle $P$ of mass $m$ is moving on a horizontal surface with speed $2u$ when it collides directly with a particle $Q$ of mass $3m$ which is moving in the same direction with speed $u$.
The coefficient of restitution between the particles is $\frac{3}{5}$.

   (a) Show that the speed of $Q$ immediately after the collision is $\dfrac{7u}{5}$.

   (b) Find the speed of $P$ immediately after the collision.

   (c) Find the kinetic energy lost in the collision.

**10** A particle $A$ of mass $m$ is moving on a horizontal surface with speed $4u$ when it collides directly with a particle $B$ of mass $2m$ moving in the opposite direction with speed $u$.
The direction of motion of $A$ is reversed by the collision.
The coefficient of restitution between the particles is $e$.

   Show that $e > \frac{1}{5}$.

**11** A particle of mass $3m$ moving with speed $2u$ on a horizontal surface collides directly with a particle of mass $4m$ which is at rest.
The coefficient of restitution between the particles is $e$.

   Given that the particles move off in the same direction after the collision, find the range of values for $e$.

# D Collision with a fixed plane surface (answers p 136)

In the last section we saw that when a movable object collides with a fixed object Newton's law of restitution can be used to find the ratio of the separation speed to the approach speed. However, when the collision is with a fixed object, momentum is not conserved.

   **D1** An object of mass $2\,\text{kg}$ is moving on a smooth horizontal surface with a speed of $4\,\text{m s}^{-1}$ towards a smooth wall. It collides directly with the wall and rebounds.

   (a) If the coefficient of restitution between the object and the wall is $0.75$, find the speed of the object after the collision.

   (b) Find the impulse exerted by the wall on the object.

   (c) Find the kinetic energy lost in the collision.

Consider an object which is dropped from a height $h\,\text{m}$ above ground level and falls vertically to the ground. Assuming air resistance can be ignored, mechanical energy is conserved as the object falls.

   **D2** (a) What happens to the object if the collision with the ground is perfectly elastic ($e = 1$)?

   (b) What happens if the collision is inelastic ($e = 0$)?

   (c) What happens if $0 < e < 1$?

**D3** A ball of mass 0.4 kg is dropped from a height of 2 m above ground level.

(a) Use the principle of conservation of energy to calculate the speed at which the ball reaches the ground.

(b) If the coefficient of restitution between the ball and the ground is 0.4, find the speed of the ball immediately after the collision.

(c) Find the impulse exerted by the ground on the ball during the collision.

(d) Find the energy lost during the collision.

(e) Use the principle of conservation of energy to find the maximum height reached by the ball after its first bounce.

**K** When a moving object collides with a fixed object, the fixed object exerts an impulse on the moving object, causing its direction to be reversed. Unless the collision is perfectly elastic, energy is lost during the collision.

---

### Example 7

A ball is dropped from a height $h$ m above ground level.
Given that the coefficient of restitution between the ball and the ground is $\frac{1}{2}$, show that the maximum height reached by the ball after its second bounce is $\frac{1}{16}h$.

### Solution

*Energy is conserved as the ball rises or drops.*
*The speed of the ball is zero when the ball is at its maximum height.*
*As energy is conserved, the ball reaches the ground at the same speed as it left it.*
*The maximum height reached by the ball reduces after each bounce.*

Let $m$ be the mass of the ball and $v$ its speed when it first hits the ground.

Loss in p.e. = gain in k.e.
$$mgh = \tfrac{1}{2}mv^2$$
$$\Rightarrow \quad v = \sqrt{2gh}$$

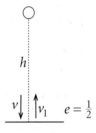

Let $v_1$ be the speed of the ball as it leaves the ground after its first bounce.

Apply Newton's law of restitution: $\quad v_1 = \tfrac{1}{2}v = \tfrac{1}{2}\sqrt{2gh}$

Energy is conserved until the second bounce so the ball hits the ground with speed $v_1$. If it leaves with speed $v_2$, then by Newton's law,
$$v_2 = \tfrac{1}{2}v_1 = \tfrac{1}{4}\sqrt{2gh}$$

The k.e. of the ball as it leaves the ground after the second bounce is $\tfrac{1}{2}mv_2^2$.

Let $H$ be the maximum height reached after the second bounce.

Gain in p.e. = loss in k.e.
$$mgH = \tfrac{1}{2}mv_2^2 = \tfrac{1}{2}m\left(\tfrac{1}{4}\sqrt{2gh}\right)^2 = \tfrac{1}{16}mgh$$
$$\Rightarrow \quad H = \tfrac{1}{16}h$$

---

**Exercise D** (answers p 136)

**1** A particle of mass 1.5 kg moving at a speed of 8 m s$^{-1}$ collides with a wall which is perpendicular to the direction of motion.
The coefficient of restitution between the particle and the wall is 0.6.

(a) Find the speed of the particle after the impact.

(b) Find the magnitude of the impulse exerted by the wall on the particle.

**2** A ball of mass 2 kg moving at a speed of 5 m s$^{-1}$ collides with a wall that is perpendicular to the direction of motion.
The ball rebounds with a speed of 3 m s$^{-1}$.

(a) Find the coefficient of restitution between the ball and the wall.

(b) Find the magnitude of the impulse exerted by the wall on the ball.

**3** A smooth ball of mass 0.5 kg collides directly with a wall and rebounds with a speed of 3 m s$^{-1}$.
The coefficient of restitution between the ball and the wall is 0.75.

(a) Find the speed of the ball before the collision.

(b) Find the kinetic energy lost in the collision.

**4** A particle of mass $m$ is moving on a smooth horizontal surface with a speed $u$ towards a fixed plane. It collides directly with the plane and rebounds.
The coefficient of restitution between the particle and the plane is $\frac{4}{5}$.

Find the kinetic energy lost in the collision.

**5** A ball of mass 0.5 kg is dropped from a height of 3 m above ground level.

(a) Find the speed at which the ball reaches the ground.

(b) The coefficient of restitution between the ball and the ground is 0.6.
Find the speed of the ball immediately after it bounces.

(c) Find the maximum height reached by the ball after the first bounce.

**6** A ball is dropped from a height $H$ above ground level.
It bounces and reaches a maximum height $\dfrac{H}{2}$.

Find the coefficient of restitution between the ball and the ground.

**7** A ball is thrown vertically downwards with a speed of 5 m s$^{-1}$ from a height of 1 m above ground level.
The ball bounces and reaches a maximum height of 1 m.

Find the coefficient of restitution between the ball and the ground.

**\*8** A particle is projected vertically downwards with a speed $u$ from a height $h$ above ground level.
The coefficient of restitution between the particle and the ground is $e$.

Find an expression for the maximum height reached by the particle after its second bounce.

## E Successive impacts (answers p 137)

Some problems involve two movable objects and a fixed object, or more than two movable objects. In these situations you may need to consider what conditions must be met in order for further collisions to occur. The speed and direction of each object after each collision will determine whether or not another collision will occur.

**E1** Two particles $A$ and $B$, each of mass $1\,\text{kg}$, lie on a smooth surface in a straight line perpendicular to a wall as shown. Initially $B$ is at rest, and $A$ is projected towards it with a speed of $5\,\text{m}\,\text{s}^{-1}$. The coefficient of restitution between $A$ and $B$ is $0.8$ and the coefficient of restitution between $B$ and the wall is $0.6$.

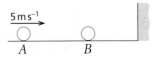

(a) The first collision takes place between $A$ and $B$.

    (i) Find the speed of $B$ after this collision.

    (ii) Find the speed of $A$ after this collision.

    (iii) Draw a sketch showing the speeds of the particles after this collision.

(b) The second collision takes place between $B$ and the wall.

    (i) Find the speed of $B$ after this collision.

    (ii) Draw a sketch showing the speeds of the particles after this collision.

(c) (i) Explain why there will be another collision between $A$ and $B$.

    (ii) Find the speeds of $A$ and $B$ after this collision.

(d) Will there be another collision?
Explain your answer.

**E2** Three particles $A$, $B$ and $C$, of masses $1\,\text{kg}$, $2\,\text{kg}$ and $1\,\text{kg}$ respectively, lie on a straight line on a smooth horizontal surface. $A$ is moving towards $B$ with a speed of $4\,\text{m}\,\text{s}^{-1}$ and $B$ is moving in the opposite direction with a speed of $2\,\text{m}\,\text{s}^{-1}$. $C$ is at rest. The coefficient of restitution between $A$ and $B$ and between $B$ and $C$ is $\frac{1}{3}$.

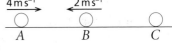

(a) The first collision takes place between $A$ and $B$.

    (i) Find the speed of $B$ after this collision.

    (ii) Find the speed of $A$ after this collision.

(b) Draw a sketch showing the speeds of the three particles after this collision.

(c) The second collision takes place between $B$ and $C$.

    (i) Find the speed of $B$ after this collision.

    (ii) Find the speed of $C$ after this collision.

(d) (i) Draw a sketch showing the speeds of the three particles after this collision.

    (ii) Will there be another collision? If so, which particles will collide?
Explain your answer.

## Example 8

A small smooth ball $A$ of mass $m$ is moving on a horizontal table with speed $u$ when it collides directly with another small smooth ball $B$ of mass $4m$ which is at rest on the table. The coefficient of restitution between $A$ and $B$ is $e$. The direction of motion of $A$ is reversed by the collision.

(a) Find, in terms of $e$ and $u$, the speeds of $A$ and $B$ immediately after the collision.

(b) Show that $e > \frac{1}{4}$.

After the collision, $B$ hits a vertical wall that is perpendicular to the direction in which $B$ is travelling. The coefficient of restitution between $B$ and the wall is $\frac{1}{2}$. After rebounding from the wall, $B$ collides with $A$.

(c) Find the range of possible values of $e$.

## Solution

(a) Let the speeds of $A$ and $B$ after the collision be $x$ and $y$.
We know that $A$ is reversed by the collision, so $x$ is shown in the opposite direction from $y$.

From conservation of momentum, $m(-x) + 4my = mu$

$$\Rightarrow \quad -x + 4y = u \quad (1)$$

From Newton's law of restitution, $\quad x + y = eu \quad (2)$

$(1) + (2)$:
$$5y = u + eu$$
$$\Rightarrow \quad y = \tfrac{1}{5}(1 + e)u$$

$4 \times (2) - (1)$:
$$5x = 4eu - u$$
$$\Rightarrow \quad x = \tfrac{1}{5}(4e - 1)u$$

(b) The direction of $A$ is reversed, so $x > 0$, from which $4e - 1 > 0$, so $e > \frac{1}{4}$.

(c) $B$ rebounds from the wall with speed $\frac{1}{2}y = \frac{1}{10}(1 + e)u$.

$B$ catches up and collides with $A$ if this speed is greater than the speed of $A$.

So $\frac{1}{10}(1 + e)u > \frac{1}{5}(4e - 1)u$

$$1 + e > 2(4e - 1)$$
$$1 + e > 8e - 2$$
$$3 > 7e$$
$$e < \tfrac{3}{7}$$

From (b) we already have $e > \frac{1}{4}$, so the range for $e$ is $\frac{1}{4} < e < \frac{3}{7}$.

---

## Exercise E (answers p 137)

**1** $A$, $B$, $C$ are three identical balls, each of mass $m$, in line with one another on a horizontal surface. $B$ and $C$ are stationary. The coefficient of restitution between any pair of balls is $\frac{1}{2}$. $A$ is moving with speed $u$ when it collides with $B$, which then goes on to collide with $C$. Show that there is a further collision between $A$ and $B$.

**2** A ball $A$ of mass $1\,\text{kg}$ is moving on a horizontal surface with a speed of $4\,\text{m s}^{-1}$ when it collides directly with a stationary ball $B$ of mass $10\,\text{kg}$. The coefficient of restitution between the balls is $\frac{1}{2}$.

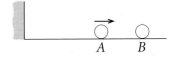

(a) Show that the direction of $A$ is reversed by the collision and find the speeds of the balls after the collision.

Ball $A$ then hits a vertical wall directly and rebounds. The coefficient of restitution between $A$ and the wall is $e$.

(b) Given that $A$ subsequently collides again with $B$, find the range of possible values of $e$.

**3** Three balls $A$, $B$, $C$ of masses $m$, $3m$ and $5m$ are in a straight line on a horizontal surface. The coefficient of restitution between $A$ and $B$ is $\frac{1}{4}$ and between $B$ and $C$ is $\frac{1}{2}$. $B$ and $C$ are stationary. $A$ moves towards $B$ with speed $u$ and collides with $B$.

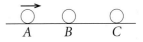

(a) Find, in terms of $u$, the speeds of $A$ and $B$ after the collision.

$B$ now collides with $C$.

(b) Show that there is then a further collision between $A$ and $B$.

**4** A ball $A$ of mass $m$ is moving with speed $u$ on a horizontal surface when it collides directly with a stationary ball $B$ of mass $2m$. The coefficient of restitution between $A$ and $B$ is $\frac{3}{4}$.

(a) Show that the motion of $A$ is reversed by the collision and find, in terms of $u$, the speeds of $A$ and $B$ after the collision.

Ball $B$ then hits a vertical wall directly and rebounds. The coefficient of restitution between $B$ and the wall is $e$. Subsequently $B$ collides with $A$ again.

(b) Find the range of possible values of $e$.

**5** Three balls $A$, $B$, $C$ of masses $5m$, $m$ and $5m$ are in a straight line on a horizontal surface. $A$ and $C$ are stationary. The coefficient of restitution between $A$ and $B$ and between $B$ and $C$ is $e$. Ball $B$ is between $A$ and $C$ and moving towards $C$ with speed $u$ when it collides with $C$.

(a) Given that the motion of $B$ is reversed as a result of the collision, show that $e > \frac{1}{5}$.

(b) Find, in terms of $e$ and $u$, the speeds of $B$ and $C$ after the first collision.

$B$ now collides with $A$. After the collision, $B$ moves towards $C$ with speed $\frac{1}{4}u$.

(c) Find the value of $e$.

(d) Is there a further collision between $B$ and $C$? Give the reason for your answer.

**6** A ball $A$ of mass $m$ is moving with speed $u$ when it collides with a stationary ball $B$ of mass $km$. The coefficient of restitution between $A$ and $B$ is $e$. The direction of $A$ is reversed. $A$ then collides directly with a vertical wall. The coefficient of restitution between $A$ and the wall is also $e$. After rebounding from the wall, $A$ collides with $B$ again.

Show that $k > \dfrac{1+2e}{e^2}$.

## Key points

- Momentum and impulse are vector quantities.
  Momentum of an object = mass × velocity
  Impulse of a force = force × time
  Impulse of force acting on an object = change in momentum of the object
  Momentum and impulse are both measured in N s (newton second).    (p 87)

- If an object of mass $m_1$ travelling with velocity $\mathbf{u}_1$ collides with an object
  of mass $m_2$ travelling with velocity $\mathbf{u}_2$, and if $\mathbf{v}_1$ and $\mathbf{v}_2$ are the velocities
  of the objects immediately after the collision, then
  $$m_1\mathbf{u}_1 + m_2\mathbf{u}_2 = m_1\mathbf{v}_1 + m_2\mathbf{v}_2$$
  This is called the principle of conservation of momentum.    (p 90)

- If two objects moving on the same straight line collide then
  $$\text{separation speed} = e \times \text{approach speed}$$
  where $e$ is a constant called the **coefficient of restitution** for the objects.

  The coefficient of restitution satisfies the inequality $0 \le e \le 1$.
  In a perfectly elastic collision $e = 1$ and mechanical energy is conserved.
  If the collision is not perfectly elastic some mechanical energy is converted
  into another form such as heat or sound.
  In an inelastic collision, where the particles coalesce, $e = 0$.    (pp 93–94)

- When a moving object collides with a fixed object, the fixed object exerts
  an impulse on the moving object, causing its direction to be reversed.
  Unless the collision is perfectly elastic, energy is lost during the collision.    (p 99)

## Mixed questions (answers p 138)

1   **i** and **j** are perpendicular unit vectors in a horizontal plane. A ball of mass 0.4 kg
    is travelling with velocity $(4\mathbf{i} - \mathbf{j})\,\text{m s}^{-1}$ when it is struck by a bat. The impulse
    of the bat on the ball is $(10\mathbf{i} + 5\mathbf{j})\,\text{N s}$. Find

    (a) the velocity of the ball immediately after being struck

    (b) the speed of the ball immediately after being struck

    (c) the kinetic energy gained by the ball as a result of the impact

2   A ball $A$ of mass $m$, moving on a horizontal surface with speed $u$, collides with
    a stationary ball $B$ of mass $6m$. After the collision, $A$ is moving in the opposite
    direction with speed $\frac{1}{2}u$.

    (a) Find the coefficient of restitution between $A$ and $B$.

    (b) Show that the kinetic energy lost in the collision is $\frac{3}{16}mu^2$.

**3** A ball $A$, of mass $0.8\,\text{kg}$, is moving with velocity $(4\mathbf{i} + 8\mathbf{j})\,\text{m s}^{-1}$ on a horizontal surface, where $\mathbf{i}$ and $\mathbf{j}$ are perpendicular horizontal unit vectors. The ball is struck by a rod and immediately afterwards its velocity is $10\mathbf{i}\,\text{m s}^{-1}$.

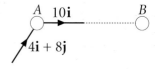

(a) Find the magnitude of the impulse exerted by the rod on the ball and the angle between the direction of the impulse and the vector $\mathbf{i}$.

Subsequently the ball collides directly with a stationary ball $B$ of mass $2\,\text{kg}$. After this collision, $A$ is at rest.

(b) Find the coefficient of restitution between $A$ and $B$.

**4** A ball $A$ of mass $m$ is moving with speed $u$ on a horizontal surface when it collides with a ball $B$ of mass $3m$ moving with speed $\frac{1}{2}u$ in the same direction. The coefficient of restitution between $A$ and $B$ is $e$.

(a) Find, in terms of $e$ and $u$, the speed of each ball after the collision.

(b) Show that it is impossible for the motion of $A$ to be reversed by the collision.

**5** Two identical snooker balls $A$ and $B$ of mass $m$ are positioned on a horizontal table along a line at right angles to the cushion at the edge of the table, as shown in the diagram. The coefficient of restitution between the two balls is $0.8$. The coefficient of restitution between a ball and the cushion is $0.5$.

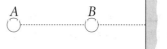

Ball $A$ is struck so that it moves with speed $u$ towards $B$. It collides with $B$, causing $B$ to hit the cushion and rebound.

(a) Show that there is then another collision between $A$ and $B$.

(b) Find, in terms of $u$, the speed of each ball after this second collision.

(c) Show that $B$ then hits the cushion again, but that there is no further collision between $A$ and $B$.

**6** A particle of mass $0.5\,\text{kg}$ is acted upon by a single variable force $\mathbf{F}$ newtons. The velocity $\mathbf{v}\,\text{m s}^{-1}$ of the particle at time $t$ seconds is given by $\mathbf{v} = t^2\mathbf{i} + (2t - 1)\mathbf{j}$.

(a) Show that when $t = 3$ the magnitude of $\mathbf{F}$ is $\sqrt{10}$ newtons.

At time $t = 5$ the particle receives an impulse of $(8\mathbf{i} - 5\mathbf{j})\,\text{N s}$.

(b) Find the velocity of the particle immediately after the impulse.

**7** A ball $A$ of mass $m$ is moving with speed $u$ on a horizontal surface when it collides directly with another ball $B$ of mass $2m$ moving with speed $u$ in the opposite direction. The coefficient of restitution between $A$ and $B$ is $e$. As a result of the collision the motions of both balls are reversed.

(a) Show that $e > \frac{1}{2}$.

Subsequently ball $A$ hits a vertical wall directly and rebounds. The coefficient of restitution between $A$ and the wall is $\frac{1}{6}$.

(b) Given that $A$ collides with $B$ again, find the range of possible values of $e$.

**8** A particle of mass 0.5 kg is acted upon by a single variable force **F** newtons. The velocity $\mathbf{v}\,\mathrm{m\,s^{-1}}$ of the particle at time $t$ seconds is given by $\mathbf{v} = 3t\mathbf{i} + (t^2 - 4)\mathbf{j}$.

(a) Find the magnitude of **F** when $t = 2$.

When $t = 6$, the particle receives an impulse of magnitude $3\sqrt{5}\,\mathrm{N\,s}$ in the direction of the vector $\mathbf{i} - 2\mathbf{j}$.

(b) Find the velocity of the particle immediately after the impulse.

**9** $A$, $B$, $C$ are three identical balls, each of mass $m$, in line with one another on a horizontal surface. $B$ and $C$ are stationary. The coefficient of restitution between any pair of balls is $e$, where $e < 1$. $A$ is moving with speed $u$ when it collides with $B$, which then goes on to collide with $C$.

(a) Show that the speed of $B$ after the second collision is $\frac{1}{4}(1 - e^2)u$.

(b) Hence show that there will be a further collision between $A$ and $B$.

**10** A ball of mass 0.2 kg is struck by a bat at a point which is 1.4 m above horizontal ground. Before being struck, the velocity of the ball is $(10\mathbf{i} + 4\mathbf{j})\,\mathrm{m\,s^{-1}}$, where the unit vectors **i** and **j** are respectively horizontal and vertical. After being struck, the velocity of the ball is $(20\mathbf{i} + 14\mathbf{j})\,\mathrm{m\,s^{-1}}$.

(a) Calculate the magnitude of the impulse exerted by the bat on the ball.

(b) Calculate the kinetic energy of the ball immediately after being struck.

The ball now moves under gravity until it hits the ground.

(c) Find the speed with which the ball hits the ground.

(d) Find the angle at which the ball hits the ground.

**11** A ball of mass $m$ is travelling with speed $u$ when it collides directly with a ball of mass $2m$ moving in the opposite direction with speed $2u$. The coefficient of restitution between the two balls is $e$.

Show that the kinetic energy lost as a result of the collision is $3mu^2(1 - e^2)$.

**12** A ball of mass 0.5 kg is projected from a point on horizontal ground with velocity $(15\mathbf{i} + 35\mathbf{j})\,\mathrm{m\,s^{-1}}$. The unit vectors **i** and **j** are horizontal and vertical respectively. When the ball reaches a height of 40 m, it receives an impulse of $(5\mathbf{i} + 6\mathbf{j})\,\mathrm{N\,s}$. Find the speed of the ball

(a) immediately after it receives the impulse

(b) as it strikes the horizontal ground

**13** A shell of mass 20 kg is fired from a point on horizontal ground with velocity $(15\mathbf{i} + 80\mathbf{j})\,\mathrm{m\,s^{-1}}$, where the unit vectors **i** and **j** are horizontal and vertical respectively. There is an internal explosion after 5 seconds in which the shell splits into two parts $A$ and $B$ of masses 5 kg and 15 kg respectively. Immediately after the explosion $A$ has a velocity of $10\mathbf{j}\,\mathrm{m\,s^{-1}}$.

(a) Find the height at which the explosion occurs.

(b) Find the velocity of $B$ immediately after the explosion.

(c) Find the speed with which $B$ hits the ground.

**\*14** A ball is dropped from a point $h$ metres above a fixed elastic horizontal surface. The coefficient of restitution between the ball and the surface is $e$.

(a) Show that the maximum height reached by the ball after rebounding from the surface is $e^2h$.

(b) The time between being dropped and hitting the surface for the third time is $T$ seconds. Show that $T = \sqrt{\dfrac{2h}{g}}\,(1 + 2e + 2e^2)$.

**\*15** Three balls $A$, $B$, $C$ of masses $3m$, $2m$, $m$ respectively are in a straight line on a horizontal surface. The coefficient of restitution between any pair of balls is $e$. $B$ and $C$ are initially at rest. $A$ is moving towards $B$ with speed $u$ when it collides with $B$. $B$ then collides with $C$.

(a) Show that the speed of $B$ after its collision with $C$ is $\frac{1}{5}u(1 + e)(2 - e)$.

There is a further collision between $A$ and $B$.

(b) Show that $e^2 - 3e + 1 > 0$ and hence find the range of possible values of $e$.

## Test yourself (answers p 139)

**1** $\mathbf{i}$ and $\mathbf{j}$ are unit vectors at right angles to each other in a horizontal plane. A ball of mass $0.4\,\text{kg}$ is travelling with velocity $(5\mathbf{i} - 15\mathbf{j})\,\text{m s}^{-1}$ when it is hit by a bat which gives it an impulse of $(6\mathbf{i} + 12\mathbf{j})\,\text{N s}$. Find the speed of the ball immediately after being struck.

**2** A particle $A$ of mass $m$ is moving with speed $3u$ on a smooth horizontal table when it collides directly with a particle $B$ of mass $2m$ which is moving in the opposite direction with speed $u$. The direction of motion of $A$ is reversed by the collision. The coefficient of restitution between $A$ and $B$ is $e$.

(a) Show that the speed of $B$ immediately after the collision is $\frac{1}{3}(1 + 4e)u$.

(b) Show that $e > \frac{1}{8}$.

Subsequently $B$ hits a wall fixed at right angles to the line of motion of $A$ and $B$. The coefficient of restitution between $B$ and the wall is $\frac{1}{2}$. After $B$ rebounds from the wall there is a further collision between $A$ and $B$.

(c) Show that $e < \frac{1}{4}$.                                                    Edexcel

**3** The unit vectors $\mathbf{i}$ and $\mathbf{j}$ lie in a vertical plane, $\mathbf{i}$ being horizontal and $\mathbf{j}$ vertical. A ball of mass $0.1\,\text{kg}$ is hit by a bat which gives it an impulse of $(3.5\mathbf{i} + 3\mathbf{j})\,\text{N s}$. The velocity of the ball immediately after being hit is $(10\mathbf{i} + 25\mathbf{j})\,\text{m s}^{-1}$.

(a) Find the velocity of the ball immediately before it is hit.

In the subsequent motion the ball is modelled as a particle moving freely under gravity. When it is hit the ball is $1\,\text{m}$ above horizontal ground.

(b) Find the greatest height of the ball above the ground in the subsequent motion.

The ball is caught when it is again $1\,\text{m}$ above the ground.

(c) Find the distance from the point where the ball is hit to the point where it is caught.                                                    Edexcel

# 6 Moments

In this chapter you will solve problems involving the equilibrium of a rigid body.

---

### Key points from Mechanics 1

- The normal reaction, of magnitude $R$, is the force at right angles to a surface which the surface exerts on an object in contact with it.

- A rough surface can offer a friction force parallel to the surface. This friction force has a maximum magnitude given by $F_{max} = \mu R$, where $\mu$ is the coefficient of friction.

- When the magnitude $F$ of the friction force on an object is at its maximum, so that the object is about to move, the object is said to be in limiting equilibrium. If the object is in equilibrium but not limiting equilibrium, then $F < \mu R$.

---

## A Moment of a force (answers p 140)

The moment of a force about a point is the product of the magnitude of the force and the perpendicular distance from the point to the line of action of the force.

Moment of force $F$ about $O = Fd$

The units of a moment are newton metres (N m).

A spanner is used to loosen a nut.
A force $F$, of magnitude 8 N, is applied to the spanner.

Moment of $F$ about $A = 8 \times 0.2 = 1.6$ N m anticlockwise

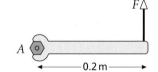

**A1** The same force $F$ is now applied to the spanner as shown.

(a) Will the moment of $F$ be more than, less than or the same as before?

(b) What is the perpendicular distance, $d$, from the point $A$ to the line of action of $F$?

(c) Find the moment of $F$ about $A$.

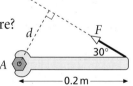

**A2** A force $P$, of magnitude 10 N, is applied to a spanner as shown.

(a) Find the moment of $P$ about $A$.

(b) The point of application of the force is moved, so that it is 0.15 m from $A$, and $P$ is still applied at 45° to the spanner. Find the moment of $P$ about $A$.

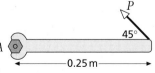

Anticlockwise moments are taken as positive and clockwise moments as negative.

**A3** Find the moment of each force about $O$.

(a)

(b)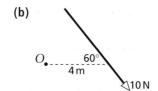

(c)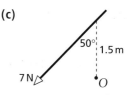

**A4** $ABCD$ is a square lamina of side 4 m.
A force of 5 N acts at vertex $A$ and a force of 8 N acts
at vertex $B$ as shown.

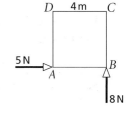

   (a) (i) Show that the moment of the 5 N force about $D$ is 20 N m.

      (ii) Find the moment of the 8 N force about $D$.

      (iii) Find the total moment of the forces about $D$.

   (b) Explain why the total moment of the forces about $B$ is zero.

   (c) Find the total moment of the forces about $A$.

   (d) Find the total moment of the forces about $C$.

**A5** $AB$ is a light rod of length 10 m. Forces act on the rod as shown.

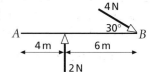

   (a) Show that the moment of the 4 N force about $A$ is $-20$ N m.

   (b) Find the moment of the 2 N force about $A$.

   (c) Find the total moment of the forces about $A$.

The resultant moment of a set of forces about a point is equal to the sum
of the moments of the individual forces about that point.
Anticlockwise moments are taken as positive and clockwise moments as negative.

---

**Example 1**

Forces of 4 N and 6 N act on the lamina $ABCD$ as shown.

Find the total moment of these forces about $O$.

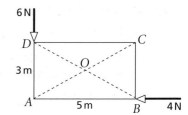

**Solution**

*The line of action of the 4 N force is 1.5 m from $O$ and
the line of action of the 6 N force is 2.5 m from $O$.*

Moment of 4 N force about $O$ = $4 \times 1.5 = 6$ N m clockwise

Moment of 6 N force about $O$ = $6 \times 2.5 = 15$ N m anticlockwise

*The total moment is the sum of the moments of the individual forces.
Remember anticlockwise moments are positive and clockwise moments are negative.*

Total moment = $15 - 6 = 9$ N m

---

**1** Find the moment of each force about $O$.

**(a)**

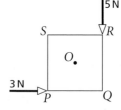

**(b)**

**(c)**

**2** $PQRS$ is a square lamina of side 5 m with centre $O$.
Forces of 3 N and 5 N act as shown.
Find the total moment of these forces about

**(a)** $P$          **(b)** $S$          **(c)** $O$

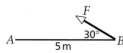

**3** A force of magnitude $F$ N acts on a light rod $AB$
of length 5 m as shown.
The moment of $F$ about $A$ is 15 N m.
Find the value of $F$.

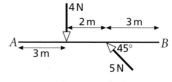

**4** $AB$ is a light rod of length 8 m.
Forces act on the rod as shown.
Find the total moment of these forces about

**(a)** $A$          **(b)** $B$

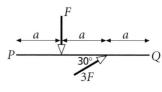

**5** $PQ$ is a light rod of length $3a$ metres.
Forces of magnitude $F$ N and $3F$ N act on the rod
as shown.
Find, in terms of $F$ and $a$, the total moment about

**(a)** $P$          **(b)** $Q$

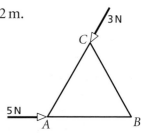

**6** $ABC$ is a light rigid equilateral triangular framework of side 2 m.
Forces act on the framework as shown.
Find the total moment of these forces about

**(a)** $A$          **(b)** $B$          **(c)** $C$

**7** $ABCD$ is a light rigid rectangular framework with centre $O$.
Forces of magnitude $F$ N and $3F$ N act on the framework as shown.
The total moment of these forces about $C$ is 28 N m.
Find the total moment of these forces about $O$.

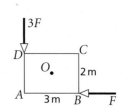

## B Equilibrium of a rigid body (answers p 140)

**B1** A uniform rod of weight 30 N rests horizontally in equilibrium on two smooth supports at $A$ and $B$ as shown. The rod is in equilibrium, so the resultant force is zero and the total moment about any point is zero.

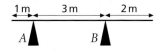

(a) Draw a force diagram for the rod.

(b) Use the fact that the total moment of all the forces about $A$ is zero to show that the reaction at $B$ is 20 N.

(c) Use the fact that the total moment of all the forces about $B$ is zero to find the reaction at $A$.

(d) Find the resultant of the forces vertically to check that they are in equilibrium.

**B2** A uniform rod $AD$ of weight 15 N and length 4 m hangs in equilibrium in a horizontal position.
It is held in position by two light vertical cables attached at $B$ and $C$ as shown.
A particle of weight 5 N is fixed to the rod at $D$.

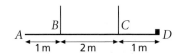

(a) Draw a force diagram for the rod.

(b) Find the tension in the cable at $B$.

(c) Find the tension in the cable at $C$.

In the questions above, all of the forces involved were parallel. The same method can be applied to systems of coplanar forces, where the forces are not all parallel.

 For a system of coplanar forces in equilibrium, the total moment about any point equals zero and the total component of forces in any direction equals zero.

A drawbridge of mass 500 kg and length 6 m is pivoted at point $P$ and is held in a horizontal position by a cable attached at point $Q$ as shown.

Assume that the drawbridge can be modelled as a uniform rod and that the cable is light.

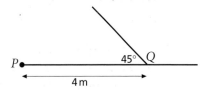

The force diagram for the drawbridge is shown.
The reaction at the pivot can no longer be assumed to be vertical, so we represent it by the horizontal and vertical components $X$ and $Y$ newtons. The reaction at the pivot is the resultant of these two components.

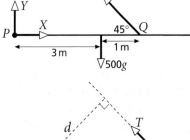

The moments of the forces $X$ and $Y$ about $P$ are zero because the lines of action of the forces pass through $P$. So taking moments about $P$ will allow us to find the tension in the cable, $T$ newtons.

This diagram shows the perpendicular distance $d$ from $P$ to the line of action of $T$.

**B3 (a)** Explain why the moment of $T$ about the point $P$ is $4T\sin 45°$.

  **(b)** By taking moments about $P$, show that $1500g = 4T\sin 45°$.

  **(c)** Find, to 3 s.f., the value of $T$.

**B4 (a)** Resolve the forces vertically to find the value of $Y$.

  **(b)** Resolve the forces horizontally to find the value of $X$.

  **(c)** Find the magnitude and direction of the reaction at $P$.

When a rigid body is freely hinged at a point, a reaction force will act at that point. Since the direction of the reaction is not known, it can be represented by its horizontal and vertical components.

**B5** A uniform shelf $AB$ of mass $2\,\text{kg}$ is freely hinged at the wall at $A$, and held in a horizontal position by a force applied at $B$ as shown.

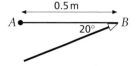

  **(a)** Sketch a force diagram for the shelf.

  **(b)** By taking moments about $A$, find the magnitude of the force at $B$ in newtons.

  **(c)** Find the magnitude and direction of the reaction at the wall.

Imagine a ladder leaning against a wall as shown. The wall and the ground are both modelled as smooth and the ladder is uniform.

**D** **B6 (a)** Sketch a diagram showing the forces acting on the ladder.

  **(b)** Describe what happens to the ladder.

This is clearly not a good model for the case where the ladder is stationary. The model can be improved by treating the ground as rough but the wall as smooth.

**D** **B7 (a)** Sketch a diagram showing the forces acting on the ladder in this case.

  **(b)** Describe what could happen to the ladder in this case.

A ladder of length $4\,\text{m}$ and weight $100\,\text{N}$ rests in equilibrium at $60°$ to the horizontal with one end against a smooth wall. The base rests on rough horizontal ground. The force diagram for the ladder is shown. We need to find the values of the reaction forces and the friction force.

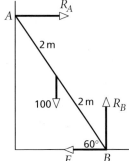

Resolving the forces vertically gives $R_B = 100$.

Resolving the forces horizontally gives $R_A = F$.

We have not been told that the ladder is in limiting equilibrium, so we cannot use $F = \mu R$ to find the friction force and hence the reaction at the wall.

Taking moments about a point will give a third equation which can be used to solve the problem.

**D** **B8** Explain why taking moments about $B$ will allow you to find $R_A$ directly.

The diagrams below show the perpendicular distance from the point $B$ to the line of action of the two required forces.

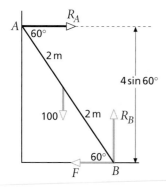 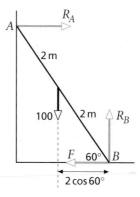

$$M(B): R_A \times 4\sin 60° = 100 \times 2\cos 60° \implies R_A = \frac{50\cos 60°}{\sin 60°}$$

The forces in newtons on the ladder are, to 3 s.f., $R_A = 28.9$, $R_B = 100$ and $F = 28.9$.

**D** **B9** A man now climbs up the ladder.
What happens to the forces on the ladder as he does so?

**B10** This is the force diagram for the ladder when a man of weight 750 N has climbed a distance of $x$ m up the ladder.

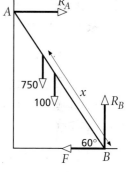

(a) Resolve the forces vertically to find the value of $R_B$ in newtons.

(b) Resolve the forces horizontally to write down an equation relating $R_A$ and $F$.

(c) By taking moments about $B$, find an equation relating $R_A$ and $x$.

(d) Given that the coefficient of friction is 0.4, find the maximum value of the friction force and hence the value of $R_A$ when the ladder is in limiting equilibrium.

(e) Use your equation from (c) to find the value of $x$ when the ladder is in limiting equilibrium.
State the maximum distance the man can climb up the ladder before it slips.

**B11** A uniform rod $AB$ of length $4a$ and weight $W$ rests with the end $A$ on rough horizontal ground. The rod is supported by a smooth peg at $C$, where $AC = 3a$.
The rod makes an angle $\alpha$ with the horizontal, where $\tan \alpha = \frac{3}{4}$.

(a) Draw a force diagram for the rod.

(b) By taking moments about $A$, show that the magnitude of the reaction at $C$ is $\frac{8}{15}W$.

(c) Resolve the forces horizontally to find the magnitude of the friction force.

(d) Resolve the forces vertically to find the magnitude of the reaction at $A$.

(e) Given that the rod is in limiting equilibrium, show that the coefficient of friction between the rod and the ground is $\frac{24}{43}$.

## Example 2

A uniform rod $AB$ of length $4\,\text{m}$ and weight $20\,\text{N}$ rests in equilibrium with the end $A$ on rough horizontal ground. The rod is supported at $60°$ to the horizontal by a smooth peg at $C$ where $AC = 3\,\text{m}$.

Show that $\mu \geq \dfrac{\sqrt{3}}{5}$, where $\mu$ is the coefficient of friction between the rod and the ground.

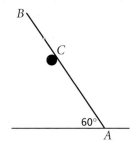

## Solution

*Sketch a force diagram showing all of the forces acting on the rod. The peg is smooth so the reaction at the peg is normal to the rod at the point of contact.*

*Take moments about A.*

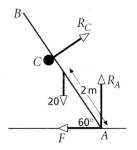

$$\text{M}(A): \quad 20 \times 2 \cos 60° = 3R_C$$

$$\Rightarrow \qquad R_C = \tfrac{40}{3} \times \tfrac{1}{2} = \tfrac{20}{3}$$

*The remaining forces can be found by resolving the forces on the rod vertically and horizontally.*

*The diagram shows the vertical and horizontal components of $R_C$.*

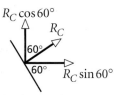

Resolve forces vertically. $\quad R_A + R_C \cos 60° = 20$

$$\Rightarrow \qquad R_A = 20 - \tfrac{20}{3} \times \tfrac{1}{2} = \tfrac{50}{3}$$

Resolve forces horizontally. $\quad F = R_C \sin 60° = \tfrac{20}{3} \times \dfrac{\sqrt{3}}{2} = \dfrac{10\sqrt{3}}{3}$

For equilibrium $F \leq \mu R_A$. $\qquad \dfrac{10\sqrt{3}}{3} \leq \tfrac{50}{3}\mu$

$$\Rightarrow \qquad \mu \geq \dfrac{10\sqrt{3}}{50}$$

$$\Rightarrow \qquad \mu \geq \dfrac{\sqrt{3}}{5}$$

## Exercise B (answers p 141)

**1** A uniform rod $AB$ of length $4\,\text{m}$ and weight $60\,\text{N}$ is pivoted at $A$ and held in a horizontal position by a light cable attached at $C$ as shown.

(a) Draw a force diagram for the rod.

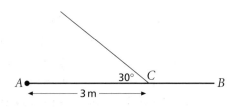

(b) Show that the moment about $A$ of the tension $T$ newtons in the cable is $3T \sin 30°$.

(c) Find the magnitude of $T$.

**2** A uniform rod $AB$ of length $2\,\text{m}$ and weight $W\,\text{N}$ is hinged at $A$ and held at an angle of $60°$ to the horizontal by a smooth support at $C$ as shown.
Find, in terms of $W$, the magnitude of the reaction at $C$.

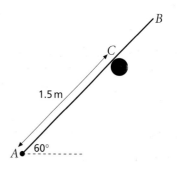

**3** A uniform ladder of length $5\,\text{m}$ and mass $12\,\text{kg}$ leans against a smooth wall with its base on rough ground as shown.
The ladder is in limiting equilibrium.

(a) Draw a force diagram for the ladder.

(b) Taking $g$ as $9.8\,\text{m s}^{-2}$, find the magnitude of the reaction at the wall.

(c) Find the magnitude of the friction force.

(d) Find the coefficient of friction between the ladder and the ground.

**4** A uniform flagpole is attached to a wall by a hinge, and is held in position by a light horizontal cable attached at its mid-point as shown. The length of the flagpole is $1.5\,\text{m}$ and its weight is $2\,\text{kg}$.

(a) Draw a force diagram for the flagpole.

(b) Find the tension in the cable.

(c) Find the magnitude and direction of the reaction at the hinge.

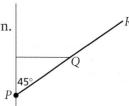

**5** A uniform rod $AB$ of length $2l$ and weight $W$ is freely hinged at $B$ to a fixed support. A horizontal force of magnitude $4W$ is applied at $A$ to keep the rod in equilibrium at an angle $\theta$ to the vertical as shown.

(a) Draw a force diagram for the rod.

(b) Write down the horizontal and vertical components of the reaction of the hinge on the rod at $B$.

(c) Find the magnitude and direction of the reaction at the hinge.

(d) Find the value of $\theta$.

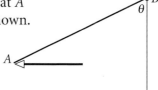

**6** A scaffold pole of length $3\,\text{m}$ and mass $10\,\text{kg}$ leans against a smooth fence of height $1.6\,\text{m}$.
One end of the pole rests on rough ground at $60°$ to the horizontal as shown.
The coefficient of friction between the pole and the ground is $\mu$.

(a) Draw a diagram to show the forces acting on the pole.

(b) Calculate the magnitude of the frictional force acting on the base of the pole.

(c) Find the minimum value of $\mu$ for the pole to remain at rest.

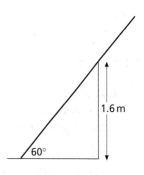

**7** A uniform ladder of length 6 m and weight 150 N is leaning at an angle of 20° to the vertical against a smooth wall with its base resting on rough horizontal ground. A man of weight 800 N climbs up the ladder.

Given that the coefficient of friction is 0.3, find the maximum distance that the man can climb up the ladder before it slips.

**8** A horizontal rod $AB$ of length $2a$ and weight $W$ rests with the end $A$ against a rough vertical wall.
The rod is held in position by a light string $BC$ attached to the rod at $B$ as shown. The string is inclined at an angle $\theta$ to the horizontal, where $\sin\theta = \frac{3}{5}$.
The coefficient of friction between the rod and the wall is $\mu$.
Show that $\mu \geq \frac{3}{4}$.

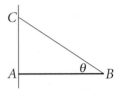

---

### Key points

- The resultant moment of a set of forces about a point is equal to the sum of the moments of the individual forces about that point.
  Anticlockwise moments are taken as positive and clockwise moments as negative. (p 109)

- For a system of coplanar forces in equilibrium, the total moment about any point equals zero and the total component of forces in any direction equals zero. (p 111)

---

## Mixed questions (answers p 142)

**1** A uniform rod $AB$ of length $2a$ and mass $m$ is freely hinged at $A$ to a fixed support.
A horizontal force is applied at $B$ to keep the rod in equilibrium at 30° to the vertical.

Find the magnitude of the force applied at $B$.

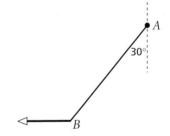

**2** A uniform ladder $AB$ of length $2a$ and weight $W$ has the end $A$ on rough horizontal ground. The coefficient of friction between the ladder and the ground is $\frac{1}{4}$. The other end $B$ of the ladder rests against a smooth vertical wall.
A man of weight $8W$ stands at the top of the ladder.
To prevent the ladder from slipping, another man applies a horizontal force of magnitude $P$ to the base of the ladder.
The ladder rests in equilibrium in a vertical plane perpendicular to the wall and makes an angle $\alpha$ with the horizontal, where $\tan\alpha = 3$.

Find, in terms of $W$, the range of values of $P$ for which the ladder remains in equilibrium.

**1** A uniform ladder of mass $m$ and length $2l$ is leaning at an angle $\alpha$ to the vertical against a smooth wall with its base resting on rough horizontal ground. The coefficient of friction between the ladder and the ground is $\frac{3}{5}$. A man of mass $4m$ climbs up the ladder.

Given that the man reaches the top of the ladder, show that $\tan\alpha \leq \frac{2}{3}$.

**2** A straight log $AB$ has weight $W$ and length $2a$. A cable is attached to one end $B$ of the log. The cable lifts the end $B$ off the ground. The end $A$ remains in contact with the ground, which is rough and horizontal. The log is in limiting equilibrium. The log makes an angle $\alpha$ to the horizontal, where $\tan\alpha = \frac{5}{12}$. The cable makes an angle $\beta$ to the horizontal, as shown. The coefficient of friction between the log and the ground is $0.6$. The log is modelled as a uniform rod and the cable as light.

**(a)** Show that the normal reaction on the log at $A$ is $\frac{2}{5}W$.

**(b)** Find the value of $\beta$.

The tension in the cable is $kW$.

**(c)** Find the value of $k$. Edexcel

**3** A uniform ladder, of weight $W$ and length $2a$, rests in equilibrium with one end $A$ on a smooth horizontal floor and the other end $B$ on a rough vertical wall. The ladder is in a vertical plane perpendicular to the wall. The coefficient of friction between the wall and the ladder is $\mu$. The ladder makes an angle $\theta$ with the floor, where $\tan\theta = 2$. A horizontal light inextensible string $CD$ is attached to the ladder at the point $C$, where $AC = \frac{1}{2}a$. The string is attached to the wall at the point $D$, with $BD$ vertical, as shown. The tension in the string is $\frac{1}{4}W$.

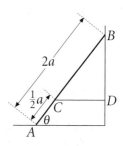

By modelling the ladder as a rod,

**(a)** find the magnitude of the force of the floor on the ladder,

**(b)** show that $\mu \geq \frac{1}{2}$.

**(c)** State how you have used the modelling assumption that the ladder is a rod. Edexcel

**4** A uniform rod $AB$ of length $2a$ and weight $W$ is freely hinged at $A$ to a vertical wall. The rod is held in a horizontal position by a light string attached to the rod at $B$. The string is inclined at an angle $\theta$ to the horizontal, where $\tan\theta = \frac{3}{4}$. A particle of weight $2W$ is attached to the rod at $D$, where $BD = \frac{1}{2}a$ as shown. The rod remains horizontal and in equilibrium.

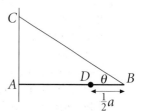

Show that the reaction at the hinge has magnitude $\dfrac{\sqrt{73}W}{3}$.

# Answers

## 1 Projectiles

Answers are given to three significant figures where appropriate.

### A Motion of a projectile (p 6)

**A1 (a)** The speed of the ball decreases from its initial value of $15\,\mathrm{m\,s^{-1}}$ as the ball moves upwards. The ball is at its maximum height when the speed of the ball reaches zero. The speed of the ball then increases as the ball returns to the ground. The ball reaches the ground at a speed of $15\,\mathrm{m\,s^{-1}}$.

**(b)** $9.8\,\mathrm{m\,s^{-2}}$ vertically downwards

**(c) (i)** Using $s = ut + \frac{1}{2}at^2$,
$$s = 15 \times 1 + \tfrac{1}{2}(-9.8) \times 1^2 = 10.1$$

**(ii)** $v = u + at$ gives $v = 15 - 9.8 \times 1 = 5.2$

**(d) (i)** $s = 15t - 4.9t^2$    **(ii)** $v = 15 - 9.8t$

**(e) (i)** $0\,\mathrm{m\,s^{-1}}$

**(ii)** $v^2 = u^2 + 2as$ gives $0 = 15^2 + 2(-9.8)s$
$$\Rightarrow s = 11.5$$
Maximum height reached is 11.5 m.

**A2 (a) (i)** $u = 0$, $a = -9.8$ gives $s = 0 + \frac{1}{2}(-9.8)t^2$
$$\Rightarrow s = -4.9t^2$$

**(ii)**

| $t$ | 0 | 1 | 2 | 3 | 4 |
|---|---|---|---|---|---|
| $y$ | 0 | −4.9 | −19.6 | −44.1 | −78.4 |

**(b) (i)** $v_y = 0 - 9.8t \Rightarrow v_y = -9.8t$

**(ii)**

| $t$ | 0 | 1 | 2 | 3 | 4 |
|---|---|---|---|---|---|
| $v_y$ | 0 | −9.8 | −19.6 | −29.4 | −39.2 |

**A3** Stones, snowballs, hockey balls, cricket balls thrown from the outfield and basketballs are all situations that can reasonably be modelled as projectiles.
If the motion of the object is affected by wind or spin it cannot be modelled as a projectile.
Polishing half of a cricket ball can accentuate swing when it is bowled, and it cannot then be modelled as a projectile.

**A4 (a)** Horizontal motion: $u = 10$, $a = 0$, $s = x$
$$s = ut + \tfrac{1}{2}at^2 \text{ gives } x = 10t$$

**(b)** Vertical motion: $u = 0$, $a = -9.8$, $s = y$
$$s = ut + \tfrac{1}{2}at^2 \text{ gives } y = \tfrac{1}{2}(-9.8)t^2 \Rightarrow y = -4.9t^2$$

**A5 (a)** When $t = 3$, $s = (10 \times 3)\mathbf{i} - (4.9 \times 3^2)\mathbf{j}$
$$= 30\mathbf{i} - 44.1\mathbf{j}$$

**(b)**

| $t$ | 0 | 1 | 2 | 3 | 4 |
|---|---|---|---|---|---|
| $s$ | 0 | $10\mathbf{i} - 4.9\mathbf{j}$ | $20\mathbf{i} - 19.6\mathbf{j}$ | $30\mathbf{i} - 44.1\mathbf{j}$ | $40\mathbf{i} - 78.4\mathbf{j}$ |

**(c)** (and A6(e))

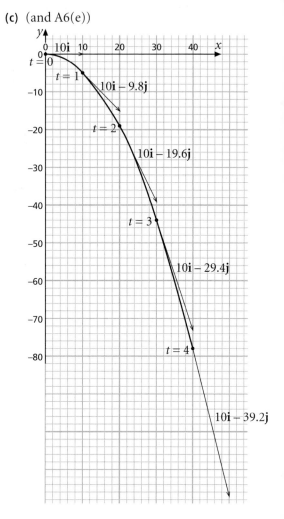

**A6 (a)** The initial horizontal velocity of the ball is $10\,\mathrm{m\,s^{-1}}$, and there is no horizontal acceleration, so the horizontal velocity $v_x$ is constant.

**(b)** Vertical motion: $u = 0$, $a = -9.8$, $v = v_y$
$v = u + at$ gives $v_y = -9.8t$

**(c)** $\mathbf{v} = v_x\mathbf{i} + v_y\mathbf{j}$ gives $\mathbf{v} = 10\mathbf{i} - 9.8t\mathbf{j}$

**(d)**

| $t$ | 0 | 1 | 2 | 3 | 4 |
|---|---|---|---|---|---|
| $\mathbf{v}$ | $10\mathbf{i}$ | $10\mathbf{i} - 9.8\mathbf{j}$ | $10\mathbf{i} - 19.6\mathbf{j}$ | $10\mathbf{i} - 29.4\mathbf{j}$ | $10\mathbf{i} - 39.2\mathbf{j}$ |

**(e)** See A5(c).

**A7 (a)** In A2(a) the ball has moved vertically; this displacement is the same as the vertical component of displacement in A5(b). In each case the initial vertical velocity of the ball was zero and the ball moved under gravity. In A5(b) the initial horizontal velocity caused the ball to be displaced horizontally as well as vertically.

**(b)** In A2(b) the velocity of the ball is always vertical; this velocity is the same as the vertical component of the velocity in A6(d). In both cases the ball had no initial vertical component of velocity, so the vertical velocities are caused by the acceleration due to gravity.
The initial horizontal velocity of the ball in A6(d) caused the constant horizontal velocity.

**A8 (a) (i)** Horizontal motion: $u_x = 10$, $a = 0$
$s = ut + \frac{1}{2}at^2$ gives $x = 10t$
Vertical motion: $u_y = 15$, $a = -9.8$
$s = ut + \frac{1}{2}at^2$ gives $y = 15t - 4.9t^2$
Combine the components of displacement:
$\mathbf{s} = 10t\mathbf{i} + (15t - 4.9t^2)\mathbf{j}$

**(ii)**

| $t$ | 0 | 0.5 | 1 | 1.5 |
|---|---|---|---|---|
| $\mathbf{s}$ | 0 | $5\mathbf{i} + 6.275\mathbf{j}$ | $10\mathbf{i} + 10.1\mathbf{j}$ | $15\mathbf{i} + 11.475\mathbf{j}$ |

| 2 | 2.5 | 3 |
|---|---|---|
| $20\mathbf{i} + 10.4\mathbf{j}$ | $25\mathbf{i} + 6.875\mathbf{j}$ | $30\mathbf{i} + 0.9\mathbf{j}$ |

**(iii) (and (b)(iii))**

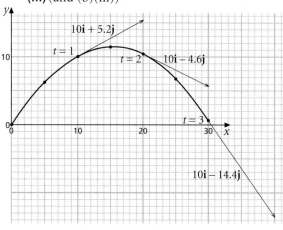

**(b) (i)** Horizontal motion: $v = u + at$ gives
$v_x = 10$
Vertical motion: $v = u + at$ gives
$v_y = 15 - 9.8t$
Combine the components of velocity:
$\mathbf{v} = 10\mathbf{i} + (15 - 9.8t)\mathbf{j}$

**(ii)**

| $t$ | 1 | 2 | 3 |
|---|---|---|---|
| $\mathbf{v}$ | $10\mathbf{i} + 5.2\mathbf{j}$ | $10\mathbf{i} - 4.6\mathbf{j}$ | $10\mathbf{i} - 14.4\mathbf{j}$ |

**(iii)** See A8 (a)(iii).

### Exercise A (p 11)

**1 (a)** Horizontal motion: $v_x = u_x = 12$
Vertical motion: $v_y = 0 - (9.8 \times 2) = -19.6$
Combine the components: $\mathbf{v} = 12\mathbf{i} - 19.6\mathbf{j}$

**(b)** $(12\mathbf{i} - 39.2\mathbf{j})\,\mathrm{m\,s^{-1}}$

**2 (a)**

| $t$ | 0 | 1 | 2 | 3 | 4 |
|---|---|---|---|---|---|
| $\mathbf{s}$ | 0 | $10\mathbf{i} + 15.1\mathbf{j}$ | $20\mathbf{i} + 20.4\mathbf{j}$ | $30\mathbf{i} + 15.9\mathbf{j}$ | $40\mathbf{i} + 1.6\mathbf{j}$ |

**(b) (and (c) and (d))**

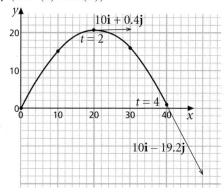

**(c)** $(10\mathbf{i} + 0.4\mathbf{j})\,\mathrm{m\,s^{-1}}$

**(d)** $(10\mathbf{i} - 19.2\mathbf{j})\,\mathrm{m\,s^{-1}}$

**3 (a)** $(4\mathbf{i} - 12.6\mathbf{j})\,\mathrm{m\,s^{-1}}$     **(b)** $(8\mathbf{i} - 5.6\mathbf{j})\,\mathrm{m}$

**4 (a)** $13.4\,\mathrm{m\,s^{-1}}$    **(b)** $63.4°$     **(c)** $9.68\,\mathrm{m\,s^{-1}}$

   **(d)** $51.7°$ below the horizontal

**5 (a)** $66.4\,\mathrm{m}$     **(b)** $16\,\mathrm{m}$

**6 (a)** $60\,\mathrm{m}$     **(b)** $1.225\,\mathrm{m}$

**7 (a)** $\mathbf{v} = 5\mathbf{i} + (6 - 9.8t)\mathbf{j}$

   **(b)** The speed is least when $6 - 9.8t = 0$
      $\Rightarrow t = 0.612$
      The speed is least $0.612\,\mathrm{s}$ after the ball is thrown.

   **(c)** $5\,\mathrm{m\,s^{-1}}$

## B Projectile problems (p 12)

**B1 (a)** Horizontal component $= 15\cos 30°$
      Vertical component $= 15\sin 30°$

   **(b)** $y = 15t\sin 30° - \tfrac{1}{2}gt^2 \Rightarrow y = 7.5t - 4.9t^2$

   **(c)** At $A$, $y = 0$ so $7.5t - 4.9t^2 = 0$
      $\Rightarrow t(7.5 - 4.9t) = 0 \Rightarrow t = 0$ or $1.53$
      $t = 0$ at $O$, so at $A$ $t = 1.53$
      The time of flight is $1.53\,\mathrm{s}$.

   **(d)** $x = 15t\cos 30°$

   **(e)** $19.9\,\mathrm{m}$

**B2 (a)** $v_y = 15\sin 30° - gt \Rightarrow v_y = 7.5 - 9.8t$

   **(b)** At maximum height $v_y = 0 \Rightarrow 7.5 - 9.8t = 0$
      $\Rightarrow t = 0.765\,\mathrm{s}$

   **(c)** The time when the particle is at its maximum height is half of the time of flight because of the symmetry of the path of the projectile.

   **(d)** $2.87\,\mathrm{m}$

**B3 (a)** When the particle is at its maximum height, the horizontal distance travelled is half of the range, i.e. $9.9\,\mathrm{m}$.

   **(b)** When the projectile is at its maximum height, the vertical component of the velocity is zero, so the direction of the velocity is horizontal.

**B4 (a)** $t = \dfrac{x}{15\cos 30°}$

**(b)** $y = 15\sin 30° \dfrac{x}{15\cos 30°} - \tfrac{1}{2}g\dfrac{x^2}{15^2\cos^2 30°}$

    $\Rightarrow y = x\tan 30° - \dfrac{gx^2\sec^2 30°}{450}$

    $\Rightarrow y = x\tan 30° - \dfrac{gx^2}{450}(1 + \tan^2 30°)$

   **(c)** When $x = 3$, $y = 1.47$

   **(d)** When $y = 2$,
      $2 = x\tan 30° - \dfrac{gx^2}{450}(1 + \tan^2 30°)$
      $\Rightarrow 0.029x^2 - 0.577x + 2 = 0$
      $\Rightarrow x = 4.47$ and $15.4$

**B5 (a)** Since the particle hits the ground when $y = 0$,
      $10t\sin 20° - \tfrac{1}{2}gt^2 = 0$
      $\Rightarrow t(10\sin 20° - 4.9t) = 0 \Rightarrow t = 0$ or $0.698$
      Initially $t = 0$, so the time of flight is $0.698\,\mathrm{s}$.

   **(b)** $x = 10t\cos 20° \Rightarrow x = 6.559$
      The range is $6.56\,\mathrm{m}$.

   **(c)** The particle is at its maximum height when
      $t = 0.35 \Rightarrow y = 0.5968$
      The maximum height is $0.597\,\mathrm{m}$.

### Exercise B (p 15)

**1 (a)** $2.62\,\mathrm{s}$      **(b)** $40.2\,\mathrm{m}$

**2 (a)** $2.04\,\mathrm{s}$      **(b)** $8.16\,\mathrm{m}$

**3** $2.33\,\mathrm{m}$

**4 (a)** $3.6\,\mathrm{m}$      **(b)** $19.2\,\mathrm{m}$

**5 (a)** $1.02\,\mathrm{s}$      **(b)** $7.14\,\mathrm{m}$

**6 (a)** The time of flight is the time when $y = 0$, and
      $y = Vt\sin\alpha - \tfrac{1}{2}gt^2 \Rightarrow Vt\sin\alpha - \tfrac{1}{2}gt^2 = 0$
      $\Rightarrow t(V\sin\alpha - \tfrac{1}{2}gt) = 0$
      $\Rightarrow t = 0$ or $t = \dfrac{2V\sin\alpha}{g}$

      Initially $t = 0$, so time of flight $t = \dfrac{2V\sin\alpha}{g}$.

   **(b)** $x = R$ when $t = \dfrac{2V\sin\alpha}{g}$.

      $x = Vt\cos\alpha$ so $R = V \times \dfrac{2V\sin\alpha}{g} \times \cos\alpha$

      $\Rightarrow R = \dfrac{2V^2\sin\alpha\cos\alpha}{g}$

**7 (a)** $4.13\,\mathrm{m}$      **(b)** $22.0\,\mathrm{m}$

**8** $23.3°$

**9** $29.3 \, \text{m s}^{-1}$ at $56.9°$ to the horizontal

**10** $7.73 \, \text{m s}^{-1}$ at $49.7°$ to the horizontal

**11** The angle of projection is $14.2°$. The range is $121 \, \text{m}$.

**12** (a) $0.714 \, \text{s}$    (b) $0.5 \, \text{m}$    (c) $0.639 \, \text{s}$

**13** The speed of release is $16.1 \, \text{m s}^{-1}$. It is in the air for $1.89 \, \text{s}$.

**14** $x = ut\cos\theta$

$\Rightarrow t = \dfrac{x}{u\cos\theta}$

$y = ut\sin\theta - \frac{1}{2}gt^2$

$y = u\sin\theta \times \dfrac{x}{u\cos\theta} - \frac{1}{2}g\left(\dfrac{x}{u\cos\theta}\right)^2$

$y = x\tan\theta - \dfrac{gx^2}{2u^2}\sec^2\theta$

$y = x\tan\theta - \dfrac{gx^2}{2u^2}(1 + \tan^2\theta)$

## C Release from a given height

### Exercise C (p 18)

**1** (a) $1.80 \, \text{s}$    (b) $17.7 \, \text{m}$

**2** (a) $\mathbf{v} = (21\cos 40°)\mathbf{i} + (21\sin 40° - 9.8t)\mathbf{j}$

  (b) $\mathbf{s} = (21t\cos 40°)\mathbf{i} + (21t\sin 40° - 4.9t^2 + 2)\mathbf{j}$

  (c) $46.6 \, \text{m}$

**3** $1.53 \, \text{s}$

**4** (a) $0.391 \, \text{s}$    (b) $30.7$    (c) $6.33 \, \text{m}$

**5** (a) $182 \, \text{m}$    (b) $14.4 \, \text{m}$

**6** $\dfrac{U^2}{2g} + h$

**7** (a) $5.23 \, \text{m}$

  (b) Jill's stone lands in the water after $1.92 \, \text{s}$. Jack's stone lands in the water after $0.96 \, \text{s}$. Jack's stone lands in the water first.

  (c) Jill's stone lands $9.58 \, \text{m}$ away. Jack's stone lands $3.66 \, \text{m}$ away. Jill's stone lands $5.92 \, \text{m}$ further.

**8** The object hits the target when $Ut\cos 45° = 20$ and $Ut\sin 45° - 4.9t^2 + 1 = 0$.

So $t = \dfrac{20}{U\cos 45°}$

Substituting, $20\tan 45° - \dfrac{4.9 \times 400}{U^2\cos^2 45°} + 1 = 0$

$\Rightarrow 21 = \dfrac{3920}{U^2}$   $\Rightarrow U = 13.7$

The object leaves the catapult at $13.7 \, \text{m s}^{-1}$.

## Mixed questions (p 20)

**1** (a) (i) $7.35 \, \text{m}$    (ii) $2.45 \, \text{s}$

  (b) (i) $5.51 \, \text{m}$    (ii) $2.12 \, \text{s}$

  (c) When the stone is projected at $60°$ to the horizontal, the vertical component of the velocity is $12\sin 60°$, which is less than $12$, so the height reached and the time in the air will be less.

**2** (a) $2.67 \, \text{s}$    (b) $53.5 \, \text{m}$    (c) $33.0 \, \text{m s}^{-1}$

**3** (a) $6.14 \, \text{m}$    (b) $7.82 \, \text{m}$

  (c) The shot can be modelled as a particle. Air resistance is negligible. The shot travels in a vertical plane.

**4** (a) The particle is at maximum height when $v_y = 0$

So $V\sin\alpha - gt = 0 \Rightarrow t = \dfrac{V\sin\alpha}{g}$

$y = Vt\sin\alpha - \frac{1}{2}gt^2$

So $y = V\sin\alpha \dfrac{V\sin\alpha}{g} - \frac{1}{2}g\dfrac{V^2\sin^2\alpha}{g^2}$

$\Rightarrow y = \dfrac{V^2\sin^2\alpha}{g} - \dfrac{V^2\sin^2\alpha}{2g} = \dfrac{V^2\sin^2\alpha}{2g}$

  (b) $20.9 \, \text{m s}^{-1}$

**5** (a) $2 \, \text{s}$

  (b) When $t = 2$, $y = 2.4 \, \text{m}$ so he does score a goal.

  (c) $13.2 \, \text{m s}^{-1}$ at $40.7°$ below the horizontal

**6** (a) $a = \dfrac{R}{T}, b = \dfrac{Tg}{2}$    (b) $\dfrac{gT^2}{8}$

**7** (a) $1.77 \, \text{s}$    (b) $11.8 \, \text{m}$

**8** $76.0°$

**9 (a)** 11.7 m

**(b)** 2.61 s

**(c)** 37.0 m

**(d)** 18.2 m s$^{-1}$

**(e)** 39.0° below the horizontal

**10 (a)** At $A$, $y = 0$ so $0 = 5Ut - \frac{1}{2}gt^2$

$\Rightarrow 0 = t(5U - \frac{1}{2}gt) \Rightarrow t = 0$ or $\frac{10U}{g}$

$t = 0$ at $O$, so at $A$ $t = \frac{10U}{g}$

**(b)** $\frac{20U}{g}$

**(c)** $\sqrt{29}\,U$

**(d) (i)** $\frac{4U}{g}, \frac{6U}{g}$      **(ii)** $\frac{12U^2}{g}$

### Test yourself (p 23)

**1 (a)** 4.13 m      **(b)** 1.83 m

**(c)** Air resistance or spin

**2 (a)** $x = 4ut$, $y = 2ut - \frac{1}{2}gt^2$

At $A$, $y = 0$ so $t(2u - 4.9t) = 0$

$\Rightarrow t = \frac{2u}{4.9}$ ($t = 0$ at start)

At $A$, $x = 245$ so $245 = 4u \times \frac{2u}{4.9} \Rightarrow u = 12.25$

**(b)** 5 s

**(c)** 54.8 m s$^{-1}$

**(d)** 30 m

**3 (a)** 2.81 s      **(b)** 25.3 m      **(c)** 18.0 m s$^{-1}$

**4 (a)** $x = \frac{4ut}{5}$, when $t = T$, $x = 8 \Rightarrow 8 = \frac{4uT}{5}$

$\Rightarrow uT = 10$

**(b)** 7

**(c)** −1.75

# 2 Variable acceleration

## A Motion in one dimension

### Exercise A (p 24)

**1 (a)** $v = 12t^3 - 2t$,   $a = 36t^2 - 2$

**(b)** $v = 3t^2 + 8t$,   $a = 6t + 8$

**(c)** $v = 1 - t^{-2}$,   $a = 2t^{-3}$

**2 (a)** $0.25t^2 + 0.5t^3 + c$

**(b) (i)** $c = 1$

$x = 0.25t^2 + 0.5t^3 + 1$

**(ii)** 6

**3 (a) (i)** $6t^2 - 6$      **(ii)** $\frac{1}{2}t^4 - 3t^2$

**(iii)** $13\frac{1}{2}$

**(b) (i)** $4t^3 - 6t$      **(ii)** $\frac{1}{5}t^5 - t^3$

**(iii)** $21\frac{3}{5}$

**(c) (i)** $3t^2 - t^{-\frac{1}{2}}$      **(ii)** $\frac{1}{4}t^4 - \frac{4}{3}t^{\frac{3}{2}}$

**(iii)** 13.3 (to 3 s.f.)

**4 (a) (i)** $3t + \frac{4}{3}\sqrt{t^3} + 4$

**(ii)** $\frac{3}{2}t^2 + \frac{8}{15}\sqrt{t^5} + 4t$

**(b)** Speed = 13.8 m s$^{-1}$ (to 3 s.f.)

Position = 17.0 m (to 3 s.f.)

**5 (a)** $t = 0$, $\frac{1}{2}$      **(b)** 0.125 m

**6 (a)** $v = -\frac{1}{4}t^3 + c$

$v = 16$ when $t = 0 \Rightarrow c = 16$

So $v = -\frac{1}{4}t^3 + 16$.

When $t = 4$, $v = -\frac{1}{4} \times 4^3 + 16 = 0$,

so the object is at rest when $t = 4$.

**(b)** 48 m

**7 (a)** $p = -\frac{5}{2}$,   $q = 7$

**(b)** $x = -\frac{5}{6}t^3 + \frac{7}{2}t^2 - \frac{7}{3} \Rightarrow x = \frac{1}{3}$ when $t = 4$

## B Motion in two dimensions 1 (p 27)

**B1** When $t = 1$, $0.1t^3 = 0.1$ and $6t - t^2 = 5$

So   $\mathbf{r} = 0.1\mathbf{i} + 5\mathbf{j}$

$t = 2$, $\mathbf{r} = 0.8\mathbf{i} + 8\mathbf{j}$

$t = 3$, $\mathbf{r} = 2.7\mathbf{i} + 9\mathbf{j}$

$t = 4$, $\mathbf{r} = 6.4\mathbf{i} + 8\mathbf{j}$

$t = 5$, $\mathbf{r} = 12.5\mathbf{i} + 5\mathbf{j}$

**B2**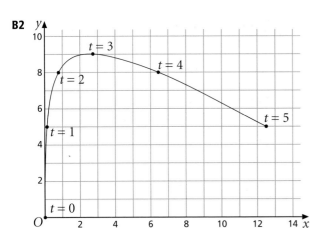

**B3** When $t = 0$, $\mathbf{v} = 0\mathbf{i} + (6 - 0)\mathbf{j} = 6\mathbf{j}$
$t = 1$, $\mathbf{v} = 0.3\mathbf{i} + 4\mathbf{j}$
$t = 2$, $\mathbf{v} = 1.2\mathbf{i} + 2\mathbf{j}$
$t = 3$, $\mathbf{v} = 2.7\mathbf{i}$
$t = 4$, $\mathbf{v} = 4.8\mathbf{i} - 2\mathbf{j}$
$t = 5$, $\mathbf{v} = 7.5\mathbf{i} - 4\mathbf{j}$

**B4** $t = 0$, $\mathbf{a} = -2\mathbf{j}$
$t = 1$, $\mathbf{a} = 0.6\mathbf{i} - 2\mathbf{j}$
$t = 2$, $\mathbf{a} = 1.2\mathbf{i} - 2\mathbf{j}$
$t = 3$, $\mathbf{a} = 1.8\mathbf{i} - 2\mathbf{j}$
$t = 4$, $\mathbf{a} = 2.4\mathbf{i} - 2\mathbf{j}$
$t = 5$, $\mathbf{a} = 3\mathbf{i} - 2\mathbf{j}$

**B5** (a) $t = 0$, $\mathbf{r} = 0\mathbf{i} + 0\mathbf{j}$
$t = 1$, $\mathbf{r} = 0.5\mathbf{i} + 4.8\mathbf{j}$
$t = 2$, $\mathbf{r} = 2\mathbf{i} + 8.4\mathbf{j}$
$t = 3$, $\mathbf{r} = 4.5\mathbf{i} + 9.6\mathbf{j}$
$t = 4$, $\mathbf{r} = 8\mathbf{i} + 7.2\mathbf{j}$
$t = 5$, $\mathbf{r} = 12.5\mathbf{i}$

(b) $t\mathbf{i} + (5 - 0.6t^2)\mathbf{j}$

(c) $t = 0$, $\mathbf{v} = 0\mathbf{i} + 5\mathbf{j}$
$t = 1$, $\mathbf{v} = \mathbf{i} + 4.4\mathbf{j}$
$t = 2$, $\mathbf{v} = 2\mathbf{i} + 2.6\mathbf{j}$
$t = 3$, $\mathbf{v} = 3\mathbf{i} - 0.4\mathbf{j}$
$t = 4$, $\mathbf{v} = 4\mathbf{i} - 4.6\mathbf{j}$
$t = 5$, $\mathbf{v} = 5\mathbf{i} - 10\mathbf{j}$
The results at $t = 0, 1, 2, 3, 4, 5$ are reasonable because they are tangent vectors.

(d) The velocity is in the $\mathbf{i}$-direction when
$5 - 0.6t^2 = 0 \Rightarrow 0.6t^2 = 5 \Rightarrow t = 2.89$
(to 3 s.f.)

(e) $\mathbf{i} - 1.2t\mathbf{j}$

(f) $t = 0$, $\mathbf{a} = \mathbf{i}$
$t = 1$, $\mathbf{a} = \mathbf{i} - 1.2\mathbf{j}$
$t = 2$, $\mathbf{a} = \mathbf{i} - 2.4\mathbf{j}$
$t = 3$, $\mathbf{a} = \mathbf{i} - 3.6\mathbf{j}$
$t = 4$, $\mathbf{a} = \mathbf{i} - 4.8\mathbf{j}$
$t = 5$, $\mathbf{a} = \mathbf{i} - 6\mathbf{j}$
The acceleration vectors are all directed towards the 'inside' of the curve, as expected.

**B6** (a) $\mathbf{v} = 10t\mathbf{i} + 4\mathbf{j}$
$\mathbf{a} = 10\mathbf{i}$

(b) $\mathbf{v} = (4t - 3)\mathbf{i} + 12t^2\mathbf{j}$
$\mathbf{a} = 4\mathbf{i} + 24t\mathbf{j}$

(c) $\mathbf{v} = (3t^2 - 2)\mathbf{i} - 4t^3\mathbf{j}$
$\mathbf{a} = 6t\mathbf{i} - 12t^2\mathbf{j}$

**B7** (a) $3t^{-\frac{1}{2}}\mathbf{i} + (4 - 24t^2)\mathbf{j}$

(b) $-\frac{3}{2}t^{-\frac{3}{2}}\mathbf{i} - 48t\mathbf{j}$

**B8** (a) $8\mathbf{i} + 3\mathbf{j}$

(b) $v = |\mathbf{v}| = \sqrt{8^2 + 3^2} = 8.5440\ldots$
Speed = $8.54\,\text{m s}^{-1}$ (to 3 s.f.)

(c) Angle = $\tan^{-1}\frac{3}{8} = 20.6°$ (to 3 s.f.)

(d) $3\mathbf{i} + 2t\mathbf{j}$

(e) When $t = 2$, $\mathbf{a} = 3\mathbf{i} + 4\mathbf{j}$
$a = |\mathbf{a}| = \sqrt{3^2 + 4^2} = 5$
Acceleration = $5\,\text{m s}^{-2}$

(f) Angle = $\tan^{-1}\frac{4}{3} = 53.1°$ (to 3 s.f.)

**Exercise B** (p 31)

**1** (a) $(5 - 2t)\mathbf{i} + 3t^2\mathbf{j}$

(b) $\sqrt{1^2 + 12^2} = 12.04\ldots$
Speed = $12.0\,\text{m s}^{-1}$ (to 3 s.f.)

(c) $-2\mathbf{i} + 6t\mathbf{j}$

(d) $\sqrt{(-2)^2 + 12^2} = 12.16\ldots$
Acceleration = $12.2\,\text{m s}^{-2}$ (to 3 s.f.)

**2** (a) $(1 + 3t^2)\mathbf{i} - 8t\mathbf{j}$

(b) $36.9\,\text{m s}^{-2}$ (to 3 s.f.)

**3** (a) $32t\mathbf{i} + (3t^2 - 48)\mathbf{j}$

(b) $3t^2 - 48 = 0 \Rightarrow t = 4$

(c) $32t = -(3t^2 - 48) \Rightarrow 3t^2 + 32t - 48 = 0$
$\Rightarrow (3t - 4)(t + 12) = 0 \Rightarrow t = \frac{4}{3}$

**4 (a)** $(3t^2 - 14t)\mathbf{i} + (2t - 6)\mathbf{j}$

**(b)** $2t - 6 = 0 \implies t = 3$

**(c)** $15\,\mathrm{m\,s^{-1}}$

**(d)** The $\mathbf{i}$-component of $\mathbf{v} = 0$
So $3t^2 - 14t = 0 \implies t(3t - 14) = 0$
$\implies t = 0$ or $4\frac{2}{3}$

**(e)** At $t = 0$, speed $= 6\,\mathrm{m\,s^{-1}}$
At $t = 4\frac{2}{3}$, speed $= 3\frac{1}{3}\,\mathrm{m\,s^{-1}}$

**5 (a)** $(t^2 - 4)\mathbf{i} + (12t - 3t^2)\mathbf{j}$

**(b)** When $t = 2$, the horizontal component
of $\mathbf{v} = 2^2 - 4 = 0$.
As the horizontal component of $\mathbf{v}$ is 0, the
velocity is vertical.

**(c)** $12t - 3t^2 = 0 \implies 3t(4 - t) = 0 \implies t = 0, t = 4$

**6 (a)** $6t^2\mathbf{i} + (2t + 4)\mathbf{j}$

**(b) (i)** $1\,\mathrm{s}$

**(ii)** Acceleration $= 12t\mathbf{i} + 2\mathbf{j}$
Magnitude of acceleration $= 12.2\,\mathrm{m\,s^{-2}}$
(to 3 s.f.)

**7 (a)** $0.4t\mathbf{i} + (2 - 0.2t)\mathbf{j}$

**(b)** $2\,\mathrm{m\,s^{-1}}$

**(c) (i)** $\mathbf{a} = \dfrac{\mathrm{d}\mathbf{v}}{\mathrm{d}t} = 0.4\mathbf{i} - 0.2\mathbf{j}$, which is constant

**(ii)** $0.447\,\mathrm{m\,s^{-2}}$ (to 3 s.f.)

**(d) (i)** $10\,\mathrm{s}$

**(ii)** $4\,\mathrm{m\,s^{-1}}$

**(iii)** $22.4\,\mathrm{m}$ (to 3 s.f.)

**8 (a)** $4.12\,\mathrm{m}$ (to 3 s.f.)      **(b)** $2.5\,\mathrm{m\,s^{-1}}$

**(c)** $1.25\,\mathrm{m\,s^{-2}}$

## C Motion in two dimensions 2 (p 33)

**C1** $\mathbf{r} = \int \mathbf{v}\,\mathrm{d}t = \int (6t^2\mathbf{i} + (4t - 3)\mathbf{j})\,\mathrm{d}t$
$= 2t^3\mathbf{i} + (2t^2 - 3t)\mathbf{j} + \mathbf{c}$
When $t = 0$, $\mathbf{r} = 2\times0^3\mathbf{i} + (2\times0^2 - 3\times0)\mathbf{j} + \mathbf{c} = \mathbf{c}$
so $\mathbf{c} = \mathbf{i} + \mathbf{j}$
so $\mathbf{r} = (2t^3 + 1)\mathbf{i} + (2t^2 - 3t + 1)\mathbf{j}$

**C2** $\mathbf{r} = \int \mathbf{v}\,\mathrm{d}t = \int \left(t^{\frac{1}{2}}\mathbf{i} + t^{-\frac{1}{2}}\mathbf{j}\right)\mathrm{d}t = \frac{2}{3}t^{\frac{3}{2}}\mathbf{i} + 2t^{\frac{1}{2}}\mathbf{j} + \mathbf{c}$
When $t = 0$, $\mathbf{r} = \mathbf{0}$, so $\mathbf{c} = \mathbf{0}$
So $\mathbf{r} = \frac{2}{3}t^{\frac{3}{2}}\mathbf{i} + 2t^{\frac{1}{2}}\mathbf{j}$

**C3** $\mathbf{v} = \int \mathbf{a}\,\mathrm{d}t = \int (3(t^2 - 4)\mathbf{i} + (t + 2)\mathbf{j})\,\mathrm{d}t$
$= 3(\frac{1}{3}t^3 - 4t)\mathbf{i} + (\frac{1}{2}t^2 + 2t)\mathbf{j} + \mathbf{c}$
When $t = 0$, $\mathbf{v} = 0\mathbf{i} + 0\mathbf{j} + \mathbf{c} = 2\mathbf{i} - \mathbf{j} \implies \mathbf{c} = 2\mathbf{i} - \mathbf{j}$
so $\mathbf{v} = 3(\frac{1}{3}t^3 - 4t)\mathbf{i} + (\frac{1}{2}t^2 + 2t)\mathbf{j} + 2\mathbf{i} - \mathbf{j}$
$\implies \mathbf{v} = (t^3 - 12t + 2)\mathbf{i} + (\frac{1}{2}t^2 + 2t - 1)\mathbf{j}$

## Exercise C (p 34)

**1** $(4t^2 - 2t^3)\mathbf{i} + (2t^2 + t^3)\mathbf{j}$

**2** $(2 + 2t + \frac{5}{2}t^2)\mathbf{i} + (2t^2 + \frac{1}{3}t^3)\mathbf{j}$

**3 (a)** $(\frac{1}{2}t^2 - t)\mathbf{i} + (\frac{1}{4}t^4 - \frac{1}{2}t^2 + 5)\mathbf{j}$

**(b)** $(\frac{1}{6}t^3 - \frac{1}{2}t^2)\mathbf{i} + (\frac{1}{20}t^5 - \frac{1}{6}t^3 + 5t)\mathbf{j}$

**4 (a)** $\mathbf{v} = (3t^3 + 2t + 1)\mathbf{i} + (4t^3 - t + 1)\mathbf{j}$
$\mathbf{r} = (\frac{3}{4}t^4 + t^2 + t)\mathbf{i} + (t^4 - \frac{1}{2}t^2 + t)\mathbf{j}$

**(b)** $\mathbf{v} = (\frac{1}{4}t^4 - 2t)\mathbf{i} + (\frac{2}{3}t^3 + 4)\mathbf{j}$
$\mathbf{r} = (\frac{1}{20}t^5 - t^2 + 1)\mathbf{i} + (\frac{1}{6}t^4 + 4t + 1)\mathbf{j}$

**(c)** $\mathbf{v} = \frac{2}{3}t^{\frac{3}{2}}\mathbf{i} - 4t\mathbf{j}$
$\mathbf{r} = \frac{4}{15}t^{\frac{5}{2}}\mathbf{i} - 2t^2\mathbf{j}$

**5 (a)** $0, 3$      **(b)** $((3 - 2t)\mathbf{i} + 24t^2\mathbf{j})\,\mathrm{m\,s^{-2}}$

**(c)** $((\frac{3}{2}t^2 - \frac{1}{3}t^3)\mathbf{i} + 2t^4\mathbf{j})\,\mathrm{m}$

**6** $109\,\mathrm{m}$ (to 3 s.f.)

## D Using Newton's laws in one dimension (p 35)

**D1 (a)** $6t - 6t^2$

**(b)** $6 - 12t$

**(c)** $F = m(6 - 12t) = 2.5(6 - 12t) = 15 - 30t$

**(d)** $F = -45 \implies |F| = 45\,\mathrm{N}$

**(e)** $2.5(6 - 12t) = 0 \implies t = 0.5\,\mathrm{s}$

**D2 (a)** N2L: $F = ma \implies 6\sqrt{t} - 2 = 0.4a$
$\implies a = 15\sqrt{t} - 5$

**(b)** $15\sqrt{t} - 5 = 0 \implies \sqrt{t} = \frac{1}{3} \implies t = \frac{1}{9}$

**(c)** $v = \int a\,\mathrm{d}t = \int (15\sqrt{t} - 5)\,\mathrm{d}t = 10t^{\frac{3}{2}} - 5t + c$
$v = 0$ when $t = 0 \implies c = 0$
so $v = 10t^{\frac{3}{2}} - 5t$

**(d)** Displacement $= \int v\,\mathrm{d}t = \int (10t^{\frac{3}{2}} - 5t)\,\mathrm{d}t$
$= 4t^{\frac{5}{2}} - \frac{5}{2}t^2 + c$
Displacement $= 0$ when $t = 0 \implies c = 0$
So displacement $= 4t^{\frac{5}{2}} - \frac{5}{2}t^2$

**(e)** The particle is at rest when $10t^{\frac{3}{2}} - 5t = 0$.

So $5t(2t^{\frac{1}{2}} - 1) = 0$

$\Rightarrow t^{\frac{1}{2}} = \frac{1}{2}$ (or $t = 0$)

$\Rightarrow t = \frac{1}{4}$

**(f)** When $t = 0$, $F = -2\,\text{N}$

When $t = 4$, $F = 1\,\text{N}$

## Exercise D (p 36)

**1 (a)** $2t^2 - 6t$     **(b)** $\frac{2}{3}t^3 - 3t^2$     **(c)** $4.5\,\text{s}$

**(d)** $\frac{1}{6}t^4 - t^3$     **(e)** $6\,\text{s}$     **(f)** $36\,\text{m s}^{-1}$

**2 (a)** $10 - 8t$

**(b)** $5 - 4t$

**(c)** $1.25\,\text{s}$

**(d) (i)** $0\,\text{s}, 2.5\,\text{s}$

    **(ii)** When $t = 0$, force $= 5\,\text{N}$

        When $t = 2.5$, force $= -5\,\text{N}$

**3 (a)** $30 - 5kt$

**(b)** $30t - \frac{5}{2}kt^2$

**(c)** $15t^2 - \frac{5}{6}kt^3$

**(d) (i)** When $t = 4$, $x = 0 \Rightarrow 240 - \dfrac{160k}{3} = 0$

        $\Rightarrow k = 4.5$

    **(ii)** $v = 30t - \frac{45}{4}t^2$

        When $t = 4$, velocity $= -60\,\text{m s}^{-1}$

**4 (a)** $30\sqrt{t}$     **(b)** $20t^{\frac{3}{2}} + 2$

**(c)** $2.25\,\text{s}$     **(d)** $8t^{\frac{5}{2}} + 2t$

**(e)** $65.25\,\text{m}$

**5** Acceleration $= \dfrac{\mathrm{d}v}{\mathrm{d}t} = 8t - 3$

  Force $= 12t - 4.5$

**6** Acceleration $= \dfrac{\mathrm{d}^2x}{\mathrm{d}t^2} = -6 - 3t$

  Force $= 0.05(-6 - 3t) = -0.3 - 0.15t$

  Magnitude $= \lvert -0.3 - 0.15t \rvert$

## E Using Newton's laws in two dimensions
(p 37)

**E1 (a)** $(10t - 2)\mathbf{i} + 6t^2\mathbf{j}$

**(b)** $\mathbf{F} = m\mathbf{a}$ from which $\mathbf{F} = 3((10t - 2)\mathbf{i} + 6t^2\mathbf{j})$

                 $= (30t - 6)\mathbf{i} + 18t^2\mathbf{j}$

                 $= 6(5t - 1)\mathbf{i} + 18t^2\mathbf{j}$

**(c)** When $t = 1$, $\mathbf{F} = 6(5(1) - 1)\mathbf{i} + 18(1)^2\mathbf{j}$

              $= 24\mathbf{i} + 18\mathbf{j}$

    $\lvert \mathbf{F} \rvert = \sqrt{24^2 + 18^2} = \sqrt{900} = 30$

**E2 (a)** $\mathbf{F} = m\mathbf{a}$ from which $15t^2\mathbf{i} = 2.5\mathbf{a}$

                      $\Rightarrow \mathbf{a} = 6t^2\mathbf{i}$

**(b)** $\mathbf{v} = \int 6t^2\mathbf{i}\,\mathrm{d}t = 2t^3\mathbf{i} + \mathbf{c}$

**(c)** When $t = 0$, $\mathbf{v} = 2(0)^3\mathbf{i} + \mathbf{c} = \mathbf{c}$

    Also, when $t = 0$, $\mathbf{v} = 3\mathbf{i} - 2\mathbf{j} \Rightarrow \mathbf{c} = 3\mathbf{i} - 2\mathbf{j}$

    So $\mathbf{v} = 2t^3\mathbf{i} + 3\mathbf{i} - 2\mathbf{j} = (2t^3 + 3)\mathbf{i} - 2\mathbf{j}$

**(d)** $\mathbf{r} = \int \mathbf{v}\,\mathrm{d}t = (\frac{1}{2}t^4 + 3t)\mathbf{i} - 2t\mathbf{j} + \mathbf{c}$

    When $t = 0$, $\mathbf{r} = 0 \Rightarrow \mathbf{c} = 0$

                    $\Rightarrow \mathbf{r} = (\frac{1}{2}t^4 + 3t)\mathbf{i} - 2t\mathbf{j}$

**(e)** When $t = 2$, $\mathbf{r} = 14\mathbf{i} - 4\mathbf{j}$

    Distance from origin $= \sqrt{14^2 + (-4)^2} = 14.6\,\text{m}$

## Exercise E (p 39)

**1** $(1.6 - 2t)\mathbf{i} + 0.4(t - t^2)\mathbf{j}$

**2 (a)** $(10 - 2t)\mathbf{i} + 7\mathbf{j}$     **(b)** $(2 - 0.4t)\mathbf{i} + 1.4\mathbf{j}$

**3 (a)** $(2t^2 - 4)\mathbf{i} + (4t + 6)\mathbf{j}$

**(b)** $(\frac{2}{3}t^3 - 4t + 4)\mathbf{i} + (2t^2 + 6t)\mathbf{j}$

**4 (a)** $3t^2\mathbf{i} + (2t - 2)\mathbf{j}$     **(b)** $6t\mathbf{i} + 2\mathbf{j}$

**(c)** $12t\mathbf{i} + 4\mathbf{j}$     **(d)** $24.3\,\text{N}$ (to 3 s.f.)

**5** $\mathbf{F} = t\mathbf{i} + (2 - 3t)\mathbf{j}$

  Magnitude $= 13.9\,\text{N}$ (to 3 s.f.)

**6** $\mathbf{F} = 3\mathbf{i} + 9t\mathbf{j}$

## Mixed questions (p 40)

**1 (a)** $\frac{2}{3}\,\text{s}$            **(b)** $17.9\,\text{m s}^{-1}$ (to 3 s.f.)

**(c)** $\frac{1}{3}\,\text{s}$            **(d)** $8.25\,\text{m s}^{-2}$ (to 3 s.f.)

**2 (a)** $2$                **(b)** $36\,\text{m}$

**3 (a)** $-2t^{-\frac{3}{2}}\mathbf{i} + 2\mathbf{j}$     **(b)** $2.02\,\text{N}$ (to 3 s.f.)

**4 (a) (i)** $12 - 6t$        **(ii)** $0$

**(b)** $16\,\text{m}$

**(c)** $112\,\text{m}$

**5 (a)** $(\frac{1}{4}t^4 + \frac{3}{2}t^2 + 2)\mathbf{i} + (t - 2t^2 + 1)\mathbf{j}$

**(b)** $(6t^2 + 6)\mathbf{i} - 8\mathbf{j}$

**(c)** $31.0\,\text{N}$ at $14.9°$ below the $\mathbf{i}$-direction

**6 (a)** $(3t^2 - 12t)\mathbf{i} + 10t\mathbf{j}$

**(b)** $(6t - 12)\mathbf{i} + 10\mathbf{j}$

**(c) (i)** $|\mathbf{a}| = \sqrt{(6t-12)^2 + 10^2}$

$|\mathbf{a}|$ is minimum when $6t - 12 = 0$
$\Rightarrow t = 2$

**(ii)** $10\,\text{m s}^{-2}$

## Test yourself (p 41)

**1 (a)** $8t\mathbf{i} + (5 - 2t)\mathbf{j}$

**(b)** Acceleration $= \dfrac{\mathrm{d}v}{\mathrm{d}t} = 8\mathbf{i} - 2\mathbf{j}$, which is constant
Magnitude $= 8.25\,\text{m s}^{-2}$ (to 3 s.f.)

**2 (a)** $\left(\frac{3}{2}t^2 + 1\right)\mathbf{i} + (2 - t)\mathbf{j}$

**(b)** $\left(\frac{1}{2}t^3 + t\right)\mathbf{i} + \left(2t - \frac{1}{2}t^2\right)\mathbf{j}$

**3 (a)** $3t^2 - 9t + 6$      **(b)** $0.5\,\text{m}$

**4 (a)** $(8t - 6)\mathbf{i} + 4t\mathbf{j}$      **(b)** $1.5\,\text{s}$

**5 (a)** $4.02\,\text{N}$      **(b)** $67\mathbf{i} + 28\mathbf{j}$

# 3 Centre of mass

## A Centre of mass of a system of particles (p 42)

**A1 (a)** Resolve vertically: $3g = R$

**(b)** M(support): $2g \times x = g(2 - x)$
$\Rightarrow 2gx = 2g - gx$
$\Rightarrow 3x = 2 \Rightarrow x = \frac{2}{3}$
The centre of mass is $\frac{2}{3}\,\text{m}$ from $A$.

**A2 (a)** $19.6\,\text{N m}$ clockwise

**(b)** $3g \times \frac{2}{3} = 19.6\,\text{N m}$ clockwise

**A3 (a)** $39.2\,\text{N m}$ anticlockwise

**(b)** $3g \times \left(2 - \frac{2}{3}\right) = 39.2\,\text{N m}$ anticlockwise

**A4 (a)** $2g \times 1 - g \times 1 = 9.8\,\text{N m}$ anticlockwise

**(b)** $3g \times \frac{1}{3} = 9.8\,\text{N m}$ anticlockwise

### Exercise A (p 44)

**1 (a)** $1.125\,\text{m}$   **(b)** $1.15\,\text{m}$   **(c)** $0.84\,\text{m}$   **(d)** $0.5\,\text{m}$

**2 (a)** $3.4\,\text{m}$      **(b)** $3.75\,\text{m}$ from $A$

**3** $30$

**4** $6$

**5** $2.25\,\text{m}$

**6** $4.25\,\text{m}$

## B A system of particles in a plane

### Exercise B (p 46)

**1 (a)** $(3.25, 1.75)$      **(b)** $(4, 3.7)$

**(c)** $(3.2, 2.6)$      **(d)** $(3.4, 1.8)$

**2** $(1.4, 2)$

**3 (a)** $0.53\,\text{m}$ (to 2 d.p.)      **(b)** $2\,\text{m}$

**4 (a)** $(1.5, 1.5)$      **(b)** $(1.5, 1)$

**5 (a)** $8$      **(b)** $0.625$

**6 (a)** $1.2\,\text{m}$      **(b)** $2\,\text{m}$

**(c)** $1\,\text{m}$ from $PQ$, $1.5\,\text{m}$ from $PS$

**7** $p = 8, q = 4$

## C  Centre of mass by symmetry (p 48)

**C1 (a)** $(2, 1)$

**(b)** The lines $x = 2$ and $y = 1$ are lines of symmetry of the system. The centre of mass lies at the point of intersection of these lines as the masses are symmetrically distributed about this point.

**C2 (a)** The centre of the circle

**(b)** The centre of the square

**(c)** The centre of the rectangle

### Exercise C (p 48)

**1 (a)** $(2.5, 2.5)$    **(b)** $(1.5, 1.6)$

**2 (a)** $(2.5, 3)$    **(b)** $(3.5, 2.5)$

**(c)** $(-0.5, 0.5)$    **(d)** $(2.5, 1.5)$

## D  Centres of mass of special shapes (p 49)

**D1 (a)** Length of median $= \sqrt{8^2 - 3^2} = \sqrt{55}$
$= 7.42\,\mathrm{m}$ (to 3 s.f.)

**(b)** $\frac{1}{3} \times 7.42 = 2.47\,\mathrm{m}$ (to 3 s.f.) from $PR$

### Exercise D (p 51)

**1** $4.24\,\mathrm{m}$ (to 3 s.f.)

**2** $4.71\,\mathrm{m}$ (to 3 s.f.)

**3 (a)** $(1, 1)$    **(b)** $(4, 1)$

**4** $5.73\,\mathrm{m}$ (to 3 s.f.)

**5** $3.25\,\mathrm{m}$ (to 3 s.f.)

**6 (a)** $(3.40, 3.40)$ (to 3 s.f.)

**(b) (i)** $(-3.40, 3.40)$ (to 3 s.f.)

**(ii)** Each quadrant can be replaced by a particle of the same mass positioned at the centre of mass of the quadrant. The centre of mass of these particles will lie on the line joining them, so the centre of mass of the semicircular lamina lies on the line joining the centres of mass of $OAB$ and $OBC$.

**(iii)** $(0, 3.40)$ (to 3 s.f.)

**(iv)** Distance of centre of mass $=$

$$\frac{2r\sin\alpha}{3\alpha} = \frac{2 \times 8 \times \sin\frac{\pi}{2}}{3 \times \frac{\pi}{2}} = 3.40 \text{ (to 3 s.f.)}$$

The centre of mass of the semicircular lamina lies on its line of symmetry at $(0, 3.40)$ (to 3 s.f.).

## E  Centre of mass of a composite body (p 52)

**E1 (a)** $(1, 2)$    **(b)** $(5, 1)$

**E2 (a)** $8a\,\mathrm{kg}$    **(b)** $12a\,\mathrm{kg}$

**E3** Using $M\bar{x} = \sum mx$, $20a\bar{x} = 8a \times 1 + 12a \times 5$
$\Rightarrow 20\bar{x} = 68 \Rightarrow \bar{x} = 3.4$

Using $M\bar{y} = \sum my$, $20a\bar{y} = 8a \times 2 + 12a \times 1$
$\Rightarrow 20\bar{y} = 28 \Rightarrow \bar{y} = 1.4$

The centre of mass is at $(3.4, 1.4)$.

**E4 (a)**

|  | Area | Distance from $AE$ | Distance from $AC$ |
|---|---|---|---|
| $ABDE$ | $24\,\mathrm{m}^2$ | $3\,\mathrm{m}$ | $2\,\mathrm{m}$ |
| $BCD$ | $8\,\mathrm{m}^2$ | $7\frac{1}{3}\,\mathrm{m}$ | $1\frac{1}{3}\,\mathrm{m}$ |
| Lamina | $32\,\mathrm{m}^2$ | $\bar{x}\,\mathrm{m}$ | $\bar{y}\,\mathrm{m}$ |

**(b)** Using $M\bar{x} = \sum mx$, $32\bar{x} = 24 \times 3 + 8 \times 7\frac{1}{3}$
$\Rightarrow 32\bar{x} = 130\frac{2}{3} \Rightarrow \bar{x} = 4.08$ (to 3 s.f.)
Using $M\bar{y} = \sum my$, $32\bar{y} = 24 \times 2 + 8 \times 1\frac{1}{3}$
$\Rightarrow 32\bar{y} = 58\frac{2}{3} \Rightarrow \bar{y} = 1.83$ (to 3 s.f.)
The centre of mass of the lamina is at $(4.08, 1.83)$ to 3 s.f.

**E5 (a)**

|  | Area | Distance from $AD$ | Distance from $AB$ |
|---|---|---|---|
| $ABCD$ | $24\,\mathrm{m}^2$ | $3\,\mathrm{m}$ | $2\,\mathrm{m}$ |
| $EFGH$ | $4\,\mathrm{m}^2$ | $3\,\mathrm{m}$ | $1.5\,\mathrm{m}$ |
| Lamina | $20\,\mathrm{m}^2$ | $x_L\,\mathrm{m}$ | $y_L\,\mathrm{m}$ |

**(b) (i)** Using $M\bar{x} = \sum mx$, $24 \times 3 = 4 \times 3 + 20x_L$
$\Rightarrow 72 = 12 + 20x_L$

**(ii)** Using $M\bar{y} = \sum my$, $24 \times 2 = 4 \times 1.5 + 20y_L$
$\Rightarrow 48 = 6 + 20y_L$

**(iii)** $20x_L = 60 \Rightarrow x_L = 3$
$20y_L = 42 \Rightarrow y_L = 2.1$
The centre of mass is at $(3, 2.1)$.

**Exercise E** (p 55)

**1 (a)** $(2.5, 1)$  **(b)** $(4, 2.5)$  **(c)** $(2.75, 1.25)$

**2 (a)** $(0.83, 0.83)$ (to 2 d.p.)

  **(b)** $(1.86, 1)$ (to 2 d.p.)

  **(c)** $(2, 1.3)$

  **(d)** $(2, 1.27)$ (to 2 d.p.)

**3 (a)** $AD$ is a line of symmetry of the lamina.

  **(b)** $(2.71, 2.71)$ (to 2 d.p.)

**4 (a)**

|  | Length | Distance from $AC$ | Distance from $AB$ |
|---|---|---|---|
| Side $AB$ | 0.3 m | 0.15 m | 0 m |
| Side $BC$ | 0.5 m | **0.15 m** | 0.2 m |
| Side $AC$ | 0.4 m | **0 m** | 0.2 m |
| Triangle | **1.2 m** | $\bar{x}$ m | $\bar{y}$ m |

  **(b)** 0.1 m  **(c)** 0.15 m

**5 (a)** 0.14 m (to 2 d.p.)  **(b)** 0.4 m

**6 (a)** $(1.33, 1.33)$ (to 2 d.p.)

  **(b)** $(1.5, 1.25)$

  **(c)** $(1.32, 1.34)$ (to 2 d.p.)

**7 (a)** $(2.17, 2)$ (to 2 d.p.)

  **(b)** $(3.95, 1.98)$ (to 2 d.p.)

**8** 0.75 m

**9 (a)** Using $M\bar{y} = \Sigma my$,
   $(1.5 + 4 + 2)\bar{y} = 1.5 \times 1 + 4 \times 2 + 2 \times 2$
   $\Rightarrow 7.5\bar{y} = 13.5 \Rightarrow \bar{y} = 1.8$
   So the centre of mass is 1.8 m from $AB$.

  **(b)** 1.1 m

**10 (a)** 0.225 m  **(b)** 0.45 m

**11** 1.52 cm (to 2 d.p.)

## F Equilibrium (p 57)

**F1 (a)** It would not stay in this position because the weight of the lamina, acting at its centre of mass, has a resultant moment about $A$, causing the lamina to rotate.

  **(b)** Again, the lamina will not stay in this position, because there is still a resultant moment of the weight of the lamina about $A$.

  **(c)** When the centre of mass of the lamina is vertically below $A$, the moment of the weight about $A$ is zero, and so the lamina is in equilibrium.

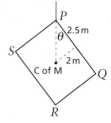

  **(d)** $\theta = \tan^{-1}\frac{1}{2} = 26.6°$ (to 3 s.f.)

**F2 (a) (i)** 2 m  **(ii)** 2.5 m

  **(b) (i)**

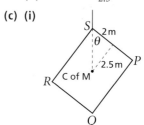

  **(ii)** $\theta = \tan^{-1}\frac{2}{2.5} = 38.7°$ (to 3 s.f.)

  **(c) (i)**

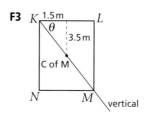

  **(ii)** $51.3°$ (to 3 s.f.)

**F3**

  $\theta = \tan^{-1}\frac{3.5}{1.5} = 66.8°$ (to 3 s.f.)

**F4 (a)**

|  | Area | Distance from $AG$ | Distance from $AB$ |
|---|---|---|---|
| $ABFG$ | 9 m² | 1.5 m | 1.5 m |
| $CDEF$ | 3 m² | 4.5 m | 2.5 m |
| Lamina | 12 m² | $\bar{x}$ m | $\bar{y}$ m |

   $12\bar{x} = 9 \times 1.5 + 3 \times 4.5 \Rightarrow 12\bar{x} = 27$
   $\Rightarrow \bar{x} = 2.25$

  **(b)** $12\bar{y} = 9 \times 1.5 + 3 \times 2.5 \Rightarrow 12\bar{y} = 21$
   $\Rightarrow \bar{y} = 1.75$

**(c) (i)**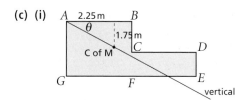

**(ii)** $\theta = \tan^{-1} \frac{1.75}{2.25} = 38°$ to the nearest degree

**F5 (a)** The friction force must be equal to the component of the weight acting down the plane. If the angle is increased further once the friction force has reached its limiting value, the component of the weight acting down the plane will be greater than the friction force and the lamina will slip.

**(b)** If the centre of mass of the lamina is vertically above a point of contact with the plane, there is no resultant moment on the lamina and it will not tip. If the angle is increased so that the centre of mass is not vertically above a point of contact, then there will be a resultant moment acting on the lamina, causing it to tip over.

**(c)** $\tan \theta = \frac{1}{2} \Rightarrow \theta = 26.6°$
The lamina will tip when the plane makes an angle of 26.6° (to 3 s.f.) with the horizontal.

### Exercise F (p 60)

**1 (a)** $G$ is the point of intersection of the lines of symmetry of the framework.

**(b)**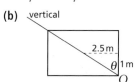

$\theta = \tan^{-1} \frac{2.5}{1} = 68.198... = 68°$ to the nearest degree

**2 (a) (i)** 1.5 m  **(ii)** 1 m

**(b)** 56.3° (to 3 s.f.)

**(c)** 71.6° (to 3 s.f.)

**3 (a)**

|  | Area | Distance from $AB$ | Distance from $AD$ |
|---|---|---|---|
| Rectangle | $6\,m^2$ | 1.5 m | 1 m |
| Triangle | $6\,m^2$ | 1 m | $3\frac{1}{3}$ m |
| Lamina | $12\,m^2$ | $\bar{y}$ m | $\bar{x}$ m |

$12\bar{y} = 6 \times 1.5 + 6 \times 1 \Rightarrow 12\bar{y} = 15$
$\Rightarrow \bar{y} = 1.25$

**(b)** 2.17 m (to 3 s.f.)  **(c)** 18.1° (to 3 s.f.)

**4 (a) (i)** 2 m  **(ii)** 5.18 m (to 3 s.f.)

**(b)** 68.9° (to 3 s.f.)

**5 (a) (i)** 0.1875 m  **(ii)** 0.1 m

**(b)** 58.0° (to 3 s.f.)

**6** 3

**7** 28°

### Mixed questions (p 62)

**1** 2.48 cm (to 3 s.f.)

**2 (a)**

|  | Mass | Distance from $AB$ | Distance from $AD$ |
|---|---|---|---|
| Rectangle | $3m$ | $\frac{1}{2}a$ | $2a$ |
| Particle A | $m$ | 0 | 0 |
| Particle B | $2m$ | 0 | $4a$ |
| Lamina | $6m$ | $\bar{y}$ | $\bar{x}$ |

$6m\bar{y} = 3m \times \frac{1}{2}a + m \times 0 + 2m \times 0 \Rightarrow 6\bar{y} = \frac{3}{2}a$
$\Rightarrow \bar{y} = \frac{1}{4}a$

**(b)** $\frac{7}{3}a$  **(c)** 24°

**3 (a)** $\frac{22}{21}a$  **(b)** $\frac{37}{21}a$  **(c)** $m = \frac{26}{21}M$

**4 (a)** 3.5 m  **(b)** 1.78 m (to 3 s.f.)

**5** 55°

**6 (a)** 4.85 cm (to 3 s.f.)  **(b)** 28°

### Test yourself (p 63)

**1 (a)** Using $M\bar{y} = \Sigma my$,
$(1 + 3 + m) \times 3 = 1 \times 3 + 3 \times 1 + m \times 6$
$\Rightarrow 12 + 3m = 6 + 6m \Rightarrow m = 2$

**(b)** 5

**2** **(a)** 8.59 cm (to 3 s.f.)    **(b)** 8.59 cm (to 3 s.f.)

**(c)** 53°

**3** **(a)**

|  | Area | Distance from $BC$ |
|---|---|---|
| $ABC$ | 1200 cm² | 10 cm |
| $ADE$ | 300 cm² | 20 cm |
| Lamina | 900 cm² | $\bar{y}$ |

Using $M\bar{y} = \sum my$,
$1200 \times 10 = 300 \times 20 + 900\bar{y}$
$\Rightarrow 12000 = 6000 + 900\bar{y} \Rightarrow \bar{y} = 6\frac{2}{3}$

**(b)** 22.6° (to 1 d.p.)

**4** **(a)** The line joining the mid-point of $AE$ to point $C$, which is at a distance $2a$ from $AB$, is a line of symmetry.

**(b)** $\dfrac{19a}{5}$

**(c)** $\dfrac{4}{15}$

# 4 Work, energy and power

## A Work (p 64)

**A1** You will do twice as much work.

**A2** Work done $= 40 \times 10 = 400\,$J

**A3** **(a)** $Fd\,$J

**(b)** **(i)**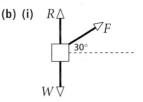

**(ii)** The horizontal component, $F\cos 30°$, of the force $F$

**(iii)** $Fd\cos 30°\,$J

**A4** **(a)** 0 J

**(b)** $25 \times 10 \times \cos 40° = 192\,$J (to 3 s.f.)

**A5** $2500 \times 50 = 125\,000\,$J

### Exercise A (p 66)

**1** 120 J

**2** 150 000 J

**3** **(a)** 32.9 J (to 3 s.f.)

**(b)** **(i)** The magnitude of the horizontal component of the force is now less.

**(ii)** 26.8 J (to 3 s.f.)

**4** 350 N

**5** 2120 J (to 3 s.f.)

**6** **(a)** 468 J (to 3 s.f.)    **(b)** 72.3 J (to 3 s.f.)

**7** 5 m

## B Kinetic energy (p 66)

**B1** **(a)** $u = 0, v = 20, s = 100$
Using $v^2 = u^2 + 2as$, $20^2 = 0^2 + 200a$
$\Rightarrow a = 2\,\text{m s}^{-2}$

**(b)** $F = ma = 2000 \times 2 = 4000\,$N

**(c)** Work done $= Fs = 4000 \times 100 = 400\,000\,$J

**B2** (a) Using $v^2 = u^2 + 2as$ with $u = 0$,
$v^2 = 2as \Rightarrow a = \dfrac{v^2}{2s}$

(b) $F = ma = \dfrac{mv^2}{2s} \Rightarrow Fs = \frac{1}{2}mv^2$

**B3** (a) (i) $u = 15$, $v = 30$, $s = 200$
Using $v^2 = u^2 + 2as$, $30^2 = 15^2 + 400a$
$\Rightarrow a = 1.6875\,\text{m s}^{-2}$

(ii) $F = ma = 2500 \times 1.6875 = 4218.75\,\text{N}$
Work done $= Fs = 4218.75 \times 200$
$= 843\,750\,\text{J}$

(b) (i) $\frac{1}{2}mu^2 = \frac{1}{2} \times 2500 \times 15^2 = 281\,250\,\text{J}$

(ii) $\frac{1}{2}mv^2 = \frac{1}{2} \times 2500 \times 30^2 = 1\,125\,000\,\text{J}$

(iii) Change in k.e. $= 1\,125\,000 - 281\,250$
$= 843\,750\,\text{J}$

**B4** (a) $v^2 = u^2 + 2as \Rightarrow v^2 - u^2 = 2as$
$\Rightarrow a = \dfrac{v^2 - u^2}{2s}$

(b) $F = ma = \dfrac{m(v^2 - u^2)}{2s} \Rightarrow Fs = \frac{1}{2}mv^2 - \frac{1}{2}mu^2$

**B5** $\frac{1}{2} \times 10 \times 18^2 - 0 = 1620\,\text{J}$

**B6** $40F = -1620 \Rightarrow F = -40.5$
The magnitude of the force is 40.5 N.

**B7** (a) $150 - 80 = 40a \Rightarrow a = 1.75\,\text{m s}^{-2}$
$v^2 = u^2 + 2as$ gives $v^2 = 0 + 2 \times 1.75 \times 5 = 17.5$
so $v = 4.18\,\text{m s}^{-1}$ (to 3 s.f.)

(b) Gain in k.e. $= \frac{1}{2}mv^2 - \frac{1}{2}mu^2 = \frac{1}{2} \times 40 \times 17.5 - 0$
$= 350\,\text{J}$

(c) Work done $= 150 \times 5 = 750\,\text{J}$

(d) Work done by resistance $= -80 \times 5 = -400\,\text{J}$

(e) (i) Resultant force $= 150 - 80 = 70\,\text{N}$

(ii) Work done by resultant $= 70 \times 5 = 350\,\text{J}$
The sum of the work done by the 150 N force and the work done by the 80 N force is equal to the work done by the resultant force. The work done by the resultant is equal to the gain in kinetic energy of the box.

**Exercise B** (p 69)

**1** $225\,000\,\text{J}$

**2** (a) $1755\,\text{J}$ (b) $1755\,\text{J}$

**3** $315\,000\,\text{J}$

**4** (a) $1\,200\,000\,\text{J}$ (b) $12\,000\,\text{N}$

**5** $15\,\text{m s}^{-1}$

**6** (a) $600\,000\,\text{J}$ (b) $500\,\text{N}$

**7** $7\,\text{m s}^{-1}$

**8** (a)

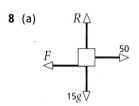

(b) 44.1 N

(c) (i) 1000 J (ii) −882 J

(d) 3.97 m s$^{-1}$ (to 3 s.f.)

**9** 120 J (to 3 s.f.)

## C Potential energy (p 70)

**C1** (a) 0 J

(b) As the ball drops, its speed, and hence its kinetic energy, increases.

(c) $u = 0$, $a = 9.8$, $s = 2$
$v^2 = u^2 + 2as$ gives $v^2 = 0 + 2 \times 9.8 \times 2 = 39.2$
so $v = 6.26\,\text{m s}^{-1}$ (to 3 s.f.)
k.e. $= \frac{1}{2}mv^2 = \frac{1}{2} \times 0.1 \times 39.2 = 1.96\,\text{J}$

(d) (i) The weight of the ball

(ii) Work done $= Fs = 0.1 \times 9.8 \times 2 = 1.96\,\text{J}$

**C2** The weight of the particle is $mg\,\text{N}$ and the distance moved is $h\,\text{m}$.
Work done $= Fs = mgh\,\text{J}$

**C3** (a) $\frac{1}{2}mv^2 - \frac{1}{2}mu^2$

(b) $mga - mgb$

(c) Using $v^2 = u^2 + 2as$, $v^2 = u^2 + 2g(a - b)$
$\Rightarrow$ gain in k.e. $= \frac{1}{2}m(u^2 + 2g(a - b)) - \frac{1}{2}mu^2$
$= \frac{1}{2}mu^2 + mg(a - b) - \frac{1}{2}mu^2$
$= mga - mgb = $ loss in p.e.

**C4** (a) $\frac{1}{2} \times 0.1 \times 8^2 = 3.2\,\text{J}$

(b) As the ball moves upwards, its speed, and hence its kinetic energy, decreases until it reaches its maximum height, at which point its speed and kinetic energy are zero. The ball then moves downwards with increasing speed and hence increasing kinetic energy.

(c) Using $v^2 = u^2 + 2as$, $v^2 = 8^2 + 2\times(-g)\times x$
$\Rightarrow v^2 = 64 - 2gx$

(d) As the ball's height increases, its potential energy increases. It has maximum potential energy when it is at its maximum height. As the ball drops, its potential energy decreases.

(e) p.e. $= 0.1gx$ J

(f) k.e. $+$ p.e. $= \frac{1}{2}\times 0.1\times(64 - 2gx) + 0.1gx$
$= 3.2 - 0.1gx + 0.1gx = 3.2$ J
The sum of the k.e. and p.e. is independent of $x$ and hence constant.

**C5** Gain in p.e. $= 18\times 9.8\times 2.5 = 441$ J

**C6** (a) Loss in p.e. $= 5\times 9.8\times 10 = 490$ J

(b) (i) $\sin 25° = \dfrac{10}{d}$
$\Rightarrow d = \dfrac{10}{\sin 25°}$

(ii) Only the component of the weight acting down the plane does work.
Work done $= 5g\sin 25°\times\dfrac{10}{\sin 25°} = 490$ J
The loss of potential energy when the particle slides down the plane is the same as when it falls the same distance vertically.

**Exercise C** (p 73)

1  313.6 J

2  864 J (to 3 s.f.)

3  588 000 J

4  (a) 200 000 J    (b) −25 000 J    (c) 73 500 J

5  (a) 1470 J    (b) −1200 J

6  (a)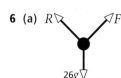

26g

(b) 41.7 N (to 3 s.f.)

(c) −167 J (to 3 s.f.)

(d) 585 J (to 3 s.f.)

7  (a) 1440 J    (b) −398 J (to 3 s.f.)

(c) 304 J (to 3 s.f.)

# D Conservation of energy (p 74)

**D1** (a) (i) $u = 8$, $v = 0$, $a = -9.8$
$v^2 = u^2 + 2as$ gives $0 = 8^2 - 2\times 9.8\times s$
so $s = 3.27$ m (to 3 s.f.)

(ii) Gain in p.e. $= 0.2\times 9.8\times 3.27 = 6.4$ J

(b) (i) $0\,\mathrm{m\,s^{-1}}$

(ii) Loss in k.e. $= \frac{1}{2}\times 0.2\times 8^2 - 0 = 6.4$ J
The loss in k.e. is equal to the gain in p.e.

**D2** (a) (i) $h = 10\sin 30° = 5$

(ii) Loss in p.e. $= 15\times 9.8\times 5 = 735$ J

(b) (i) Using $F = ma$, $15g\sin 30° = 15a$
$\Rightarrow a = 9.8\sin 30° = 4.9\,\mathrm{m\,s^{-2}}$

(ii) $u = 0$, $s = 10$, $a = 4.9$
$v^2 = u^2 + 2as$ gives $v^2 = 2\times 4.9\times 10 = 98$
So $v = 9.90\,\mathrm{m\,s^{-1}}$ (to 3 s.f.)

(iii) Gain in k.e. $= \frac{1}{2}\times 15\times 98 = 735$ J
The gain in k.e. is equal to the loss in p.e.

**D3** (a) (i) $h = 10\sin 25° = 4.23$ m (to 3 s.f.)

(ii) Loss in p.e. $= 15\times 9.8\times 4.23 = 621$ J (to 3 s.f.)

(b) (i) Using $F = ma$, $15g\sin 25° - 50 = 15a$
So $a = 0.808\,\mathrm{m\,s^{-2}}$ (to 3 s.f.)

(ii) $u = 0$, $s = 10$, $a = 0.808$
$v^2 = u^2 + 2as$ gives $v^2 = 2\times 0.808\times 10 = 16.2$
So $v = 4.02\,\mathrm{m\,s^{-1}}$ (to 3 s.f.)

(iii) Gain in k.e. $= \frac{1}{2}\times 15\times 16.2 = 121$ J (to 3 s.f.)
The gain in k.e. is less than the loss in p.e. in this case.

**D4** (a) Total gain in energy $=$ gain in k.e. $-$ loss in p.e.
$= 121 - 621 = -500$ J
There is an overall energy loss of 500 J.

(b) Work done by resisting force $= -50\times 10$
$= -500$ J
The work done by the resisting force is equal to the change in energy of the box.

**D5** (a) At its maximum height the speed, and hence the kinetic energy of the stone, is zero.
Gain in p.e. $=$ loss in k.e.
$0.2\times 9.8\times h = \frac{1}{2}\times 0.2\times 5^2$
So $h = 1.28$ m (to 3 s.f.)

**(b)** When it hits the water, the stone is a vertical distance of 30 m below its starting point.
Gain in k.e. = loss in p.e.
$\frac{1}{2} \times 0.2 \times v^2 - \frac{1}{2} \times 0.2 \times 5^2 = 0.2 \times 9.8 \times 30$
$\Rightarrow v^2 = 613 \Rightarrow v = 24.8\,\text{m s}^{-1}$ (to 3 s.f.)

**(c)** Each term in the energy equation contains the mass, so it cancels out and was not required.

**(d)** The stone can be treated as a particle and there is no air resistance.

**D6 (a)** The only external force doing work is gravity, so mechanical energy is conserved. The normal reaction does no work as it is perpendicular to the direction of motion.

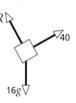

**(b)** $\frac{1}{2} \times 0.1 \times 10^2 = 5\,\text{J}$

**(c)** 5 J

**(d)** 5 J

**(e)** When the ball is at its maximum distance $d$ up the slope, the increase in height is $d \sin 40°$.
Increase in p.e. $= 0.1 \times 9.8 \times d \sin 40° = 5$
So $d = 7.94\,\text{m}$ (to 3 s.f.)

**D7 (a)** Gravity is not the only external force doing work; the resistance also does work, so the principle of conservation of mechanical energy does not apply.

**(b)** $-40 \times 2.5 = -100\,\text{J}$

**(c)** $16 \times 9.8 \times 2.5 \sin 35° = 225\,\text{J}$ (to 3 s.f.)

**(d)** Work done = gain in p.e. + gain in k.e.
$-100 = -225 +$ gain in k.e.
$\Rightarrow$ gain in k.e. $= 125\,\text{J}$

**(e)** $\frac{1}{2} \times 16 \times v^2 = 125 \Rightarrow v = 3.95\,\text{m s}^{-1}$ (to 3 s.f.)

**Exercise D** (p 77)

**1 (a)** 5.88 J

**(b)** k.e. = 5.88 J, $v = 7.67\,\text{m s}^{-1}$ (to 3 s.f.)

**2 (a)** 2.94 J

**(b)** $12.9\,\text{m s}^{-1}$ (to 3 s.f.)

**(c) (i)** 11.25 J      **(ii)** 11.5 m (to 3 s.f.)

**3** $4.02\,\text{m s}^{-1}$ (to 3 s.f.)

**4 (a)** 2940 J      **(b)** 240 J      **(c)** −2700 J

**5 (a)** 17 640 J

**(b)** 1920 J

**(c)** −15 720 J

**(d)** It has been assumed that there is no air resistance acting. Air resistance would also help to slow the boy down.

**6 (a)** 9.3 J      **(b)** 1.86 N

**7 (a)** −15 J      **(b)** 3 N

**(c)** 0.177 (to 3 s.f.)

## E Power (p 78)

**E1 (a)** 750 J

**(b)** 750 J

**(c)** They have both done the same amount of work, but Tim's push had more power, as he did the work in a shorter time.

**E2** Tim's push: power $= \frac{750}{10} = 75\,\text{W}$

Alison's push: power $= \frac{750}{15} = 50\,\text{W}$

**E3 (a)** $1000 \times 9.8 \times 25 = 245\,000\,\text{J}$

**(b)** $\frac{245\,000}{40} = 6125\,\text{W}$

**E4 (a)** $950 \times 18 = 17\,100\,\text{W}$

**(b)** $\frac{5000}{15} = 333\,\text{N}$ (to 3 s.f.)

**E5** The power is constant, so when the speed decreases the driving force increases.

**E6 (a)** $0\,\text{m s}^{-2}$      **(b)** 1200 N

**(c)** $\frac{45\,000}{1200} = 37.5\,\text{m s}^{-1}$

**E7 (a)** $\frac{45\,000}{25} = 1800\,\text{N}$

**(b)** $F = ma \Rightarrow 1800 - 1200 = 1500a$
$\Rightarrow a = 0.4\,\text{m s}^{-2}$

**E8 (a)** $F = 1200 + 1500g \sin \alpha = 2180\,\text{N}$

**(b)** $\frac{45\,000}{2180} = 20.6\,\text{m s}^{-1}$ (to 3 s.f.)

**E9 (a) (i)** $40 \times 35 = 1400\,\text{N}$

**(ii)** Max. power = resistance × max. speed
$= 1400 \times 35 = 49\,000\,\text{W}$

**(b) (i)** $40 \times 20 = 800\,\text{N}$

**(ii)** $\frac{49\,000}{20} = 2450\,\text{N}$

**(iii)** $F = ma \Rightarrow 2450 - 800 = 2500a$
$\Rightarrow a = 0.66\,\text{m s}^{-2}$

**Exercise E** (p 82)

**1** $54\,000\,\text{W}$

**2** (a) $970.2\,\text{J}$      (b) $485.1\,\text{W}$

**3** $7056\,\text{W}$

**4** $30\,\text{m}\,\text{s}^{-1}$

**5** $0.347\,\text{m}\,\text{s}^{-2}$ (to 3 s.f.)

**6** (a) $5\,600\,000\,\text{W}$      (b) $31.7\,\text{m}\,\text{s}^{-1}$ (to 3 s.f.)

**7** (a) $1875\,\text{N}$      (b) $0.04\,\text{m}\,\text{s}^{-2}$

**8** $1770\,\text{N}$ (to 3 s.f.)

**9** (a) (i) $2500\,\text{N}$      (ii) $1.28\,\text{m}\,\text{s}^{-2}$ (to 3 s.f.)

    (b) At maximum speed, driving force = resistance
       Power = driving force × velocity = $25v \times v$
       So $45\,000 = 25v^2 \implies v^2 = 1800$
       So $v = 42.4\,\text{m}\,\text{s}^{-1}$ (to 3 s.f.)

## Mixed questions (p 84)

**1** (a) (i) $10.1\,\text{m}\,\text{s}^{-1}$ (to 3 s.f.)

       (ii) $6.57\,\text{m}\,\text{s}^{-1}$ (to 3 s.f.)

    (b) If the track is smooth the only external force
       doing work is the weight of the ball, so the
       principle of conservation of mechanical
       energy can be applied. If the track were rough,
       the friction force would be doing work,
       causing the ball to lose energy, and its speed at
       $C$ would be lower.

**2** (a) $7.32\,\text{m}\,\text{s}^{-1}$ (to 3 s.f.)    (b) $335.2\,\text{W}$

**3** (a) $52.16$              (b) $3\,\text{s}$

    (c) $48\,\text{m}$            (d) $23.6\,\text{m}\,\text{s}^{-1}$ (to 3 s.f.)

**4** (a) $40$               (b) $0.738\,\text{m}\,\text{s}^{-2}$ (to 3 s.f.)

## Test yourself (p 85)

**1** $35\,000\,\text{N}$

**2** (a) $3.67\,\text{m}$ (to 3 s.f.)     (b) $0.271$ (to 3 s.f.)

**3** (a) $51\,688\,\text{W}$         (b) $36.92\,\text{m}\,\text{s}^{-1}$

**4** (a) $0.8$              (b) $81.7$ (to 3 s.f.)

    (c) The resistance to motion may be dependent
       on the speed of the car.

**5** (a) $1437$           (b) $0.570\,\text{m}\,\text{s}^{-2}$ (to 3 s.f.)

# 5 Momentum

## A Momentum and impulse (p 86)

**A1** (a) $0.5(2\mathbf{i} + 6\mathbf{j}) = (\mathbf{i} + 3\mathbf{j})\,\text{kg}\,\text{m}\,\text{s}^{-1}$

     (b) $2(3\mathbf{i} - 5\mathbf{j}) = (6\mathbf{i} - 10\mathbf{j})\,\text{kg}\,\text{m}\,\text{s}^{-1}$

**A2** (a) Initial momentum $= 0.2(5\mathbf{i} - 2\mathbf{j})$
                           $= (\mathbf{i} - 0.4\mathbf{j})\,\text{kg}\,\text{m}\,\text{s}^{-1}$
       Final momentum $= 0.2(3\mathbf{i} + 4\mathbf{j})$
                         $= (0.6\mathbf{i} + 0.8\mathbf{j})\,\text{kg}\,\text{m}\,\text{s}^{-1}$

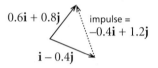

     (b) Impulse $= (0.6\mathbf{i} + 0.8\mathbf{j}) - (\mathbf{i} - 0.4\mathbf{j})$
                   $= (-0.4\mathbf{i} + 1.2\mathbf{j})\,\text{N}\,\text{s}$

**A3** (a) $3(\mathbf{i} + 2\mathbf{j}) = (3\mathbf{i} + 6\mathbf{j})\,\text{N}\,\text{s}$

     (b) $(3\mathbf{i} + 6\mathbf{j})\,\text{N}\,\text{s}$

     (c) $(3\mathbf{i} + 6\mathbf{j}) \div 0.2 = (15\mathbf{i} + 30\mathbf{j})\,\text{m}\,\text{s}^{-1}$

**A4** (a) $0.5(8\mathbf{i} - 6\mathbf{j}) = (4\mathbf{i} - 3\mathbf{j})\,\text{N}\,\text{s}$

     (b) $5(2\mathbf{i} + \mathbf{j}) = (10\mathbf{i} + 5\mathbf{j})\,\text{N}\,\text{s}$

     (c) $(4\mathbf{i} - 3\mathbf{j}) + (10\mathbf{i} + 5\mathbf{j}) = (14\mathbf{i} + 2\mathbf{j})\,\text{N}\,\text{s}$

     (d) $(14\mathbf{i} + 2\mathbf{j}) \div 0.5 = (28\mathbf{i} + 4\mathbf{j})\,\text{m}\,\text{s}^{-1}$

### Exercise A (p 88)

**1** $\left(3\mathbf{i} - \tfrac{1}{3}\mathbf{j}\right)\text{m}\,\text{s}^{-1}$

**2** (a) $30\mathbf{j}\,\text{N}\,\text{s}$         (b) $(-4\mathbf{i} + 61\mathbf{j})\,\text{m}\,\text{s}^{-1}$

**3** $(12\mathbf{i} - 14\mathbf{j})\,\text{N}\,\text{s}$

**4** $1\,\text{m}\,\text{s}^{-1}$

**5** $(6.4\mathbf{i} + 0.4\mathbf{j})\,\text{m}\,\text{s}^{-1}$

**6** $6.71\,\text{N}$ (to 3 s.f.)

**7** Magnitude $= 1.77\,\text{N}\,\text{s}$ (to 3 s.f.)
    Direction = 45° clockwise from the negative
    $\mathbf{i}$-direction

**8** (a) $15.6\,\text{m}\,\text{s}^{-1}$ (to 3 s.f.)   (b) $9.43\,\text{m}\,\text{s}^{-1}$ (to 3 s.f.)

**9** (a) $(8\mathbf{i} + 8\mathbf{j})\,\text{N}\,\text{s}$      (b) $(12\mathbf{i} + 6\mathbf{j})\,\text{m}\,\text{s}^{-1}$

**10** (a) $6\mathbf{i}\,\text{m}\,\text{s}^{-1}$         (b) $31.0°$ (to 3 s.f.)

## B Conservation of momentum (p 89)

**B1 (a)** Both $A$ and $B$ could continue moving forwards.
$A$ could be stationary and $B$ continue moving forwards.
$A$ could be moving backwards and $B$ forwards.

**(b)** $A$ could be stationary and the direction of $B$ reversed.
$B$ could be stationary and the direction of $A$ reversed.
The direction of $A$ could be reversed and the direction of $B$ stay the same.
The direction of $B$ could be reversed and the direction of $A$ stay the same.
The directions of both $A$ and $B$ could be reversed.

**B2 (a)** Momentum before $= 1 \times 5 + 4 \times 2.5 = 15\,\text{N}\,\text{s}$

**(b)** Momentum after $= 1 \times 2 + 4v = 2 + 4v$

**(c)** $2 + 4v = 15 \Rightarrow v = 3.25$
The 4 kg object moves at $3.25\,\text{m}\,\text{s}^{-1}$ after the collision.

**B3** Conservation of momentum:
$2 \times 6 - 1 \times 3 = 2 \times 2 + 1 \times v \Rightarrow v = 5$
The 1 kg object moves at $5\,\text{m}\,\text{s}^{-1}$ after the collision.

**B4** $3(4\mathbf{i} + 4\mathbf{j}) + 2(2\mathbf{i} - 3\mathbf{j}) = 3(2\mathbf{i} - \mathbf{j}) + 2\mathbf{v}_2$
$\Rightarrow 10\mathbf{i} + 9\mathbf{j} = 2\mathbf{v}_2$
$\Rightarrow \mathbf{v}_2 = 5\mathbf{i} + 4.5\mathbf{j}$

**B5** $3(4\mathbf{i} + 4\mathbf{j}) + 2(2\mathbf{i} - 3\mathbf{j}) = 5\mathbf{v}$
$\Rightarrow 16\mathbf{i} + 6\mathbf{j} = 5\mathbf{v} \Rightarrow \mathbf{v} = 3.2\mathbf{i} + 1.2\mathbf{j}$

### Exercise B (p 92)

**1** $8\,\text{m}\,\text{s}^{-1}$ forwards

**2** $(3.5\mathbf{i} + 2.5\mathbf{j})\,\text{m}\,\text{s}^{-1}$

**3** $3.8\,\text{m}\,\text{s}^{-1}$

**4** $(-2\mathbf{i} + 3\mathbf{j})\,\text{m}\,\text{s}^{-1}$

**5 (a)** $-18\,\text{N}\,\text{s}$

**(b)** $1.5\,\text{m}\,\text{s}^{-1}$

**(c)** $18\,\text{N}\,\text{s}$
The impulse on the 4 kg object is equal and opposite to the impulse on the 3 kg object.

**6 (a) (i)** $(-3\mathbf{i} - 4.5\mathbf{j})\,\text{N}\,\text{s}$   **(ii)** $(3\mathbf{i} + 4.5\mathbf{j})\,\text{N}\,\text{s}$

**(b)** $(-5\mathbf{i} - 8\mathbf{j})\,\text{m}\,\text{s}^{-1}$

**7 (a)** There is no external force acting on the shell, so no impulse acts on it and the momentum of the shell's constituents remains constant.

**(b)** $(35\mathbf{i} + 52.5\mathbf{j})\,\text{m}\,\text{s}^{-1}$

## C Newton's law of restitution (p 93)

**C1 (a)** $1 \times 6 + 1 \times 2 = 1 \times 3 + v \Rightarrow 8 = 3 + v \Rightarrow v = 5$

**(b) (i)** $\frac{1}{2} \times 1 \times 6^2 - \frac{1}{2} \times 1 \times 3^2 = 13.5\,\text{J}$
**(ii)** $\frac{1}{2} \times 1 \times 5^2 - \frac{1}{2} \times 1 \times 2^2 = 10.5\,\text{J}$
**(iii)** Energy has not been conserved.
3 J of energy has been lost in the collision.

**(c)** $A$ is moving towards $B$ at $6\,\text{m}\,\text{s}^{-1}$, but $B$ is moving away from $A$ at $2\,\text{m}\,\text{s}^{-1}$, so the approach speed is $6 - 2 = 4\,\text{m}\,\text{s}^{-1}$.

**(d)** $5 - 3 = 2\,\text{m}\,\text{s}^{-1}$

**C2** $0.5$

**C3 (a)** $1$

**(b) (i)** $0\,\text{m}\,\text{s}^{-1}$   **(ii)** $0$

**C4 (a)** $1 \times 5 + 2 \times 0 = v + 2 \times 3 \Rightarrow v = -1$
The 1 kg particle moves backwards at $1\,\text{m}\,\text{s}^{-1}$.

**(b)** $5\,\text{m}\,\text{s}^{-1}$

**(c)** $4\,\text{m}\,\text{s}^{-1}$

**(d)** $0.8$

**C5 (a)** $3 \times 4 - 4 \times 2 = 3 \times (-1) + 4v \Rightarrow v = 1.75$
The 4 kg object moves forwards at $1.75\,\text{m}\,\text{s}^{-1}$.

**(b)** Separation speed $= 2.75\,\text{m}\,\text{s}^{-1}$
Approach speed $= 6\,\text{m}\,\text{s}^{-1}$
$e = 0.458$ (to 3 s.f.)

**C6 (a)** $1 \times 4 + 3 \times 2 = v_A + 3v_B \Rightarrow v_A + 3v_B = 10$
**(b)** $v_B - v_A = 0.6(4 - 2) \Rightarrow v_B - v_A = 1.2$
**(c)** $v_A = 1.6$, $v_B = 2.8$

**C7 (a)** $2 \times 5 - 2 \times 3 = 2v_A + 2v_B \Rightarrow v_A + v_B = 2$
**(b)** $v_B - v_A = 0.8(5 + 3) \Rightarrow v_B - v_A = 6.4$
**(c)** $v_A = -2.2$, $v_B = 4.2$

### Exercise C (p 96)

**1 (a)** $2\,\text{m}\,\text{s}^{-1}$   **(b)** $0.2$

**2 (a) (i)** $4.25\,\text{m s}^{-1}$  **(ii)** $0.875$

**(b) (i)** $1\,\text{m s}^{-1}$  **(ii)** $0.4$

**3** The 4 kg particle moves forwards at $3.95\,\text{m s}^{-1}$.
The 1 kg particle moves forwards at $6.2\,\text{m s}^{-1}$.

**4 (a)** The 2 kg ball moves forwards at $1.5\,\text{m s}^{-1}$.
The 1 kg ball moves forwards at $3\,\text{m s}^{-1}$.

**(b)** Each ball receives an impulse of $3\,\text{N s}$.

**(c)** $2.25\,\text{J}$

**5** The 2 kg particle moves backwards at $\frac{4}{9}\,\text{m s}^{-1}$.
The 4 kg particle moves forwards at $\frac{11}{9}\,\text{m s}^{-1}$.

**6 (a)** $2.4\,\text{m s}^{-1}$  **(b)** $0.2$  **(c)** $76.8\,\text{J}$

**7 (a) (i)** The particles move away from each other, each with speed $\frac{1}{2}u$.

**(ii)** $\frac{3}{4}mu^2$

**(b) (i)** The particles move away from each other, each with speed $u$.

**(ii)** There is no kinetic energy lost. In a perfectly elastic collision, mechanical energy is conserved.

**8 (a)** Conservation of momentum:
$mv = mv_A + 4mv_B \Rightarrow v = v_A + 4v_B$  (1)
Restitution: $v_B - v_A = ev$  (2)
(1) + (2): $5v_B = (1 + e)v \Rightarrow v_B = \frac{1}{5}v(1 + e)$

**(b)** $\frac{1}{5}v(1 - 4e)$

**9 (a)** Conservation of momentum:
$2mu + 3mu = mv_P + 3mv_Q$
$\Rightarrow 5u = v_P + 3v_Q$  (1)
Restitution: $v_Q - v_P = e(2u - u) = \frac{3}{5}u$  (2)
(1) + (2): $4v_Q = \frac{28}{5}u \Rightarrow v_Q = \frac{7}{5}u$

**(b)** $\frac{4}{5}u$

**(c)** $\frac{6}{25}mu^2$

**10** Conservation of momentum:
$4mu - 2mu = -mv_A + 2mv_B$
$\Rightarrow 2u = -v_A + 2v_B$  (1)
Restitution: $v_A + v_B = 5eu$  (2)
$2\times(2) - (1)$: $3v_A = 10eu - 2u \Rightarrow v_A = \frac{2}{3}u(5e - 1)$
But $v_A > 0$, so $5e - 1 > 0 \Rightarrow e > \frac{1}{5}$

**11** $0 \leq e < \frac{3}{4}$

## D Collision with a fixed plane surface (p 98)

**D1 (a)** $0.75 \times 4 = 3\,\text{m s}^{-1}$

**(b)** Impulse $= -3 \times 2 - 4 \times 2 = -14\,\text{N s}$

**(c)** $\frac{1}{2} \times 2 \times 4^2 - \frac{1}{2} \times 2 \times 3^2 = 7\,\text{J}$

**D2 (a)** The object will rebound with the same speed as that with which it hits the ground and will reach a maximum height $h\,\text{m}$ above ground level.

**(b)** The object will hit the ground and will not rebound.

**(c)** The object will rebound with a lower speed than that with which it hits the ground and will reach a maximum height of less than $h\,\text{m}$ above ground level.

**D3 (a)** Gain in k.e. = loss in p.e.
$\frac{1}{2} \times 0.4v^2 = 0.4 \times 9.8 \times 2 \Rightarrow v = 6.26$ (to 3 s.f.)

**(b)** $0.4 \times 6.26 = 2.50\,\text{m s}^{-1}$ (to 3 s.f.)

**(c)** Impulse $= -0.4 \times 2.50 - 0.4 \times 6.26$
$= -3.51\,\text{N s}$ (to 3 s.f.)

**(d)** $\frac{1}{2} \times 0.4 \times 6.26^2 - \frac{1}{2} \times 0.4 \times 2.50^2$
$= 6.59\,\text{J}$ (to 3 s.f.)

**(e)** Gain in p.e. = loss in k.e.
$0.4 \times 9.8 \times h = \frac{1}{2} \times 0.4 \times 2.50^2$
$\Rightarrow h = 0.320\,\text{m}$ (to 3 s.f.)

### Exercise D (p 100)

**1 (a)** $4.8\,\text{m s}^{-1}$  **(b)** $19.2\,\text{N s}$

**2 (a)** $0.6$  **(b)** $16\,\text{N s}$

**3 (a)** $4\,\text{m s}^{-1}$  **(b)** $1.75\,\text{J}$

**4** $\frac{9}{50}mu^2$

**5 (a)** $7.67\,\text{m s}^{-1}$ (to 3 s.f.)  **(b)** $4.60\,\text{m s}^{-1}$ (to 3 s.f.)

**(c)** $1.08\,\text{m}$ (to 3 s.f.)

**6** $\dfrac{1}{\sqrt{2}}$

**7** $0.663$ (to 3 s.f.)

**8** $\dfrac{e^4}{2g}(u^2 + 2gh)$

## E Successive impacts (p 101)

**E1 (a) (i)** Conservation of momentum:
$$5 = v_A + v_B$$
Restitution: $v_B - v_A = 0.8 \times 5 = 4$
So $v_B = 4.5$

**(ii)** $v_A = 0.5$

**(iii)**

$0.5\,\text{m s}^{-1}$      $4.5\,\text{m s}^{-1}$
(A)      (B)

**(b) (i)** Restitution: $v_B = 0.6 \times 4.5 = 2.7$

**(ii)**

$0.5\,\text{m s}^{-1}$      $2.7\,\text{m s}^{-1}$
(A)      (B)

**(c) (i)** $A$ and $B$ are moving towards each other, so will collide again.

**(ii)** Conservation of momentum:
$$0.5 - 2.7 = v_A + v_B$$
Restitution:
$v_B - v_A = 0.8(0.5 + 2.7) = 2.56$
So $v_A = -2.38$, $v_B = 0.18$

**(d)** There will not be another collision. $A$ and $B$ are now moving in opposite directions away from each other. After $B$ hits the wall a second time it will be moving at $0.6 \times 0.18\,\text{m s}^{-1}$, which is too slow to catch up with $A$.

**E2 (a) (i)** Conservation of momentum:
$$4 - 2 \times 2 = v_A + 2v_B \implies v_A + 2v_B = 0$$
Restitution: $v_B - v_A = \frac{1}{3}(4 + 2) = 2$
So $v_B = \frac{2}{3}$

**(ii)** $v_A = -\frac{4}{3}$

**(b)**

$\frac{4}{3}\,\text{m s}^{-1}$    $\frac{2}{3}\,\text{m s}^{-1}$
(A)    (B)    (C)

**(c) (i)** Conservation of momentum:
$$2 \times \frac{2}{3} = 2v_B + v_C$$
Restitution: $v_C - v_B = \frac{1}{3} \times \frac{2}{3} = \frac{2}{9}$
So $v_B = \frac{10}{27}$

**(ii)** $v_C = \frac{16}{27}$

**(d) (i)**

$\frac{4}{3}\,\text{m s}^{-1}$   $\frac{10}{27}\,\text{m s}^{-1}$   $\frac{16}{27}\,\text{m s}^{-1}$
(A)    (B)    (C)

**(ii)** There will not be another collision because $C$ is moving faster than $B$, so $B$ will not catch up and collide with it, and $A$ is moving away in the opposite direction from $B$ and $C$.

### Exercise E (p 102)

**1** Collision between $A$ and $B$:
Conservation of momentum: $mu = mv_A + mv_B$
Restitution: $v_B - v_A = \frac{1}{2}u$
So $v_A = \frac{1}{4}u$, $v_B = \frac{3}{4}u$
Collision between $B$ and $C$:
Conservation of momentum: $\frac{3}{4}mu = mv_B + mv_C$
Restitution: $v_C - v_B = \frac{3}{8}u$
So $v_B = \frac{3}{16}u$, $v_C = \frac{9}{16}u$
Now $v_A = \frac{1}{4}u$ and $v_B = \frac{3}{16}u$, so $v_A > v_B$,
so $A$ will catch up and collide with $B$.

**2 (a)** Conservation of momentum:
$$4 = v_A + 10v_B$$
Restitution: $v_B - v_A = 2$
So $v_A = -\frac{16}{11}$, $v_B = \frac{6}{11}$
$v_A$ is negative, so the direction of $A$ is reversed.

**(b)** $\frac{3}{8} < e \le 1$

**3 (a)** $v_A = \frac{1}{16}u$, $v_B = \frac{5}{16}u$

**(b)** Conservation of momentum:
$$\frac{15}{16}mu = 3mv_B + 5mv_C$$
Restitution: $v_C - v_B = \frac{5}{32}u$
So $v_B = \frac{5}{256}u$
$A$ collides with $B$ if $v_A > v_B$, and $\frac{1}{16}u > \frac{5}{256}u$, so there is a further collision.

**4 (a)** Conservation of momentum:
$$mu = mv_A + 2mv_B$$
Restitution: $v_B - v_A = \frac{3}{4}u$
So $v_A = -\frac{1}{6}u$, $v_B = \frac{7}{12}u$
$v_A$ is negative, so the direction of $A$ is reversed.

**(b)** $\frac{2}{7} < e \le 1$

**5 (a)** Conservation of momentum:

$mu = -mv_B + 5mv_C \Rightarrow u = -v_B + 5v_C$

Restitution: $v_B + v_C = eu$

So $v_B = \frac{1}{6}(5e - 1)u$

$B$ is reversed, so $v_B > 0$, from which $5e - 1 > 0$

$\Rightarrow e > \frac{1}{5}$

**(b)** $v_B = \frac{1}{6}(5e - 1)u$, $v_C = \frac{1}{6}(1 + e)u$

**(c)** $\frac{4}{5}$

**(d)** There is a further collision between $B$ and $C$ if $v_B > v_C$.

$v_B = \frac{1}{4}u$, and $v_C = \frac{1}{6}(1 + e)u = \frac{3}{10}u$

$\frac{1}{4}u < \frac{3}{10}u$, so there is no further collision.

**6** First collision, between $A$ and $B$:

Conservation of momentum:

$mu = -mv_A + kmv_B \Rightarrow u = -v_A + kv_B$

Restitution: $v_A + v_B = eu$

$\Rightarrow v_B = \frac{1 + e}{1 + k}u$, $v_A = \frac{ek - 1}{1 + k}u$

$A$ collides with wall, and rebounds with speed

$v_A = \frac{ek - 1}{1 + k}eu$

$A$ will collide with $B$ again if $v_A > v_B$

$\frac{ek - 1}{1 + k}eu > \frac{1 + e}{1 + k}u$

$\Rightarrow e^2k - e > 1 + e \Rightarrow k > \frac{1 + 2e}{e^2}$

### Mixed questions (p 104)

**1 (a)** $(29\mathbf{i} + 11.5\mathbf{j})\,\mathrm{m\,s^{-1}}$   **(b)** $31.2\,\mathrm{m\,s^{-1}}$

**(c)** $191.25\,\mathrm{J}$

**2 (a)** $\frac{3}{4}$

**(b)** Total k.e. before collision $= \frac{1}{2}mu^2$

Total k.e. after collision $= \frac{1}{8}mu^2 + \frac{3}{16}mu^2$

$= \frac{5}{16}mu^2$

k.e. lost $= \frac{1}{2}mu^2 - \frac{5}{16}mu^2 = \frac{3}{16}mu^2$

**3 (a)** Magnitude $= 8\,\mathrm{N\,s}$

Direction $= 53.1°$ below the vector $\mathbf{i}$

**(b)** 0.4

**4 (a)** $v_A = \frac{1}{8}(5 - 3e)u$, $v_B = \frac{1}{8}(5 + e)u$

**(b)** If the motion is reversed, $v_A < 0$,

from which $5 - 3e < 0 \Rightarrow e > \frac{5}{3}$

But $0 \leq e \leq 1$, so $A$ must move in the same direction.

**5 (a)** First collision between $A$ and $B$:

Conservation of momentum:

$mu = mv_1 + mv_2 \Rightarrow u = v_1 + v_2$

Restitution: $v_2 - v_1 = 0.8u$

So $v_2 = 0.9u$, $v_1 = 0.1u$

$B$ collides with cushion

Restitution: $v_3 = 0.5 \times 0.9u = 0.45u$

There is a second collision between $A$ and $B$, because $A$ is moving towards the cushion with speed $0.1u$ and $B$ is moving towards $A$ with speed $0.45u$.

**(b)** After second collision:

$A$ moves away from cushion with speed $0.395u$

$B$ moves towards cushion with speed $0.045u$.

**(c)** $B$ moves towards the cushion and hits it again. It rebounds with speed $0.5 \times 0.045u = 0.0225u$. $0.0225u < 0.395u$, so $B$ will not catch up with $A$, and there will be no further collision.

**6 (a)** $\mathbf{a} = 2t\mathbf{i} + 2\mathbf{j}$, $\mathbf{F} = 0.5(2t\mathbf{i} + 2\mathbf{j}) = t\mathbf{i} + \mathbf{j}$

When $t = 3$, $\mathbf{F} = 3\mathbf{i} + \mathbf{j}$

$\Rightarrow |\mathbf{F}| = \sqrt{3^2 + 1^2} = \sqrt{10}$

**(b)** $(41\mathbf{i} - \mathbf{j})\,\mathrm{m\,s^{-1}}$

**7 (a)** Conservation of momentum:

$mu - 2mu = -mv_A + 2mv_B \Rightarrow -u = -v_A + 2v_B$

Restitution: $v_A + v_B = 2eu$

So $v_A = \frac{1}{3}(1 + 4e)u$, $v_B = \frac{1}{3}(2e - 1)u$

Direction of $A$ is reversed, so $v_A > 0$, from which $1 + 4e > 0 \Rightarrow e > -\frac{1}{4}$

Direction of $B$ is reversed, so $v_B > 0$, from which $2e - 1 > 0 \Rightarrow e > \frac{1}{2}$

So if both directions are reversed, $e > \frac{1}{2}$.

**(b)** $A$ rebounds with speed $\frac{1}{18}(1 + 4e)u$.

$A$ will collide with $B$ again if $v_A > v_B$, leading to $\frac{1}{2} < e < \frac{7}{8}$.

**8 (a)** $2.5\,\mathrm{N}$         **(b)** $(24\mathbf{i} + 20\mathbf{j})\,\mathrm{m\,s^{-1}}$

**9 (a)** First collision, between $A$ and $B$:

Conservation of momentum:

$mu = mv_1 + mv_2$

Restitution: $v_2 - v_1 = eu$

So $v_1 = \frac{1}{2}(1 - e)u$, $v_2 = \frac{1}{2}(1 + e)u$

Second collision, between $B$ and $C$:

Conservation of momentum:

$\frac{1}{2}m(1 + e)u = mv_3 + mv_4$

Restitution: $v_4 - v_3 = \frac{1}{2}e(1 + e)u$

So $v_3 = \frac{1}{4}(1 - e^2)u$

**(b)** Further collision between $A$ and $B$ if $v_1 > v_3$

$\frac{1}{2}(1-e)u > \frac{1}{4}(1-e^2)u$

$\Rightarrow 2 - 2e > 1 - e^2$

$\Rightarrow e^2 - 2e + 1 > 0$

$(e-1)^2 > 0$, which is true for all values of $e$, so there will be a further collision.

**10 (a)** $2.83\,\text{N s}$ (to 3 s.f.)

**(b)** $59.6\,\text{J}$

**(c)** $25.0\,\text{m s}^{-1}$ (to 3 s.f.)

**(d)** $36.8°$ below the horizontal (to 3 s.f.)

**11** Conservation of momentum:

$mu - 4mu = mv_A + 2mv_B \Rightarrow v_A + 2v_B = -3u$

Restitution: $v_B - v_A = 3eu$

So $v_A = -(1 + 2e)u$, $v_B = (e-1)u$

k.e. before $= \frac{1}{2}mu^2 + \frac{1}{2}(2m)(2u)^2 = \frac{9}{2}mu^2$

k.e. after $= \frac{1}{2}m(1 + 2e)^2u^2 + \frac{1}{2}(2m)(e-1)^2u^2$

$\qquad = \frac{1}{2}m(3 + 6e^2)u^2$

k.e. lost $= \frac{9}{2}mu^2 - \frac{1}{2}m(3 + 6e^2)u^2$

$\qquad = 3mu^2(1 - e^2)$

**12 (a)** $41.4\,\text{m s}^{-1}$      **(b)** $50.0\,\text{m s}^{-1}$ (to 3 s.f.)

**13 (a)** $277.5\,\text{m}$      **(b)** $(20\mathbf{i} + 38\mathbf{j})\,\text{m s}^{-1}$

**(c)** $85.3\,\text{m s}^{-1}$ (to 3 s.f.)

**14 (a)** Loss in p.e. = gain in k.e.

$mgh = \frac{1}{2}mv^2 \Rightarrow v = \sqrt{2gh}$

Restitution for first bounce: $v_1 = e\sqrt{2gh}$

After rebound, loss in k.e. = gain in p.e.

$\frac{1}{2}m(e\sqrt{2gh})^2 = mgH$

$\Rightarrow H = e^2h$

**(b)** Time taken for first drop $= \sqrt{\dfrac{2h}{g}}$

Time taken between first and second bounce

$= 2e\sqrt{\dfrac{2h}{g}}$

Ball rebounds after second bounce with speed $e^2\sqrt{2gh}$

Time taken between second and third bounce

$= 2e^2\sqrt{\dfrac{2h}{g}}$

Total time $T = \sqrt{\dfrac{2h}{g}}(1 + 2e + 2e^2)$

**15 (a)** First collision between $A$ and $B$:

Conservation of momentum:

$3mu = 3mv_1 + 2mv_2$

Restitution: $v_2 - v_1 = eu$

So $v_1 = \frac{1}{5}u(3 - 2e)$, $v_2 = \frac{3}{5}u(1 + e)$

Second collision between $B$ and $C$

Conservation of momentum:

$\frac{6}{5}mu(1 + e) = 2mv_3 + mv_4$

$\Rightarrow \frac{6}{5}u(1 + e) = 2v_3 + v_4$    (1)

Restitution: $v_4 - v_3 = \frac{3}{5}eu(1 + e)$    (2)

(1) − (2): $3v_3 = \frac{6}{5}u(1 + e) - \frac{3}{5}eu(1 + e)$

So $v_3 = \frac{1}{5}u(1 + e)(2 - e)$

**(b)** Further collision between $A$ and $B$, so

$\frac{1}{5}u(3 - 2e) > \frac{1}{5}u(1 + e)(2 - e)$

$\Rightarrow 3 - 2e > 2 + e - e^2$

$\Rightarrow e^2 - 3e + 1 > 0$

$\Rightarrow 0 < e < \dfrac{3 - \sqrt{5}}{2}$

or $0 < e < 0.382$ (to 3 s.f.)

## Test yourself (p 107)

**1** $25\,\text{m s}^{-1}$

**2 (a)** Conservation of momentum:

$3mu - 2mu = -mv_A + 2mv_B$

$\Rightarrow -v_A + 2v_B = u$    (1)

Restitution: $v_A + v_B = 4eu$    (2)

(1) + (2): $3v_B = u(1 + 4e) \Rightarrow v_B = \frac{1}{3}(1 + 4e)u$

**(b)** $v_A = \frac{1}{3}(8e - 1)u$

If $A$ is reversed, $v_A > 0$, from which $8e - 1 > 0$

$\Rightarrow e > \frac{1}{8}$

**(c)** Speed of $B$ after rebound $= \frac{1}{6}(1 + 4e)u$

$A$ and $B$ collide if $\frac{1}{6}(1 + 4e)u > \frac{1}{3}(8e - 1)u$

$\Rightarrow 1 + 4e > 16e - 2$

$\Rightarrow e < \frac{1}{4}$

**3 (a)** $(-25\mathbf{i} - 5\mathbf{j})\,\text{m s}^{-1}$      **(b)** $32.9\,\text{m}$ (to 3 s.f.)

**(c)** $51.0\,\text{m}$ (to 3 s.f.)

# 6 Moments

## A Moment of a force (p 108)

**A1** (a) Less, because the distance of the line of action from $A$ is less.

(b) $0.2 \sin 30° = 0.1\,\text{m}$

(c) $0.8\,\text{N m}$ anticlockwise

**A2** (a) $10 \times 0.25 \sin 45° = 1.77\,\text{N m}$ anticlockwise (to 3 s.f.)

(b) $10 \times 0.15 \sin 45° = 1.06\,\text{N m}$ anticlockwise (to 3 s.f.)

**A3** (a) $-5 \times 3 \sin 45° = -10.6\,\text{N m}$ (to 3 s.f.)

(b) $-10 \times 4 \sin 60° = -34.6\,\text{N m}$ (to 3 s.f.)

(c) $7 \times 1.5 \sin 50° = 8.04\,\text{N m}$ (to 3 s.f.)

**A4** (a) (i) $5 \times 4 = 20\,\text{N m}$   (ii) $32\,\text{N m}$

(iii) $52\,\text{N m}$

(b) The lines of action of both forces pass through $B$, so the total moment of the forces about $B$ is zero.

(c) $5 \times 0 + 8 \times 4 = 32\,\text{N m}$

(d) $5 \times 4 + 8 \times 0 = 20\,\text{N m}$

**A5** (a) $-4 \times 10 \sin 30° = -20\,\text{N m}$

(b) $8\,\text{N m}$

(c) Total moment $= -20 + 8 = -12\,\text{N m}$

### Exercise A (p 110)

**1** (a) $-2.54\,\text{N m}$ (to 3 s.f.) (b) $-5.79\,\text{N m}$ (to 3 s.f.)

(c) $17.3\,\text{N m}$ (to 3 s.f.)

**2** (a) $-25\,\text{N m}$     (b) $-10\,\text{N m}$     (c) $-5\,\text{N m}$

**3** 6

**4** (a) $5.68\,\text{N m}$ (to 3 s.f.) (b) $9.39\,\text{N m}$ (to 3 s.f.)

**5** (a) $2Fa\,\text{N m}$     (b) $\frac{1}{2}Fa\,\text{N m}$

**6** (a) $0\,\text{N m}$     (b) $5.20\,\text{N m}$ (to 3 s.f.)

(c) $8.66\,\text{N m}$ (to 3 s.f.)

**7** $14\,\text{N m}$

## B Equilibrium of a rigid body (p 111)

**B1** (a)

(b) $\text{M}(A):\ 30 \times 2 = R_B \times 3$
$\Rightarrow R_B = 20$
Reaction at $B = 20\,\text{N}$

(c) $\text{M}(B):\ 30 \times 1 = R_A \times 3$
$\Rightarrow R_A = 10$
Reaction at $A = 10\,\text{N}$

(d) Resolve vertically: $R_A + R_B = 30$
Substitute calculated values:
$10 + 20 = 30$, which is correct, so the forces are in equilibrium.

**B2** (a)

(b) $\text{M}(C):\ T_B \times 2 + 5 \times 1 = 15 \times 1$
$\Rightarrow T_B = 5$
Tension at $B = 5\,\text{N}$

(c) $\text{M}(B):\ T_C \times 2 = 15 \times 1 + 5 \times 3$
$\Rightarrow T_C = 15$
Tension at $C = 15\,\text{N}$

**B3** (a) The distance $d$ is $4 \sin 45°$, so the moment of $T$ about $P$ is $4T \sin 45°$.

(b) $500g \times 3 = 4T \sin 45° \Rightarrow 1500g = 4T \sin 45°$

(c) $T = 5200$ (to 3 s.f.)

**B4** (a) $Y + T \sin 45° = 500g \Rightarrow Y = 1225$

(b) $X = T \cos 45° \Rightarrow X = 3675$

(c) $R = \sqrt{1225^2 + 3675^2}$
$= 3874$

$\theta = \tan^{-1} \dfrac{1225}{3675}$
$= 18.4°$ (to 1 d.p.)

**B5** (a)

(b) $2g \times 0.25 = F \times 0.5 \sin 20° \Rightarrow F = 28.7$

(c) $X = F\cos 20° = 26.9$

$Y + F\sin 20° = 2g \Rightarrow Y = 9.8$

Magnitude of reaction $= \sqrt{26.9^2 + 9.8^2} = 28.6\,\text{N}$

Direction $= \tan^{-1}\dfrac{9.8}{26.9} = 20.0°$ to the horizontal

**B6** (a)

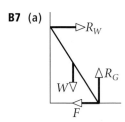

(b) There is no horizontal force to balance the reaction at the wall, $R_W$, so the ladder will slip.

**B7** (a)

(b) The ladder will remain in equilibrium if $F = R_W$. If $R_W$ is greater than the limiting value of the friction force, then the ladder will slip.

**B8** The lines of action of $F$ and $R_B$ pass through $B$, so their moments about $B$ are zero, and $R_A$ is the only unknown in the equation.

**B9** As the man climbs up the ladder, the reaction at the wall increases which causes the friction force to increase. The reaction at the ground is constant. If the friction force reaches its limiting value, then the ladder will slip.

**B10** (a) $R_B = 850$

(b) $R_A = F$

(c) $R_A \times 4\sin 60° = 100 \times 2\cos 60° + 750 \times x\cos 60°$

(d) $F_{\text{max}} = 0.4 \times 850 = 340 \Rightarrow R_A = 340$

(e) $x = 2.87$

The man can climb 2.87 m up the ladder before it slips.

**B11** (a)

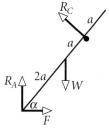

(b) $W \times 2a\cos\alpha = R_C \times 3a$

$\Rightarrow \frac{8}{5}W = 3R_C$

$\Rightarrow R_C = \frac{8}{15}W$

(c) $F = R_C\sin\alpha$

$\Rightarrow F = \frac{8}{25}W$

(d) $R_A + R_C\cos\alpha = W$

$\Rightarrow R_A = \frac{43}{75}W$

(e) $F = \mu R_A \Rightarrow \frac{8}{25}W = \frac{43}{75}\mu W$

$\Rightarrow \mu = \frac{24}{43}$

**Exercise B** (p 114)

**1** (a)

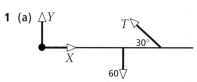

(b) The distance of $A$ from the line of action of $T$ is $3\sin 30°$, so the moment of $T$ about $A$ is $3T\sin 30°$.

(c) 80

**2** $\dfrac{W}{3}$

**3** (a)

(b) 33.9 N    (c) 33.9 N    (d) 0.289

**4 (a)**

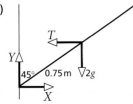

**(b)** 19.6 N

**(c)** 27.7 N at 45° to the horizontal

**5 (a)**

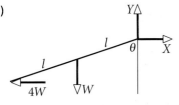

**(b)** $X = 4W$, $Y = W$

**(c)** $\sqrt{17}\,W$ at 14.0° to the horizontal

**(d)** 82.9°

**6 (a)**

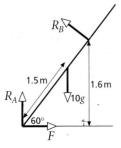

**(b)** 34.5 N          **(c)** 0.441

**7** 5.31 m

**8** M(A): $Wa = T \times 2a \sin\theta$
$\Rightarrow T = \frac{5}{6}W$

Resolve horizontally: $R = \frac{4}{5}T$
$\Rightarrow R = \frac{2}{3}W$

Resolve vertically: $F + \frac{3}{5}T = W$
$\Rightarrow F = \frac{1}{2}W$

But $F \le \mu R$, so $\frac{1}{2}W \le \frac{2}{3}W\mu$
$\Rightarrow \mu \ge \frac{3}{4}$

## Mixed questions (p 116)

**1** $\dfrac{\sqrt{3}mg}{6}$

**2** $\frac{7}{12}W \le P \le \frac{61}{12}W$

## Test yourself (p 117)

**1** Let the points of contact with the floor and wall be $A$ and $B$ respectively.

M(A): $mgl\sin\alpha + 4mg \times 2l\sin\alpha = R_B \times 2l\cos\alpha$
$\Rightarrow 9mgl\sin\alpha = 2R_B l\cos\alpha$
$\Rightarrow R_B = \frac{9}{2}mg\tan\alpha$

Resolve horizontally: $F = R_B = \frac{9}{2}mg\tan\alpha$
Resolve vertically: $R_A = 5mg$
But $F \le \mu R_A$, so $\frac{9}{2}mg\tan\alpha \le \frac{3}{5} \times 5mg$
$\Rightarrow \tan\alpha \le \frac{2}{3}$

**2 (a)** M(B): $Wa\cos\alpha = F \times 2a\sin\alpha + R_A \times 2a\cos\alpha$
$\Rightarrow \frac{12}{13}W = \frac{10}{13}F + \frac{24}{13}R_A$
Limiting equilibrium, so $F = 0.6R_A$
$\Rightarrow 12W = 6R_A + 24R_A = 30R_A$
$\Rightarrow R_A = \frac{2}{5}W$

**(b)** 68.2° (to 3 s.f.)

**(c)** 0.646 (to 3 s.f.)

**3 (a)** $\frac{7}{8}W$

**(b)** Resolve vertically: $R_A + F = W$ so $F = \frac{1}{8}W$
Resolve horizontally: $R_B = \frac{1}{4}W$
$F \le \mu R_B$ so $\frac{1}{8}W \le \frac{1}{4}\mu W$
$\Rightarrow \mu \ge \frac{1}{2}$

**(c)** The mass of the ladder is assumed to be uniformly distributed along its length and its width and depth are assumed to be negligible.

**4** Let the horizontal and vertical components of the reaction at $A$ be $X$ and $Y$ respectively.

M(A): $T \times 2a\sin\theta = Wa + 2W \times \frac{3}{2}a$
$\Rightarrow T = \frac{10}{3}W$
Resolve vertically: $T\sin\theta + Y = 3W$
$\Rightarrow Y = 3W - \frac{3}{5} \times \frac{10}{3}W \Rightarrow Y = W$
Resolve horizontally: $T\cos\theta = X$
$\Rightarrow X = \frac{4}{5} \times \frac{10}{3}W \Rightarrow X = \frac{8}{3}W$

Magnitude of reaction $= \sqrt{X^2 + Y^2} = \sqrt{\dfrac{73W^2}{9}}$
$= \dfrac{\sqrt{73}W}{3}$

# Index